THE LITERATURE OF
DEATH AND DYING

This is a volume in the Arno Press collection

THE LITERATURE OF DEATH AND DYING

Advisory Editor
Robert Kastenbaum

Editorial Board
Gordon Geddes
Gerald J. Gruman
Michael Andrew Simpson

*See last pages of this volume
for a complete list of titles*

THE

RULE AND EXERCISES

OF

HOLY DYING

Jeremy Taylor

New Introduction By Robert Kastenbaum

ARNO PRESS

A New York Times Company

New York / 1977

Reprint Edition 1977 by Arno Press Inc.

THE LITERATURE OF DEATH AND DYING
ISBN for complete set: 0-405-09550-3
See last pages of this volume for titles.

Manufactured in the United States of America

———◆———

Library of Congress Cataloging in Publication Data

Taylor, Jeremy, Bp. of Down and Connor, 1613-1667.
    The rule and exercises of holy dying.

    (The Literature of death and dying)
    Reprint of the 1819 ed. printed for Longman, Hurst,
Rees, Orme & Brown, London.
    1. Christian life--Anglican authors. 2. Sick--
Prayer-books and devotions--English. I. Title.
II. Series.
BV4500.T3 1977   248'.48'3   76-19590
ISBN 0-405-09585-6

FOREWORD

When does a person stand most in need of religious strength and guidance? Perhaps it is at that moment when death presents its claim upon life. Some observers have contended that all of the world's religions have arisen in response to the personal and social trauma of death. This sweeping generalization appears to be safely beyond conclusive proof or disproof. However, there is no questioning the close association between religious dogma and practice and a culture's mode of coming to terms with mortality.

The genius of Jeremy Taylor continues to shine through the welter of repetitive, formula-ridden expressions of the religious response to death. Taylor is precise where others meander, urgent where others plod, persistent where others falter. The force of his personality and the disciplined vigor of his prose command respect even among those who do not share the particular faith that nourishes *The Rules and Exercises of Holy Dying*. An encounter with the Rev. Dr. Taylor is formidable three centuries after he addressed himself to the problem of death—what an impression it must have made upon the faithful but anxious Christian of his own time!

For a perspective on Taylor's contribution we might begin by acknowledging the apparent "discovery" of death in the second half of the twentieth century. In the past two decades there has been a widespread increase in the expression of interest in dying, death, bereavement and related topics. This is as true in professional and scientific as in "popular" spheres. We have been telling each other that death is a "taboo" subject that should be opened to reflection and dialogue. We have been increasingly concerned about the plight of the dying person. We have either been advocating or resisting the position that death is an integral part of life, not simply the period at the end of the sentence. And we have become increasingly concerned about the morally relevant decisions that are pressing upon patients, family, and physicians.

Frequently there is the impression given that we have made a distinctive discovery: death is real, death is important. It is far more accurate, however, to acknowledge that we have simply closed a gap between our own times and the long history of our race. Cultural denial of death (parallel in some respects to the cover-up of sexuality) was evident for a relatively short period of time in our immediate and recent history. Most cultures throughout the world have expressed a more forthright attitude toward both death and sexuality, although not without elements of strategic evasion. What is happening now, in other words, is an implicit bridging between major historical traditions and the current *rediscovery* of death. It remains implicit rather than explicit because some of the most significant materials of historical interest have been unavailable, and often unknown to the person who is attempting to cope with immediate death-related problems. In this context, *Holy Dying* offers one of the most valuable opportunities for linking our death concern with its historical antecedents.

The Christian tradition had passed through several phases prior to Jeremy Taylor's day. While the early and ardent Christians could look forward to—or even seek out —a blessed, joyous departure through death to the life eternal, this view was not easily maintained by succeeding generations. Religious faith and all human resources were severely tested by the plagues, natural disasters, and warfare of the late Middle Ages. Death threatened to destroy the fabric of social organization, as when cities were devastated and the countryside left untended by onslaughts of the bubonic plague. Neither age, sex, privilege, nor piety offered much protection from the virulent modalities of death. Belief in a powerful and loving deity was daily challenged by new evidences of suffering and death. This contributed to an increased emphasis on death as *punishment*. Human wickedness and failing had brought down these dreadful but just retributions. It was during these grim times that much of the macabre and morbid shadings of death attitudes gained prominence.

Around the turn of the 15th century, a relatively new form of expression became evident. Society appeared to be recovering from its worst, most overwhelming encounters with death, but remained haunted by the memories as well as by continuing threats. This new form of expression consisted of tracts written to help people die properly. These were relatively brief essays or books intended both for priests and laymen. *The Boke of crafte of dyinge* is a typical title of the time. The literary tradition became known eventually as the *ars moriendi* (the art of dying well).

This was already a long established tradition when Taylor published his work in the middle of the 17th century. Conditions and problems of life were no longer the same as they had been either in the early days of Christianity or in the depths of the Middle Ages. Serious differences in points of doctrine existed in the church. Society in general was spinning with a heady mixture of ideas, controversies, and discoveries. The printing press was proving perhaps more revolutionary a social change agent than our own movement into television, satellites and computer networks. Yet people were still facing the prospect of their own death, or mourning the loss of loved ones. Somehow the now-old and rather primitive tracts on the craft of dying no longer seemed sufficient.

Taylor, chaplain to King Charles the First, was deeply rooted in the traditions of the past but was also a sophisticated man of his own day. He succeeded in integrating some of the more significant traditional themes into a fuller, richer, more "contemporary" view of the Christian's relationship to life and death. The book was motivated by personal impulse as well as theological purpose. Mourning the death of his own wife, Taylor dedicated the book to Lord Carbery who had recently experienced the same type of loss:

"My lord, both your lordship and myself have lately seen and felt such sorrows of death, and such sad departure of dearest friends, that it is more than high time we should think ourselves nearly concerned in the accidents. Death hath come so near to you, as to fetch a portion from your very heart; and now you cannot choose but dig your own grave, and place your coffin in your eye.... And therefore, as it is my duty, I am come to minister to your pious thoughts, and to direct your sorrows, that they may turn into virtues and advantages."

The Rule and Exercises of Holy Dying offers both logical argument and practical advice. Taylor the learned theologian and rationalist steps aside repeatedly for Taylor the humanist and minister. It is an attempt to integrate reason and faith.

Furthermore, it is also a work of art. The quality and balance of this book set it apart from the more strictly functional tracts in the *ars moriendi* tradition. *Holy Dying* can be appreciated for its literary as well as theological and humanistic merits.

Those whose acquaintance with problems of dying and death have been strongly influenced by current psychosocial approaches will have still another perspective from which to view this book. Taylor, for example, clearly recognizes some of the principles held dear by psychologists in the area of learning, personality development, and, yes, even behavior modification. He emphasizes the *continuity* of life and personality, the importance of investing each hour and day with the activities and cognitions we value. This stands against the position that one can or should miraculously transcend his previous life-style in some fantastic deathbed scene. Taylor observes quietly:

"My lord, it is a great art to die well, and to be learned by men in health, by them that can discourse and consider, by those whose understanding and acts of reason are not abated with fear or pains.... All that a sick and dying man can do, is but to exercise those virtues which he before acquired, and to perfect that repentance which was begun more early . . . if we practise imperfectly once, we shall never recover the error: for we die but once; and therefore it will be necessary that our skill be more exact, since it is not to be mended by trial, but the actions must be for ever left imperfect. . . ."

A personal note, if I may: like yourself, I am not a 17th century person. Perhaps also like yourself, I have been deeply involved in contemporary efforts to improve our understanding and care-giving in the broad realm of death-related situations. Yet Jeremy Taylor has been one of my most cherished "consultants" since the day my wife discovered a fine edition of Holy Dying in a London book shop. It is with a special delight in sharing, then, that I am pleased that the long overdue republication of this book has made use of this personal copy. I hope that you, too, will find it a challenge, a comfort, and a pleasure.

Robert Kastenbaum
University of Massachusetts-Boston
August, 1976

References

Beaty, N.L. The Craft of Dying. New Haven: Yale University Press, 1970.

Feifel, H. (ed.). The Meaning of Death. NY: McGraw-Hill, 1959.

Kastenbaum, R. Death, Society, and Human Behavior. St. Louis: Mosby, 1977.

Kastenbaum, R., & Aisenberg, R.B. The Psychology of Death. NY: Springer, 1972.

O'Connor, M. C. The Art of Dying Well. NY: Columbia University Press, 1942.

THE

RULE AND EXERCISES

OF

HOLY DYING:

IN WHICH ARE DESCRIBED

THE MEANS AND INSTRUMENTS

OF

PREPARING OURSELVES AND OTHERS RESPECTIVELY FOR A

BLESSED DEATH;

AND THE REMEDIES AGAINST THE EVILS AND TEMPTATIONS PROPER TO

THE STATE OF SICKNESS:

TOGETHER WITH

PRAYERS AND ACTS OF VIRTUE

TO BE USED BY

SICK AND DYING PERSONS,

OR BY OTHERS STANDING IN THEIR ATTENDANCE.

To which are added,

RULES FOR THE VISITATION OF THE SICK,

AND

OFFICES PROPER FOR THAT MINISTRY.

Τὸ μὲν τελευτῆσαι ἡ πεπρωμένη κατέκρινε·
Τὸ δὲ καλῶς ἀποθανεῖν, ἴδιον τοῖς σπυδάιοις ἡ φύσις ἀπένειμε.
Isoc. *ad* Demonic.

By JER. TAYLOR, D.D.

CHAPLAIN IN ORDINARY TO KING CHARLES THE FIRST.

TWENTY-NINTH EDITION.

The Rev. THOMAS THIRLWALL, M.A.

EDITOR.

LONDON:

PRINTED FOR LONGMAN, HURST, REES, ORME, AND BROWN,

PATERNOSTER-ROW.

1819.

Printed by Strahan and Spottiswoode,
Printers-Street, London.

My Lord,

I am treating your lordship as a Roman gentleman did Saint *Augustin* and his mother; I shall entertain you in a charnel house, and carry your meditation awhile into the chambers of death, where you shall find the rooms dressed up with melancholic arts, and fit to converse with your most retired thoughts, which begin with a sigh, and proceed in deep consideration, and end in a holy resolution. The sight that St. *Augustin* most noted in that house of sorrow, was the body of *Cæsar* clothed with all the dishonours of corruption that you can suppose in a six months' burial. But I know that, without pointing, your first thoughts will remember the change of a greater beauty, which is now dressing for the brightest immortality, and from her bed of darkness calls to you to dress your soul for that change which shall mingle your bones with that beloved dust, and carry your soul to the same choir, where you may both sit and sing for ever. My lord, it is your dear lady's *anniversary*, and she deserved the *biggest honour*, and the *longest memory*, and the *fairest monument*, and the most *solemn mourning*: and in order to it, give me leave (my lord) to cover her hearse with these following sheets. This book was intended first to minister to her piety; and she desired all good people should partake of the advan-

tages

tages which are here recorded: she knew how to live rarely well, and she desired to know how to die; and God taught her by an experiment. But since her work is done, and God supplied her with provisions of his own, before I could minister to her, and perfect what she desired, it is necessary to present to your Lordship those bundles of cypress which were intended to dress her closet, but come now to dress her hearse. My lord, both your lordship and myself have lately seen and felt such sorrows of death, and such sad departure of dearest friends, that it is more than high time we should think ourselves nearly concerned in the accidents. Death hath come so near to you, as to fetch a portion from your very heart; and now you cannot choose but dig your own grave, and place your coffin in your eye, when the angel hath dressed your scene of sorrow and meditation with so particular and so near an object. And therefore, as it is my duty, I am come to minister to your pious thoughts, and to direct your sorrows, that they may turn into virtues and advantages.

And since I know your lordship to be so constant and regular in your devotions, and so tender in the matter of justice, so ready in the expressions of charity, and so apprehensive of religion, and that you are a person whose work of grace is apt, and must every day grow towards those degrees, where when you arrive you shall triumph over imperfection, and choose nothing but what may please God; I could not by any compendium conduct and assist your pious purposes so well, as by that which is the great argument and the great instrument of Holy Living, the consideration and exercises of death.

My lord, it is a great art to die well, and to be learned by men in health, by them that can discourse and consider, by those whose understanding and acts of reason are not abated with fear or pains: and as the greatest part of death is passed by the preceding

years

years of our life, so also in those years are the greatest
preparations to it ; and he that prepares not for death
before his last sickness, is like him that begins to
study philosophy when he is going to dispute publicly in
the faculty. All that a sick and dying man can do, is
but to exercise those virtues which he before acquired,
and to perfect that repentance which was begun more
early. And of this (my lord) my book, I think, is
a good testimony ; not only because it represents the
vanity of a late and sick-bed repentance, but because
it contains in it so many precepts and meditations, so
many propositions and various duties, such forms of
exercise, and the degrees and difficulties of so many
graces which are necessary preparatives to a holy death,
that the very learning the duties requires study and
skill, time and understanding in the ways of godliness:
and it were very vain to say so much is necessary, and
not to suppose more time to learn them, more skill to
practise them, more opportunities to desire them, more
abilities both of body and mind than can be supposed
in a sick, amazed, timorous, and weak person ; whose
natural acts are disabled, whose senses are weak,
whose discerning faculties are lessened, whose principles are made intricate and entangled, upon whose eyes
sits a cloud, and the heart is broken with sickness, and
the liver pierced through with sorrows, and the strokes
of death. And therefore (my lord) it is intended by
the necessity of affairs, that the precepts of *dying well*
be part of the studies of them that live in health, and
the days of discourse and understanding, which in this
case hath another degree of necessity superadded ; because, in other notices, an imperfect study may be supplied by a frequent exercise and a renewed experience ; here if we practise imperfectly once, we shall
never recover the error : for we die but once ; and
therefore it will be necessary that our skill be more
exact, since it is not to be mended by trial, but the
actions must be for ever left imperfect, unless the

A 3   habit

habit be contracted with study and contemplation beforehand.

And indeed I were vain, if I should intend this book to be read and studied by dying persons: and they were vainer that should need to be instructed in those graces which they are then to exercise and to finish. For a sick bed is only a school of severe exercise, in which the spirit of a man is tried, and his graces are rehearsed: and the assistances which I have in the following pages given to those virtues which are proper to the state of sickness, are such as suppose a man in the state of grace; or they confirm a good man, or they support the weak, or add degrees, or minister comfort, or prevent an evil, or cure the little mischiefs which are incident to tempted persons in their weakness. That is the sum of the present design, as it relates to dying persons. And therefore I have not inserted any advices proper to old age, but such as are common to it and the state of sickness. For I suppose *very old age* to be *a longer sickness;* it is labour and sorrow when it goes beyond the common period of nature: but if it be on this side that period, and be healthful in the same degree it is so, I reckon it in the accounts of life; and therefore it can have no distinct consideration. But I do not think it is a station of advantage to begin the change of an evil life in: it is a middle state between *life* and *death-bed:* and therefore although it hath more of hopes than *this,* and less than *that,* yet as it partakes of either state, so it is to be regulated by the advices of that state, and judged by its sentences.

Only this: I desire that all old persons would sadly consider that their advantages in that state are very few, but their inconveniences are not few; their bodies are without strength, their prejudices long and mighty, their vices (if they have lived wicked) are habitual, the occasions of the virtues not many, the possibilities of some (in the matter of which they stand very guilty)

guilty) are past, and shall never return again, (such are, chastity, and many parts of self-denial;) that they have some temptations proper to their age, as peevishness and pride, covetousness and talking, wilfulness and unwillingness to * learn; and they think they are protected by age from learning a new, or repenting the old, and do not † leave, but change their vices : and after all this, either the day of their repentance is past, as we see it true in very many; or it is expiring, and toward the sun-set, as it is in all : and therefore although in these to recover is very possible, yet we may also remember, that in the matter of virtue and repentance *possibility* is a great way off from performance ; and how few do repent, of whom it is only *possible* that they may? and that many things more are required to reduce their *possibility* to act; a great grace, an assiduous ministry, an effective calling, mighty assistances, excellent counsel, great industry, a watchful diligence, a well-disposed mind, passionate desires, deep apprehensions of danger, quick perceptions of duty, and time, and God's good blessing, and effectual impression and seconding all this, that *to will and to do* may by him be wrought to great purposes, and with great speed.

And therefore it will not be amiss, but it is hugely necessary, that these persons who have lost their time and their blessed opportunities should have the diligence of youth, and the zeal of new converts, and take account of every hour that is left them, and pray perpetually, and be advised prudently, and study the interest of their souls carefully with diligence, and with fear ; and their old age, which in effect is nothing but a continual death-bed, dressed with some more order

---

* Vel quia nil rectum nisi quod placuit sibi ducunt:
 Vel quia turpe putant parere minoribus, et quæ
 Imberbes didicere, senes perdenda fateri.

Tenellis adhuc infantiæ suæ persuasionibus in senectute puerascunt. *Mamertus.*

and

and advantages, may be a state of hope, and labour, and acceptance, through the infinite mercies of God in Jesus Christ.

But concerning sinners really under the arrest of death, God hath made no death-bed covenant, the scripture hath recorded no promises, given no instructions, and therefore I had none to give, but only the same which are to be given to all men that are alive, because they are so, and because it is uncertain when they shall be otherwise. But then this advice I also am to insert, That they are the smallest number of Christian men, who can be divided by the characters of a *certain holiness*, or an *open villany :* and between these there are many degrees of latitude, and most are of a middle sort; concerning which we are tied to make the judgments of charity, and possibly God may do so too. But, however, all they are such to whom the *Rules of Holy Dying* are useful and applicable, and therefore no separation is to be made in this world. But where the case *is not evident*, men are to be remitted to the unerring judgment of God : where *it is evident*, we can *rejoice* or *mourn* for them that die.

In the church of *Rome* they reckon otherwise concerning sick and dying Christians than I have done : for they make profession, that from death to life, from sin to grace, a man may very certainly be changed, though the operation begin not before his last hour : and *half this* they do upon his death-bed, and the *other half* when he is in his grave : and they take away *the eternal punishment* in an instant, by a school-distinction, or the hand of the priest ; and the *temporal punishment* shall stick longer, even then when the man is no more *measured with time*, having nothing to do with any thing *of* or *under the sun ;* but that they pretend to take away too when the man is dead ; and God knows, the poor man for all this pays them both in hell. The distinction of *temporal* and *eternal* is a just measure of pain, when it refers to *this life* and

and *another :* but to dream of a punishment *temporal* when all his *time is done,* and to think of repentance when the time of grace is past, are great errors, the one in philosophy, and both in divinity, and are a huge folly in their pretence, and infinite danger if they are believed; being a certain destruction of the necessity of holy living when men dare trust them, and live at the rate of such doctrines. The secret of these is soon discovered : for by such means, though *a holy life be not* necessary, yet *a priest is ;* as if God did not appoint the priest to minister to holy living, but to excuse it, so making *the holy calling* not only to live upon the sins of the people, but upon their ruin, and the advantages of their function to spring from their eternal dangers. It is an evil craft to serve a temporal end upon the death of souls, that is an interest not to be handled but with nobleness and ingenuity, fear and caution, diligence and prudence, with great skill and great honesty, with reverence, and trembling, and severity : a soul is worth all that, and the need we have requires all that ; and therefore those doctrines that go less than all this are not friendly, because they are not safe.

I know no other difference in the visitation and treating of sick persons, than what depends upon the article of late repentance : for all churches agree in the same essential propositions, and assist the sick by the same internal ministeries. As for *external,* I mean *unction,* used in the church of *Rome,* since it is used when the man is above half dead, when he can exercise no act of understanding, it must needs be nothing : for no rational man can think that any ceremony can make a spiritual change, without a spiritual act of him that is to be changed ; nor work by way of nature, or by charm, but morally, and after the manner of reasonable creatures : and therefore I do not think that ministry at all fit to be reckoned among the advantages of sick persons. The fathers of the council of *Trent* first disputed, and after this manner at last agreed, that *extreme unction was instituted by Christ.* But afterwards, being admonished

by

by one of their theologues, that the apostles ministered
unction to infirm people before they were priests (the
priestly order, according to their doctrine, being col-
lated in the institution of the last supper) for fear that
it should be thought that this unction might be administered by him that was no priest, they blotted out
the word [*instituted*] and put in its stead [*insinuated*] this
sacrament, and that it was *published by St. James.* So
it is in their *doctrine:* and yet in their anathematisms
they curse all them that shall deny it to have been [*instituted*] *by Christ.* I shall lay no more prejudice against
it, or the weak arts of them that maintain it, but add
this only, that there being but two places of scripture
pretended for this ceremony, some chief men of their
own side have proclaimed these two invalid as to the
institution of it : for *Suarez* says, that the unction used
by the apostles in St. *Mark,* vi. 13. is not the same with
what is used in the church of *Rome,* and that it cannot
be plainly gathered from the Epistle of St. *James, Ca-
jetan* affirms, and that it did belong to the miraculous
gift of healing — not to a sacrament. The sick man's
exercise of grace formerly acquired, his perfecting
repentance begun in the days of health, the prayers and
counsels of the holy man that ministers, the giving the
holy sacrament, the ministry and assistance of angels,
and the mercies of God, the peace of conscience, and
the peace of the church, are all the assistances and preparatives that can help to dress his lamp. But if a man
shall go to buy oil when the bridegroom comes, if his
lamp be not first furnished, and then trimmed, *that* in
this life, *this* upon his death-bed, his station shall be
without-doors, his portion with unbelievers, and the
unction of the dying man shall no more strengthen his
soul than it cures his body, and the prayers for him after
his death shall be of the same force as if they should pray
that he should return to life again the next day, and live
as long as *Lazarus* in his return. But I consider, that
it is not well that men should pretend any thing will
do a man good when he dies ; and yet the same minis-

teries

teries and ten times more assistances are found for forty
or fifty years together to be ineffectual. Can extreme
unction at last cure what the holy sacrament of the
Eucharist all his life-time could not do? Can prayers
for a dead man do him more good than when he was
alive? If *all his days* the man belonged to death and
the dominion of sin, and from thence could not be
recovered by sermons, and counsels, and perpetual precepts, and frequent sacraments, by confessions and ab-
solutions, by prayers and advocations, by external ministeries and internal acts, it is but too certain that his
lamp cannot then be furnished: his extreme unction is
only then of use when it is made by the oil that burned
in his lamp in all the days of his expectation and waiting for the coming of the bridegroom.

Neither can any supply be made in this case by their
practice of praying for the dead; though they pretend
for this the fairest precedents of the church and of the
whole world. The Heathens they say did it, and the
Jews did it, and the Christians did it: some were
baptized for the dead in the days of the apostles *, and
very many were *communicated for the dead* for so
many ages after. 'Tis true they were so, and did so:
the Heathens † prayed *for an easy grave, and a perpetual spring, that saffron would rise* from their beds of
grass. The Jews prayed that the souls of their dead
might be in the garden of *Eden,* that they might have
their part in Paradise, and in the world to come; and
that they might hear the peace of the fathers of their
generation, sleeping in *Hebron.* And the Christians
prayed for a *joyful resurrection,* for *mercy at the day
of judgment,* for hastening *of the coming of Christ,
and the kingdom of God;* and they named all sorts of
persons in their prayers — all, I mean, but wicked persons — all but them that lived evil lives; they named

---

* Tertul. de Monog. S. Cyprian. l. i. Ep. 9. S. Athan. q. 33. S. Cyril. myst.
cat. 5. Epiphan. Hæres. 75. Aug. de Hæres. ca. 33. Concil. Carth. 3. c. 29.
  † Dii majorum umbris tenuem et sine pondere terram,
  Spirantésque crocos, et in urna perpetuum ver.   *Juven.* S. vii.

apostles, saints, and martyrs. And all this is so nothing to their purpose, or so much against it, that the prayers for the dead used in the church of *Rome* are most plainly condemned, because they are against the doctrines and practices of all the world, in other forms, to other purposes, relying upon distinct doctrine, until new opinions began to rise about St. *Augustin's* time, and changed the face of the proposition. *Concerning prayer for the dead, the church hath received no commandment from the Lord;* and therefore concerning it we can have no rules nor proportions, but from those imperfect revelations of the state of departed souls, and the measures of charity, which can relate only to the imperfection of their present condition, and the terrors of the day of judgment: but to think that any suppletory to an evil life can be taken from such devotions after the sinners are dead, may encourage a bad man to sin, but cannot relieve him when he hath.

But of all things in the world, methinks men should be most careful not to abuse dying people; not only because their condition is pitiable, but because they shall soon be discovered, and in the secret regions of souls there shall be an evil report concerning those men who have deceived them: and if we believe we shall go to that place where such reports are made, we may fear the shame and the amazement of being accounted impostors in the presence of angels, and all the wise holy men of the world. To be erring and innocent is hugely pitiable, and incident to mortality; that we cannot help: but to deceive or to destroy so great an interest as is that of a soul, or to lessen its advantages, by giving it trifling and false confidences, is injurious and intolerable. And therefore it were very well if all the churches of the world would be extremely curious concerning their offices and ministeries of *the visitation of the sick:* that their ministers they send be holy and prudent; that their instructions be severe and safe; that their sentences be merciful

and reasonable; that their offices be sufficient and devout; that their attendances be frequent and long; that
their deputations be special and peculiar; that the doctrines upon which they ground their offices be true, material, and holy; that their ceremonies be few, and their
advices wary; that their separation be full of caution,
their judgments not remiss, their remissions not loose
and dissolute; and that the whole ministration be made
by persons of experience and charity. For it is a sad
thing to see our dead go out of our hands: they live
incuriously, and die without regard; and the last scene
of their life, which should be dressed with all spiritual
advantages, is abused by flattery and easy propositions,
and let go with carelessness and folly.

My lord, I have endeavoured to cure some part of
the evil as well as I could, being willing to relieve the
needs of indigent people in such ways as I can; and
therefore have described the duties which every sick
man may do alone, and such in which he can be assisted by the minister: and am the more confident that
these my endeavours will be the better entertained, because they are the first entire body of directions for
sick and dying people that I remember to have been
published in the church of *England*. In the church of
Rome there have been many; but they are dressed
with such doctrines which are sometimes useless,
sometimes hurtful, and their whole design of assistance, which they commonly yield, is at the best imperfect, and the representment is too careless and
loose for so severe an employment. So that in this
affair I was almost forced to walk alone; only that I
drew the rules and advices from the fountains of scripture, and the purest channels of the primitive church,
and was helped by some experience in the cure of
souls. I shall measure the success of my labours, not
by popular noises or the sentences of curious persons,
but by the advantage which good people may receive.
My work here is not to please the speculative part of
men, but to minister to practice, to preach to the

weary, to comfort the sick, to assist the penitent, to reprove the confident, to strengthen weak hands and feeble knees, having scarce any other possibilities left me of doing alms, or exercising that charity by which we shall be judged at doomsday. It is enough for me to be an under-builder in the house of God, and I glory in the employment. I labour in the foundations, and therefore the work needs no apology for being plain, so it be strong and well laid. But (my lord) as mean as it is, I must give God thanks for the desires and the strength: and, next to him, to you, for that opportunity and little portion of leisure which I had to do it in: for I must acknowledge it publicly (and, besides my prayers, it is all the recompence I can make you) my being quiet I owe to your interest, much of my support to your bounty, and many other collateral comforts I derive from your favour and nobleness. My lord, because I much honour you, and because I would do honour to myself, I have written your name in the entrance of my book: I am sure you will entertain it, because the design related to your dear lady, and because it may minister to your spirit in the day of visitation, when God shall call for you to receive your reward for your charity and your noble piety, by which you have not only endeared very many persons, but in great degrees have obliged me to be,

My noblest Lord,

Your Lordship's most thankful

And most humble Servant,

JER. TAYLOR.

CONTENTS.

RULE AND EXERCISES

OF

HOLY DYING.

CHAP. I.

GENERAL PREPARATION TOWARDS A HOLY AND BLESSED DEATH, BY WAY OF CONSIDERATION.

SECT. I.

Consideration of the vanity and shortness of Man's Life.

A MAN *is a bubble* (said the *Greek* proverb*) which *Lucian* represents with advantages and its proper circumstances, to this purpose, saying, All the world is a storm, and men rise up in their several generations like bubbles descending *à Jove pluvio*, from God and the dew of heaven, from a tear and drop of man, from nature and providence : and some of these instantly sink into the deluge of their first parent, and are hidden in a sheet of water, having had no other business in the world but to be born, that they might

---

* Πομφόλυξ ὁ ἄνθρωπ⊙·.

B

be

be able to die : others float up and down two or three turns, and suddenly disappear, and give their place to others : and they that live longest upon the face of the waters are in perpetual motion, restless and uneasy, and being crushed with a great drop of a cloud, sink into flatness and a froth ; the change not being great, it being hardly possible it should be more a nothing than it was before. So is every man : he is born in vanity and sin ; he comes into the world like morning mushrooms, soon thrusting up their heads into the air, and conversing with their kindred of the same production, and as soon they turn into dust and forgetfulness : some of them without any other interest in the affairs of the world, but that they made their parents a little glad, and very sorrowful : others ride longer in the storm ; it may be until seven years of vanity be expired, and then peradventure the sun shines hot upon their heads, and they fall into the shades below, into the cover of death and darkness of the grave to hide them. But if the bubble stands the shock of a bigger drop, and out-lives the chances of a child, of a careless nurse, of drowning in a pail of water, of being overlaid by a sleepy servant, or such little accidents, then the young man dances like a bubble empty and gay, and shines like a dove's neck, or the image of a rainbow, which hath no substance, and whose very imagery and colours are phantastical ; and so he dances out the gaiety of his youth, and is all the while in a storm, and endures, only because he is not knocked on the head by a drop of bigger rain, or crushed by the pressure of a load of indigested meat, or quenched by the disorder of an ill-placed humour : and to preserve a man alive in the midst of so many chances and hostilities is as great a miracle as to create him ; to preserve him from rushing into nothing, and at first to draw him up from nothing, were equally the issues of an almighty power. And therefore the wise men of the world have contended who shall best fit

man's

man's condition with words signifying his vanity and short abode. *Homer* calls a man a *leaf*, the smallest, the weakest piece of a short-lived, unsteady plant. *Pindar* calls him *the dream of a shadow :* another *the dream of the shadow of smoke.* But St. *James* * spake by a more excellent spirit, saying, *Our life is but a vapour, viz.* drawn from the earth by a celestial influence, made of smoke, or the lighter parts of water, tossed with every wind, moved by the motion of a superior body, without virtue in itself, lifted up on high, or left below, according as it pleases the sun, its fosterfather. But it is lighter yet. It is but *appearing* † *;* a phantastic vapour, an apparition, nothing real : it is not so much as a mist, not the matter of a shower, nor substantial enough to make a cloud ; but it is like *Cassiopeia's* chair, or *Pelops's* shoulder, or the circles of heaven, φαινόμενα, for which you cannot have a word that can signify a verier nothing. And yet the expression is one degree more made diminutive : *a vapour* and *phantastical,* or *a mere appearance,* and this is *for a little while* neither ; the very dream, the phantasm disappears in a small time ‡, *like the shadow departeth,* or *like a tale that is told,* or *as a dream when one awaketh.* A man is so vain, so unfixt, perishing a creature, that he cannot long last; is the dream of a distracted person. The sum is not this : *that thou art a man* §, than whom there is not in the world any greater instance of heights and declensions, of lights and shadows, of misery and folly, of laughter and tears, of groans and death.

And because this consideration is of great usefulness and great necessity to many purposes of wisdom and the spirit ; all the succession of time, all the changes in nature, all the varieties of light and darkness, the

* Jam. iv. 14. ἀτμίς.　　† Φαινομένη.　　‡ πρὸς ὀλίγον.
§ Τὸ δε κεφάλαιον τῶν λόγων, ἄνθρωπ⊙ εἶ, ἢ μεταβολὴ ἰον πρὸς ὕψος, καὶ πάλιν ταπεινότητα, ζῶον ἐδὲν λαμβάνει.

B 2

ness, the thousand thousands of accidents in the world, and every contingency to every man, and to every creature, doth preach our funeral sermon, and calls us to look and see how the old Sexton *Time* throws up the earth, and digs a grave, where we must lay our sins or our sorrows, and sow our bodies, till they rise again in a fair or in an intolerable eternity. Every revolution which the sun makes about the world * divides between life and death ; and death possesses both those portions by the next morrow ; and we are dead to all those months which we have already lived, and we shall never live them over again : and still God makes little periods of our age. First we change our world, when we come from the womb to feel the warmth of the sun. Then we sleep and enter into the image of death, in which state we are unconcerned in all the changes of the world : and if our mothers or our nurses die, or a wild boar destroy our vineyards, or our king be sick, we regard it not, but during that state, are as disinterested as if our eyes were closed with the clay that weeps in the bowels of the earth. At the end of seven years, our teeth fall and die before us, representing a formal prologue to the tragedy ; and still every seven years it is odds but we shall finish the last one : and when nature, or chance, or vice, takes body in pieces, weakening some parts, and loosening others, *we taste the grave*, and the solemnities of own funerals, first, in those parts that ministered to and next, in them that served for ornament ; become short time even they that served for necessity broke useless, and entangled like the wheels of a nerals lock. *Baldness* is but a dressing to our funeral proper ornament of mourning †, and of a

* *Nihil* netur per muisquam de futuro debet promittere. Id quoque quod tenitur tempus exit, et ipsam quam premimus horam casus incidit. Volquidem lege, sed per obscurum. *Seneca.*
† Ut mortem citiùs venire credas,
  Scito jam capitis perîsse partem.

2   person

person entered very far into the regions and possession
of death: and we have many more of the same signification; grey hairs, rotten teeth, dim eyes, trembling joints, short breath, stiff limbs, wrinkled skin,
short memory, decayed appetite. Every day's necessity calls for a reparation of that portion which death
fed on all night when we lay in his lap, and slept
in his outer chambers. The very spirits of a man
prey upon the daily portion of bread and flesh, and
every meal is a rescue from one death, and lays up
for another: and while we think a thought we die;
and the clock strikes, and reckons on our portion of
eternity; we form our words with the breath of our
nostrils, we have the less to live upon for every word
we speak.

Thus nature calls us to meditate of death by those
things which are the instruments of acting it: and God
by all the variety of his providence makes us see
death every where, in all variety of circumstances,
and dressed up for all the fancies, and the expectation
of every single person. Nature hath given us one
harvest every year, but death hath two: and the spring
and the autumn send throngs of men and women to
charnel-houses; and all the summer long men are
recovering from their evils of the spring, till the dog-
days come, and then the Syrian star makes the summer
deadly; and the fruits of autumn are laid up for all
the year's provision, and the man that gathers them
eats and surfeits, and dies and needs them not, and
himself is laid up for eternity; and he that escapes till
winter, only stays for another opportunity, which the
distempers of that quarter minister to him with great
variety. Thus death reigns in all the portions of our
time. The autumn with its fruits provides disorders
for us, and the winter's cold turns them into sharp
diseases, and the spring brings flowers to strew our
hearse, and the summer gives green turf and brambles
to bind upon our graves. Calentures and surfeit,

cold

cold and agues, are the four quarters of the year, and all minister to death; and you can go no whither but you tread upon a dead man's bones.

The wild fellow in *Petronius* that escaped upon a broken table from the furies of a shipwreck, as he was sunning himself upon the rocky shore, espied a man rolled upon his floating bed of waves, ballasted with sand in the folds of his garment, and carried by his civil enemy the sea towards the shore to find a grave: and it cast him into some sad thoughts; that peradventure this man's wife in some part of the continent*, safe and warm, looks next month for the good man's return; or it may be his son knows nothing of the tempest; or his father thinks of that affectionate kiss which still is warm upon the good old man's cheek ever since he took a kind farewell, and he weeps with joy to think how blessed he shall be when his beloved boy returns into the circle of his father's arms. These are the thoughts of mortals, this the end and sum of all their designs: a dark night and an ill guide, a boisterous sea and a broken cable, an hard rock and a rough wind, dashed in pieces the fortune of a whole family, and they that shall weep loudest for the accident, are not yet entered into the storm, and yet have suffered shipwreck. Then looking upon the carcase, he knew it, and found it to be the master of the ship, who the day before cast up the accounts of his patrimony and his trade, and named the day when he thought to be at home. See how the man swims who was so angry two days since; his passions are becalmed with the storm, his accounts cast up, his cares at an end, his voyage done, and his gains are the strange events of death; which whether they be good or evil,

* Navigationes longas, et pererratis litoribus alienis, seros in patriam reditus proponimus, militiam, et castrensium laborum tarda manu pretia, procurationes, officiorûmque per officia processus, cùm interim ad latus mors est; quæ quoniam nunquam cogitatur nisi aliena, subinde nobis ingerantur mortalitatis exempla, non diutiùs quàm miramur hæsura. *Seneca.*

the

the men that are alive seldom trouble themselves concerning the interest of the dead.

But seas alone do not break our vessel in pieces:
every where we may be shipwrecked. A valiant general, when he is to reap the harvest of his crowns and
triumphs, fights unprosperously, or falls into a fever
with joy and wine, and changes his laurel into cypress,
his triumphant chariot to an hearse; dying the night
before he was appointed to perish in the drunkenness
of his festival joys. It was a sad arrest of the loose-
nesses and wilder feasts of the *French* court, when their
King (*Henry* II.) was killed really by the sportive
image of a fight. And many brides have died under
the hands of paranymphs and maidens dressing them
for uneasy joy, the new and undiscerned chains of
marriage, according to the saying of *Ben-sirach* the wise
Jew, " *The bride went into her chamber, and knew not
what should befal her there.*" Some have been paying
their vows, and giving thanks for a prosperous return to
their own house, and the roof hath descended upon
their heads, and turned their loud religion into the
deeper silence of a grave. And how many teeming
mothers have rejoiced over their swelling wombs, and
pleased themselves in becoming the channels of blessing to a family; and the midwife hath quickly bound
their heads and feet, and carried them forth to* burial?
Or else the birth-day of an heir hath seen the coffin of
the father brought into the house, and the divided
mother hath been forced to travail twice, with a painful birth, and a sadder death.

There is no state, no accident, no circumstance of
our life, but it hath been soured by some sad instance
of a dying friend: a friendly meeting often ends in
some sad mischance, and makes an eternal parting:

* Quia lex eadem manet omnes,
Gemitum dare sorte sub una,
Cognataque funera nobis
Aliena in morte dolere.
Prud. Hymn. exequ. defunctor.

B 4   and

and when the poet *Æschylus* was sitting under the walls of his house, an eagle hovering over his bald head, mistook it for a stone, and let fall his oyster, hoping there to break the shell, but pierced the poor man's skull.

Death meets us every where, and is procured by every instrument, and in all chances, and enters in at many doors; by violence and secret influence, by the aspect of a star and the stink of a mist, by the emissions of a cloud and the meeting of a vapour, by the fall of a chariot and the stumbling at a stone, by a full meal or an empty stomach, by watching at the wine, or by watching at prayers, by the sun or the moon, by a heat or a cold, by sleepless nights or sleeping days, by water * frozen into the hardness and sharpness of a dagger, or water thawed into the floods of a river, by a hair or a raisin, by violent motion or sitting still, by severity or dissolution, by God's mercy or God's anger, by every thing in providence and every thing in manners, by every thing in nature †, and every thing in chance. *Eripitur persona, manet res:* we take pains to heap up things useful to our life, and get our death in the purchase; and the person is snatched away, and the goods remain. And all this is the law and constitution of nature, it is a punishment to our sins, the unalterable event of providence, and the decree of heaven. The chains that confine us to this condition are strong as destiny, and immutable as the eternal laws of God.

I have conversed with some men who rejoiced in the death or calamity of others, and accounted it as a judgment upon them for being on the other side, and against them in the contention; but within the

---

* Aut ubi mors non est, si jugulatis aquæ? *Martial.*

† ——————————— Curret mortalibus ævum,
Nec nasci bis posse datur: fugit hora rapitque
Tartareus torrens, ac secum ferre sub umbras,
Si qua animo placuere, negat. *Sil. Ital.* l. 15.

revolution

revolution of a few months the same man met with a more uneasy and unhandsome death: which when I saw, I wept, and was afraid; for I knew that it must be so with all men *, for we also shall die, and end our quarrels and contentions by passing to a final sentence.

SECT. II.

The Consideration reduced to Practice.

IT will be very material to our best and noblest purposes, if we represent this scene of change and sorrow a little more dressed up in circumstances, for so we shall be more apt to practise those rules, the doctrine of which is consequent to this consideration. It is a mighty change that is made by the death of every person, and it is visible to us who are alive. Reckon but from the sprightfulness of youth, and the fair cheeks and the full eyes of childhood, from the vigorousness and strong flexure of the joints of five and twenty, to the hollowness and dead paleness, to the loathsomeness and horror of a three days' burial, and we shall perceive the distance to be very great and very strange. But so I have seen a rose newly springing from the clefts of its hood, and at first it was fair as the morning, and full with the dew of heaven, as a lamb's fleece: but when a ruder breath had forced open its virgin modesty, and dismantled its too youthful and unripe retirements, it began to put on darkness, and to decline to softness and the symptoms of a sickly age; it bowed the head, and broke its stalk, and at night having lost some of its leaves, and all its

* Τέθναθι κῆρα δ' ἐγὼ τότε δέξομαι, ὁππότε κεν δὴ
Ζεὺς ἐθέλῃ τελέσαι. Il. χ'.

beauty,

beauty, it fell into the portion of weeds and out-worn faces. The same is the portion of every man and every woman; the heritage of worms and serpents, rottenness and cold dishonour, and our beauty so changed, that our acquaintance quickly know us not; and that change mingled with so much horror, or else meets so with our fears and weak discoursings, that they who six hours ago tended upon us, either with charitable or ambitious services, cannot without some regret stay in the room alone where the body lies stripped of its life and honour. I have read of a fair young *German* gentleman, who living, often refused to be pictured, but put off the importunity of his friends' desire by giving way that after a few days burial, they might send a painter to his vault, and, if they saw cause for it, draw the image of *his death unto the life.***** They did so, and found his face half eaten, and his midriff and back bone full of serpents; and so he stands pictured amongst his armed ancestors. So does the fairest beauty change, and it will be as bad with you and me; and then, what servants shall we have to wait upon us in the grave? what friends to visit us? what officious people to cleanse away the moist and unwholesome cloud reflected upon our faces from the sides of the weeping vaults, which are the longest weepers for our funeral?

This discourse will be useful, if we consider and practise by the following rules and considerations respectively.

1. All the rich and all the covetous men in the world will perceive, and all the world will perceive for them, that it is but an ill recompence for all their cares, that by this time all that shall be left will be

---

* Anceps forma bonum mortalibus,
Exigui donum breve temporis:
Ut fulgor teneris, qui radiat genis,
Momento rapitur, nulláque non dies
Formosi spolium corporis abstulit.   *Seneca.*

this *, that the neighbours shall say, He died a rich man: and yet his wealth will not profit him in the grave, but hugely swell the sad accounts of doomsday. And he that kills the Lord's people with unjust or ambitious wars for an unrewarding interest, shall have this character, that he threw away all the days of his †life, that one year might be reckoned with his name, and computed by his reign or consulship: and many ‡ men, by great labours and affronts, many indignities and crimes, labour only for a pompous epitaph, and a loud title upon their marble §; whilst those into whose possessions the heirs or kindred are entered are forgotten, and lie unregarded as their ashes, and without concernment or relation, as the turf upon the face of their grave. A man may read a sermon, the best and most passionate that ever man preached, if he shall but enter into the sepulchres of kings. In the same Escurial where the *Spanish* princes live in greatness and power, and decree war or peace, they have wisely placed a cemetery where their ashes and their glory shall sleep till time shall be no more: and where our kings have been crowned, their ancestors lay interred, and they must walk over their grandsire's head to take his crown. There is an acre sown with royal seed, the copy of the greatest change, from rich to naked, from ceiled roofs to arched coffins, from *living like Gods* to *die like men.* There is enough to cool the flames of

---

* Rape, congere, aufer, posside; relinquendum est. *Martial.*

† Annos omnes prodegit, ut ex eo annus unus numeretur, et per mille indignitates laboravit in titulum sepulchri. *Seneca.*

‡ Jam eorum præbendas alii possident, et nescio utrum de iis cogitant. *Gerson.*

§ ———— Me veterum frequens
Memphis Pyramidum docet.
Me pressæ tumulo lacryma gloriæ,
Me projecta jacentium
Passim per populos busta Quiritium,
Et vilis Zephyri jocus
Jactati cineres, et procerum rogi,
Fumantúmque cadavera
Regnorum, tacito, Rufe, silentio,
Mœstum multa monent. *Lyric. Cas.* l. 2. od. 27.

lust,

lust, to abate the heights of pride, to appease the itch of covetous desires, to sully and dash out the dissembling colours of a lustful, artificial, and imaginary beauty. There the warlike and the peaceful, the fortunate and the miserable, the beloved and the despised princes mingle their dust, and pay down their symbol of mortality, and tell all the world that, when we die, our ashes shall be equal to kings, and our accounts easier, and our pains for our crowns shall be less. To my apprehension, it is a sad record which is left by *Athenæus* concerning *Ninus* the great *Assyrian* monarch, whose life and death is summed up in these words : " *Ninus* the *Assyrian* had an ocean of gold, and other riches more than the sand in the *Caspian* sea ; he never saw the stars, and perhaps he never desired it ; he never stirred up the holy fire among the *Magi*, nor touched his God with the sacred rod according to the laws ; he never offered sacrifice, nor worshipped the Deity, nor administered justice, nor spake to his people, nor numbered them : but he was most valiant to eat and drink, and having mingled his wines, he threw the rest upon the stones. This man is dead : behold his sepulchre, and now hear where *Ninus* is. Sometimes I was *Ninus*, and drew the breath of a living man, but now am nothing but clay. I have nothing but what I did eat, and what I served to myself in lust [that was and is all my portion] : the wealth with which I was [esteemed] blessed, my enemies meeting together shall bear away, as the mad *Thyades* carry a raw goat. I am gone to hell ; and when I went thither, I neither carried gold, nor horse, nor silver chariot. I that wore a mitre, am now a little heap of dust." * I know not any thing that can better represent the evil condition of a wicked man, or a changing greatness. From the

* Ἀθανασία δ' ἐκ ἔςιν ἐδ' ἂν συναγάγῃς
  Τὰ Ταντάλɐ τάλαντ' ἐκεῖνα λεγόμενα,
  Ἀλλ' ἀποθανῇ, καὶ ταῦτα καταλείψεις τινί.   Menand.

greatest

greatest secular dignity to dust and ashes his nature bears him, and from thence to hell his sins carry him, and there he shall be for ever under the dominion of chains and devils, wrath and intolerable calamity. This is the reward of an unsanctified condition, and a greatness ill gotten or ill administered.

2. Let no man extend *his thoughts*, or let *his hopes* wander towards future and far-distant events and accidental contingencies. This day is mine and yours, but *ye know not what shall be on the * morrow :* and every morning creeps out of a dark cloud, leaving behind it an ignorance and silence deep as midnight, and undiscerned as are the phantasms that make a Chrisome child to smile; so that we cannot discern what comes hereafter, unless we had a light from heaven brighter than the vision of an angel, even the spirit of prophecy. † Without revelation we cannot tell whether we shall eat to-morrow, or whether a squinancy shall choke us : and it is written in the unrevealed folds of divine predestination, that many who are this day alive shall to-morrow be laid upon the cold earth, and the women shall weep over their shroud, and dress them for their funeral. St. *James*, in his epistle, notes the folly of some men, his contemporaries, who were so impatient of the event of to-morrow, or the accidents of next year, or the good or evils of old age, that they would consult astrologers and witches, oracles and devils, what should befal them the next calends ; what should be the event of such a voyage, what God had written in his book concerning the success of battles, the election of emperors, the heir of families, the price of merchandize, the return of the *Tyrian* fleet, the rate of *Sidonian* carpets : and as they were taught by the crafty and lying demons, so they would expect the issue;

---

* Τὸ σήμερον μέλει μοι, Τὸ δ᾽ αὔριον τίς οἶδε.   Anacr.

† Quid sit futurum cras, fuge quærere, et
   Quem sors dierum cunque dabit, lucro
   Appone ————————— *Horat.*

and

and oftentimes by disposing their affairs in order towards such events, really did produce some little accidents according to their expectation; and that made
them trust the oracles in greater things, and in all.
Against this he opposes his counsel, that we should
not search after forbidden records, much less by uncertain signification: for whatsoever is disposed to
happen by the order of natural causes, or civil counsels,
may be rescinded by a peculiar decree of Providence *, or be prevented by the death of the interested
persons; who, while their hopes are full, and their
causes conjoined, and the work brought forward, and
the sickle put into the harvest †, and the first-fruits
offered and ready to be eaten, even then if they put
forth their hand to an event that stands but at the door,
at that door their body may be carried forth to burial,
before the expectation shall enter into fruition. When
Richilda, the widow of *Albert* earl of *Ebersberg*, had
feasted the Emperor *Henry* III. and petitioned in
behalf of her nephew *Welpho* for some lands formerly
possessed by the earl her husband; just as the emperor held out his hand to signify his consent, the cham-
ber-floor suddenly fell under him, and *Richilda* falling upon the edge of a bathing vessel, was bruised
to death, and stayed not to see her nephew sleep in
those lands which the emperor was reaching forth to
her, and placed at the door of restitution.

3. As our *hopes* ‡ must be confined, so must our *designs:* let us not project long designs, crafty plots, and
diggings so deep, that the intrigues of a design shall
never be unfolded till our grand-children have for-

---

* ————————— Nec Babylonios
　　Tentâris numeros, ut melius quicquid erit pati,
　　Seu pleures hyemes, seu tribuit Jupiter ultimam. *Horat.*
† Incertam frustra mortales funeris horam
　　Quæritis, et quâ sit mors aditura viâ.
　　Pœna minor certam subitò perferre ruinam;
　　Quod timeas gravius sustinuisse diu. *Catul.* eleg. 1. 29.
‡ Certa amittimus dum incerta petimus: atque hoc evenit in labore atque
in dolore, ut mors obrepat interim. *Plaut. Pseud.*

gotten

gotten our virtues or our vices. The work of our soul is cut short, facil, sweet, and plain, and fitted to the small portions of our shorter life; and as we must not trouble our inquiry, so neither must we intricate our labour and purposes, with what we shall never enjoy. This rule does not forbid us to plant orchards, which shall feed our nephews with their fruit; for by such provisions they do something towards an imaginary immortality, and do charity to their relatives: but such projects are reproved which discompose our present duty by long and future designs *; such which, by casting our labours to events at distance, make us less to remember our death standing at the door. It is fit for a man to work for his day's wages, or to contrive for the hire of a week, or to lay a train to make provisions for such a time as is within our eye, and in our duty, and within the usual periods of man's life; for whatsoever is made necessary, is also made prudent: but while we plot and busy ourselves in the toils of an ambitious war, or the levies of a great estate, night enters in upon us, and tells all the world how like fools we lived, and how deceived and miserably we died. *Seneca* tells of *Senecio Cornelius,* a man crafty in getting, and tenacious in holding a great estate, and one who was as diligent in the care of his body as of his money, curious of his health as of his possessions, that he all day long attended upon his sick and dying friend; but when he went away was quickly comforted, supped merrily, went to bed cheerfully, and on a sudden being surprised by a squinancy, scarce drew his breath until the morning, but by that time died, being snatched from the torrent of his fortune, and the swelling tide of wealth, and a likely hope bigger than the necessities of ten

---

* Quid brevi fortes jaculamur ævo
Multa? ————
Jam te premet nox, fabulæque Manes,
Et domus exilis Plutonia.————*Horat.*

men.

men. This accident was much noted then in *Rome,* because it happened in so great a fortune, and in the midst of wealthy designs; and presently it made wise men to consider, how imprudent a person he is who disposes of ten years to come, when he is not lord of to-morrow.

4. Though we must not look so far off*, and pry abroad, yet we must be busy near at hand; we must with all arts of the spirit seize upon the present, because it passes from us while we speak, and because in it all our certainty does consist. We must take our waters as out of a torrent and sudden shower, which will quickly cease dropping from above, and quickly cease running in our channels here below : this instant will never return again, and yet it may be this instant will declare or secure the fortune of a whole eternity. The old Greeks and Romans taught us the prudence of this rule, but Christianity teaches us the religion of it. † They so seized upon the present, that they would lose nothing of the day's pleasure. *Let us eat and drink, for to-morrow we shall die ;* that was their philosophy: and at their solemn feasts they would talk of death to heighten the present drinking, and that they might warm their veins with a fuller chalice, as knowing the drink that was poured upon their graves would be cold and without relish. *Break the beds, drink your wine, crown your heads with roses, and besmear your curled locks with nard ; for God bids you to remember death* ‡ : so the epigrammatist speaks the sense of their drunken principles. Something towards this signification is that of Solomon ; *there is nothing better for a man than that he should eat and drink, and that he should make his soul enjoy good in his labour ; for that is his portion ; for who shall bring him to see that which shall be after him ?* § But

---

* Ille enim ex futuro suspenditur, cui irritum est præsens. *Seneca.*
† Ætate fruere, mobili cursu fugit. *Seneca.*
‡ *Martial,* l. 2. epig. 59. § Eccles. ii. 24. iii. 22. &c.

although

although he concludes all this to be vanity, yet because it was the best thing that was then commonly known *, that they should seize upon the present with a temperate use of permitted pleasures, I had reason to say that Christianity taught us to turn this into religion. For he that by a present and a constant holiness secures the present, and makes it useful to his noblest purposes, he turns his condition into his best advantage, by making his unavoidable fate become his necessary religion.

To the purpose of this rule is that collect of *Tuscan* hieroglyphics which we have from *Gabriel Simeon.* " Our life is very short, beauty is a cozenage, money is false and fugitive; empire is odious, and hated by them that have it not, and uneasy to them that have; victory is always uncertain, and peace most commonly is but a fraudulent bargain; old age is miserable, death is the period, and is a happy one, if it be not soured by the sins of our life: but nothing continues but the effects of that wisdom which employs the present time in the acts of a holy religion, and a peaceable conscience." For they make us to live even beyond our funerals, embalmed in the spices and odours of a good name, and entombed in the grave of the Holy *Jesus,* where we shall be dressed for a blessed resurrection to the state of angels and beatified spirits.

5. Since we stay not here, being people but of a day's abode, and our age is like that of a fly, and contemporary with a gourd, we must look somewhere else for an abiding city, a place in another country to

---

* Amici dum vivimus, vivamus.

Πῖνε λέγει τὸ γλύμμα, καὶ ἔσθιε, καὶ περίκεισο
Ἄνθεα τοιαῦτοι γινόμεθ' ἐξαπίνης.

Hoc etiam faciunt ubi discubuere, tenentque
Pocula sæpe homines, et inumbrant ora coronis,
Ex animo ut dicant, brevis est hic fructus homullis;
Jam fuerit, neque post unquam revocare licebit.

Lucret. lib. iii.

fix our house in, whose walls and foundations is God, where we must find rest, or else be restless for ever. For whatsoever ease * we can have or fancy here, is shortly to be changed into sadness or tediousness : it goes away too soon, like the periods of our life ; or stays too long, like the sorrows of a sinner : its own weariness, or a contrary disturbance, is its load ; or it is eased by its revolution into vanity and forgetfulness : and where either there is sorrow or an end of joy, there can be no true felicity; which, because it must be had by some instrument, and in some period of our durations, we must carry up our affections to the mansions prepared for us above, where eternity is the measure, felicity is the state, angels are the company, the Lamb is the light, and God is the portion and in-heritance.

SECT. III.

Rules and Spiritual Arts of lengthening our days, and to take off the objection of a short time.

In the accounts of a man's life we do not reckon that portion of days in which we are shut up in the prison of the womb ; we tell our years from the day of our birth : and the same reason that makes our reckoning to stay so long, says also that then it begins too soon. For then we are beholden to others to make the account for us : for we know not of a long time, whether we be alive or no, having but some little approaches and symptoms of a life. To feed, and sleep,

---

* Quis sapiens bono
 Confidat fragili? dum licet, utere.
 Tempus sed tacitum subruit, horâque
 Semper præteritâ deterior subit. *Senec. Hippol.*

                                            and

and move a little and imperfectly, is the state of an unborn child; and when he is born, he does no more for a good while: and what is it that shall make him to be esteemed to live the life of a man? and when shall that account begin? For we should be loath to have the accounts of our age taken by the measures of a beast; and fools and distracted persons are reckoned as *civilly dead;* they are no parts of the commonwealth, nor subject to laws, but secured by them in charity, and kept from violence as a man keeps his ox: and a third part of our life is spent before we enter into an higher order, into the state of a man.

2. Neither must we think that the life of a man begins when he can feed himself, or walk alone, when he can fight or beget his like; for so he is contemporary with a camel or a cow: but he is first a man, when he comes to a certain steady use of reason, according to his proportion; and when that is, all the world of men cannot tell precisely. Some are called *at age* at fourteen, some at one-and-twenty, some never; but all men late enough, for the life a man comes upon him slowly and insensibly. But as when the sun approaching towards the gates of the morning, he first opens a little eye of heaven, and sends away the spirits of darkness, and gives light to a cock, and calls up the lark to matins, and by and by gilds the fringes of a cloud, and peeps over the eastern hills, thrusting out his golden horns, like those which decked the brows of *Moses* when he was forced to wear a veil, because himself had seen the face of God; and still while a man tells the story, the sun gets up higher, till he shews a fair face and a full light, and then he shines one whole day, under a cloud often, and sometimes weeping great and little showers, and sets quickly: so is a man's reason and his life. He first begins to perceive himself to see or taste, making little reflections upon his actions of sense, and can discourse of flies and dogs, shells and play, horses and liberty:

c 2

but

but when he is strong enough to enter into arts and little institutions, he is at first entertained with trifles and impertinent things, not because he needs them, but because his understanding is no bigger, and little images of things are laid before him, like a cockboat to a whale, only to play withal : but before a man comes to be wise, he is half dead with gouts and consumption, with catarrhs and aches, with sore eyes and a worn-out body. So that if we must not reckon the life of a man but by the accounts of his reason, he is long before his soul be dressed : and he is not to be called a man without a wise and an adorned soul, a soul at least furnished with what is necessary towards his well-being : but by that time his soul is thus furnished, his body is decayed ; and then you can hardly reckon him to be alive, when his body is possessed by so many degrees of death.

3. But there is yet another arrest. At first he wants strength of body, and then he wants the use of reason, and when that is come, it is ten to one but he stops by the impediments of vice, and wants the strengths of the *spirit ;* and we know that *Body,* and *Soul,* and *Spirit,* are the constituent parts of every Christian man. And now let us consider what that thing is which we call *years of discretion.* The young man is past his tutors, and arrived at the bondage of a caitive spirit ; he is run from discipline, and is let loose to passion ; the man by this time hath wit enough to choose his vice, to act his lust, to court his mistress, to talk confidently, and ignorantly, and perpetually, to despise his betters, to deny nothing to his appetite, to do things that when he is indeed a man he must for ever be ashamed of : For this is all the discretion that most men shew in the first stage of their manhood : they can discern good from evil ; and they prove their skill by leaving all that is good, and wallowing in the evils of folly and an unbridled appetite. And by this time the young man hath contracted vicious habits, and is a beast in manners, and therefore it will not be fitting to reckon the
beginning

beginning of his life; he is a fool in his understanding, and that is a sad death; and he is dead in trespasses and sins, and that is a sadder: so that he hath no life but a natural, the life of a beast or a tree; in all other capacities he is dead, he neither hath the intellectual nor the spiritual life, neither the life of a man nor of a Christian; and this sad truth lasts too long. For old age seizes upon most men while they still retain the minds of boys, and vicious youth, doing actions from principles of great folly and a mighty ignorance, admiring things useless and hurtful, and filling up all the dimensions of their abode with businesses of empty affairs, being at leisure to attend no virtue. They cannot pray, because they are busy, and because they are passionate; they cannot communicate, because they have quarrels and intrigues of perplexed causes, complicated hostilities, and things of the world; and therefore they cannot attend to the things of God: little considering that they must find a time to die in, when death comes, they must be at leisure for that. Such men are like sailors loosing from a port, and tost immediately with a perpetual tempest lasting till their cordage crack, and either they sink, or return back again to the same place: they did not make a voyage, though they were long at sea. The business and impertinent affairs of most men steal all their time, and they are restless in a foolish motion: but this is not the progress of a man *; he is no farther advanced in the course of a life, though he reckons many years; for still his soul is childish, and trifling like an untaught boy.

If the parts of this sad complaint find their remedy, we have by the same instruments also cured the evils and the vanity of a short life; therefore,

1. Be infinitely curious you do not set back your life in the accounts of God, by the intermingling of crimi-

---

* Bis jam Consul trigesimus instat. Et numerat paucos vix tua vita dies.

nal

nal actions, or the contracting vicious habits. There
are some vices which carry a sword in their hand,
and cut a man off before his time. There is *a sword
of the Lord,* and there is *a sword of a man,* and there
is *a sword of the devil.* Every vice of our own managing in the matter of carnality, of lust or rage, ambition or revenge, is a sword of Satan put into the hands
of a man: these are the destroying angels; sin is the
Apollyon, the *destroyer* that is gone out, not *from the
Lord,* but *from the tempter;* and we hug the poison,
and twist willingly with the vipers, till they bring us
into the regions of an irrecoverable sorrow. We use
to reckon persons as good as dead, if they have lost
their limbs and their teeth, and are confined to an
hospital, and converse with none but surgeons and
physicians, mourners and divines, those *Pollinctores,*
the dressers of bodies and souls to funeral: but it is
worse when the soul, the principle of life, is employed wholly in the offices of death: and that man was
worse than dead of whom *Seneca* tells, that being a
rich fool, when he was lifted up from the baths and set
into a soft couch, asked his slaves, *An ego jam sedeo?*
Do I now sit? the beast was drowned in sensuality
and the death of his soul, that whether he did sit or
no, he was to believe another. Idleness and every
vice is as much of death as a long disease is, or the expense of ten years: and *she that lives in pleasure is
dead while she liveth,* (saith the apostle,) and it is the
style of the Spirit concerning wicked persons, *they are
dead in trespasses and sins.* For as every sensual
pleasure, and every day of idleness and useless living
lops off a little branch from our short life; so every
deadly sin and every habitual vice does quite destroy
us: but innocence leaves us in our natural portions and
perfect period; we lose nothing of our life, if we lose
nothing of our soul's health; and therefore he that
would live a full age must avoid a sin, as he would
decline the regions of death, and the dishonours of the
grave

                                    2. If

2. If we would have our life lengthened*, let us begin betimes to live in the accounts of reason and sober
counsels, of religion and the spirit, and then we shall
have no reason to complain that our abode on earth
is so short: many men find it long enough, and indeed it is so to all senses. But when we spend in
waste what God hath given us in plenty, when we
sacrifice our youth to folly, our manhood to lust
and rage, our old age to covetousness and irreligion,
not beginning to live till we are to die, designing that
time to virtue which indeed is infirm to every thing
and profitable to nothing : then we make our lives
short, and lust runs away with all the vigorous and
healthful part of it, and pride and animosity steal the
manly portion, and craftiness and interest possess
old age; *velut ex pleno et abundanti perdimus,* we
spend as if we had too much time, and knew not what
to do with it, we fear every thing, like weak and silly
mortals ; and desire strangely, and greedily, as if we
were immortal : we complain our life is short, and yet
we throw away much of it, and are weary of many of
its parts : we complain the day is long, and the night is
long and we want company, and seek out arts to drive
the time away, and then weep because it is gone too
soon. But so the treasure of the *capitol* is but a small
estate when *Cæsar* comes to finger it, and to pay with
it all his legions ; and the revenue of all *Egypt* and
the eastern provinces was but a little sum, when they
were to support the luxury of *Mark Antony*, and feed
the riot of *Cleopatra.* But a thousand crowns is a vast
proportion to be spent in the cottage of a frugal person, or to feed a hermit. Just so is our life : it is too
short to serve the ambition of a haughty prince, or
an usurping rebel ; too little time to purchase great
wealth, to satisfy the pride of a vain-glorious fool, to

---

* Ædepol, proinde ut bene diu vivitur. *Plaut. Trinum.*
Non accepimus brevem vitam, sed fecimus; nec inopes ejus, sed prodigi
sumus. *Seneca.*

c 4

trample

trample upon all the enemies of our just or unjust interest: but for the obtaining virtue, for the purchase of sobriety and modesty, for the actions of religion, God gave us time sufficient, if we make *the outgoings of the morning and evening*, that is, our infancy and old age, to be taken into the computations of a man; which we may see in the following particulars.

1. If our childhood, being first consecrated by a forward baptism, be seconded by a holy education, and a complying obedience; if our youth be chaste and temperate, modest and industrious, proceeding through a prudent and sober manhood* to a religious old age; then we have lived our whole duration, and shall never die, but be changed in a just time to the preparations of a better and an immortal life.

2. If besides the ordinary returns of our prayers, and periodical and festival solemnities, and our seldom communions, we would allow to religion and the studies of wisdom those great shares that are trifled away upon vain sorrow, foolish mirth, troublesome ambition, busy covetousness, watchful lust, and impertinent amours, and balls, and revellings, and banquets, all that which was spent viciously, and all that time that lay fallow and without employment, our life would quickly amount to a great sum. *Tostatus Abulensis* was a very painful person, and a great clerk, and in the days of his manhood he wrote so many books, and they not ill ones, that the world computed a sheet for every day of his life; I suppose they meant, after he came to the use of reason and the state of a man: and *John Scotus* died about the two-and-thirtieth year of his age; and yet besides his public disputations, his daily lectures of divinity in public and private, the

---

* Sed potes, Publi, geminare magnâ
      Secula famâ
Quem sui raptum gemuère cives,
Hic diu vixit. Sibi quisque famam
Scribat hæredem : rapiunt avaræ
      Cætera Lunis.

books

books that he wrote, being lately collected and printed at *Lyons*, do equal the number of volumes of any two of the most voluminous fathers of the *Latin* church. Every man is not enabled to such employments, but every man is called and enabled to the works of a sober and religious life; and there are many saints of God that can reckon as many volumes of religion, and mountains of piety, as those others did of good books. St. *Ambrose* (and I think from his example, St. *Augustine*) divided every day into three *tertias* of employment: eight hours he spent in the necessities of nature and recreation; eight hours in charity and doing assistance to others, dispatching their businesses, reconciling their enmities, reproving their vices, correcting their errors, instructing their ignorances, transacting the affairs of his diocese; and the other eight hours he spent in study and prayer. If we were thus minute and curious in the spending our time, it is impossible but our life would seem very long. For so I have seen an amorous person tell the minutes of his absence from his fancied joy, and while he told the sands of his hour-glass, or the throbs and little beatings of his watch, by dividing an hour into so many members, he spun out its length by number, and so translated a day into the tediousness of a month. And if we tell our days by canonical hours of prayer, our weeks by a constant revolution of fasting days, or days of special devotion, and over all these draw a black cypress, a veil of penitential sorrow and severe mortification, we shall soon answer the calumny and objection of a short life. He that governs the day and divides the hours, hastens from the eyes and observation of a merry sinner; but loves to stand still, and behold, and tell the sighs, and number the groans, and sadly-delicious accents of a grieved penitent. It is a vast work that any man may do, if he never be idle: and it is a huge way that a man may go in virtue, if he never goes out of his way by a vicious habit or a great crime;

crime; and he that perpetually reads good books, if his parts be answerable, will have a huge stock of knowledge. It is so in all things else. Strive not to forget your time, and suffer none of it to pass undiscerned; and then measure your life, and tell me how you find the measure of its abode. However, the time we live is worth the money we pay for it; and therefore it is not to be thrown away.

3. When vicious men are dying, and scared with the affrighting truths of an evil conscience, they would give all the world for a year, for a month; nay, we read of some that called out with amazement, *inducias usque ad manè, truce but till the morning :* and if that year or some few months were given, those men think they could do miracles in it. And let us a while suppose what *Dives* would have done, if he had been loosed from the pains of hell, and permitted to live on earth one year: would all the pleasures of the world have kept him one hour from the temple? would he not perpetually have been under the hands of priests, or at the feet of the doctors, or by *Moses's* chair, or attending as near the altar as he could get, or relieving poor *Lazarus*, or praying to God, and crucifying all his sins? I have read of a melancholic person who saw hell but in a dream or vision, and the amazement was such, that he would have chosen ten times to die rather than feel again so much of that horror: and such a person cannot be fancied but that he would spend a year in such holiness, that the religion of a few months would equal the devotion of many years, even of a good man. Let us but compute the proportions. If we should spend all our years of reason so as such a person would spend that one, can it be thought that life would be short and trifling in which he had performed such a religion, served God with so much holiness, mortified sin with so great a labour, purchased virtue at such a rate, and so rare an industry? It must needs be that

I   such

such a man must die when he ought to die, and be like ripe and pleasant fruit falling from a fair tree, and gathered into baskets for the planter's use. He that hath done all his business, and is begotten to a glorious hope by the seed of an immortal spirit *, can never die too soon, nor live too long.

Xerxes wept sadly when he saw his army of 2,300,000 men, because he considered that within an hundred years all the youth of that army should be dust and ashes: and yet, as *Seneca* well observes of him, he was the man that should bring them to their graves, and he consumed all that army in two years, for whom he feared and wept the death after an hundred. Just so we do all. We complain that within thirty or forty years, a little more, or a great deal less, we shall descend again into the bowels of our mother, and that our life is too short for any great employment; and yet we throw away five-and-thirty years of our forty, and the remaining five we divide between art and nature, civility and customs, necessity and convenience, prudent counsels and religion: but the portion of the last is little and contemptible, and yet that little is all that we can prudently account of our lives. We bring that fate and that death near us, of whose approach we are so sadly apprehensive.

4. In taking the accounts of your life do not reckon by great distances, and by the periods of pleasure, or the satisfaction of your hopes, or the stating your desires; but let every intermedial day and hour pass with observation. He that reckons he hath lived but so many harvests †, thinks they come not often enough, and that they go away too soon. Some lose the day

---

* Huic neque defungi visum est, nec vivere pulchrum;
Cura fuit rectè vivere, sicque mori.

† In spe viventibus proximum quodcunque tempus elabitur, subitque aviditas temporis, et miserrimus, atque miserrima omnia efficiens, metus mortis.

Ex hac autem indigentia timor nascitur, et cupiditas futuri exedens animum. *Seneca.*

with

with longing for the night, and the night in waiting for
the day. Hope and phantastic expectations spend
much of our lives; and while with passion we look for
a coronation, or the death of an enemy, or a day of
joy, passing from fancy to possession without any intermedial notices, we throw away a precious year, and
use it but as the burthen of our time, fit to be pared
off and thrown away, that we may come at those little
pleasures which first steal our hearts, and then steal
our life.

5. A strict course of piety is the way to prolong
our lives in the natural sense, and to add good portions to the number of our years: and sin is sometimes by natural causality, very often by the anger
of God, and the divine judgment, a cause of sudden
and untimely death. Concerning which I shall add
nothing (to what I have somewhere else said * of this
article) but only the observation † of *Epiphanius;*
that for 3332 years, and even to the twentieth age, there
was not one example of a son that died before
his father, but the course of nature was kept, that
he who was first-born in the descending line did first
die, (I speak of natural death, and therefore *Abel* cannot be opposed to this observation,) till that *Terah,* the
father of *Abraham,* taught the people a new religion,
to make images of clay and worship them; and concerning him it was first remarked, that *Haran died
before his father Terah in the land of his nativity:*
God by an unheard-of judgment, and rare accident,
punishing his newly-invented crime, by the untimely
death of his son.

6. But if I shall describe a living man, a man that
hath that life that distinguishes him from a fowl or a
bird, that which gives him a capacity next to angels;
we shall find that even a good man lives not long because it is long before he is born to this life, and longer

---

* *Life of Christ,* Par. iii. Disc. 14.   † Lib. i. Tom. i. Panar. Sect. 6.

yet

yet before he hath a man's growth.* " He that can look upon death, and see its face with the same countenance with which he hears its story; that can endure all the labours of his life with his soul supporting his body; that can equally despise riches when he hath them, and when he hath them not; that is not sadder if they lie in his neighbour's trunks, nor more brag if they shine round about his own walls; he that is neither moved with good fortune coming to him, nor going from him; that can look upon another man's lands evenly and pleasedly as if they were his own, and yet look upon his own and use them too, just as if they were another man's that neither spends his goods prodigally and like a fool, nor yet keeps them avariciously and like a wretch; that weighs not benefits by weight and number, but by the mind and circumstances of him that gives them; that never thinks his charity expensive, if a worthy person be the receiver; he that does nothing for opinion's sake, but every thing for conscience, being as curious of his thoughts as of his actings in markets and theatres, and is as much in awe of himself as of the whole assembly; he that knows God looks on, and contrives his secret affairs as in the presence of God and his holy angels; that eats and drinks because he needs it, not that he may serve a lust or load his belly; he that is bountiful and cheerful to his friends, and charitable and apt to forgive his enemies; that loves his country, and obeys his prince, and desires and endeavours nothing more than that they may do honour to God." This person may reckon his life to be the life of a man, and compute his months not by the course of the sun, but by the Zodiac and circle of his virtues; because these are such things which fools and children, and birds and beasts, cannot have; these are therefore the actions of life, because they are the seeds of

* *Seneca*, de Vitâ Beatâ, *cap.* 20.

immortality.

immortality. That day in which we have done some excellent thing, we may as truly reckon to be added to our life, as were the fifteen years to the days of *Hezekiah*.

SECT. IV.

Considertion of the Miseries of Mans Life.

As our life is very *short*, so it is very *miserable*, and therefore it is well it is *short*. God in pity to mankind, lest his burthen should be insupportable, and his nature an intolerable load, hath reduced our state of misery to an abbreviature; and the greater our misery is, the less while it is like to last: the sorrows of a man's spirit being like ponderous weights, which, by the greatness of their burthen, make a swifter motion, and descend into the grave to rest and ease our wearied limbs; for then only we shall sleep quietly, when those fetters are knocked off, which not only bound our souls in prison, but also ate the flesh, till the very bones opened the secret garments of their cartilages, discovering their nakedness and sorrow.

1. Here is no place to sit down in*, but you must rise as soon as you are set; for we have gnats in our chambers, and worms in our gardens, and spiders and flies in the palaces of the greatest kings. How few men in the world are prosperous? What an infinite number of slaves and beggars, of persecuted and oppressed people, fill all corners of the earth with groans, and heaven itself with weeping, prayers, and sad remembrances? How many provinces and king-

---

* Nulla requies in terris, surgite postquam sederitis; hic est locus pulicum et culicum.

doms

doms are afflicted by a violent war, or made desolate
by popular diseases? Some whole countries are remarked with fatal evils, or periodical sicknesses.
Grand Cairo in *Egypt* feels the plague every three
years returning like a quartan-ague, and destroying
many thousand of persons. All the inhabitants of
Arabia the desert are in continual fear of being buried in huge heaps of sand; and therefore dwell in
tents and ambulatory houses, or retire to unfruitful
mountains, to prolong an uneasy and wilder life.
And all the countries round about the *Adriatic* sea
feel such violent convulsions by tempests and intolerable earthquakes, that sometimes whole cities find
a tomb, and every man sinks with his own house made
ready to become his monument, and his bed is crushed into the disorders of a grave. Was not all the
world drowned at one deluge, and breach of the divine anger? and shall not all the world* again be
destroyed by fire? Are there not many thousands
that die every night, and that groan and weep sadly
every day? But what shall we think of that great
evil, which, for the sins of men, God hath suffered
to possess the greatest part of mankind? Most of the
men that are now alive, or that have been living for
many ages, are *Jews*, *Heathens*, or *Turks*: and God
was pleased to suffer a base epileptic person, a villain and a vicious, to set up a religion which hath
filled all the nearer parts of *Asia*, and much of
Africa, and some parts of *Europe*; so that the greatest number of men and women born in so many king-
doms and provinces are infallibly made *Mahometan*,
strangers and enemies to Christ, by whom alone we
can be saved. This consideration is extremely sad,
when we remember how universal and how great an
evil it is, that so many millions of sons and daughters

* Ἔσαι καὶ Σάμ☉ ἄμμ☉, ἐσεῖται Δῆλ☉ ἄδηλ☉,
Καὶ Ῥώμη ῥύμη. Syb. Orac.

are

are born to enter into the possession of devils to eternal ages.   These evils are the miseries of great parts
of mankind, and we cannot easily consider more particularly the evils which happen to us, being the inseparable affections or incidents to the whole nature of
man.

2. We find that all the women in the world are
either born for barrenness or the pains of child-birth,
and yet this is one of our greatest blessings : but such
indeed are the blessings of this world ; we cannot be
well with, nor without many things.   Perfumes make
our heads ache ; roses prick our fingers ; and in our
very blood, where our life dwells, is the scene under
which nature acts many sharp fevers, and heavy sicknesses.   It were too sad, if I should tell how many
persons are afflicted with evil-spirits, with spectres
and illusions of the night ; and that huge multitudes
of men and women live upon man's flesh ; nay, worse
yet, upon the sins of men, upon the sins of their
sons and of their daughters, and they pay their souls
down for the bread they eat, buying this day's meal
with the price of the last night's sin.

3. Or if you please in charity to visit an hospital,
which is indeed a map of the whole world, there you
shall see the effects of *Adam's* sin, and the ruins of
human nature ;   bodies laid up in heaps, like the
bones of a destroyed town ; *hominis precarii spiritûs
et malè hærentis ;* men whose souls seem to be bor-
rowed, and are kept there by art and the force of
medicine, whose miseries are so great, that few people have charity or humanity enough to visit them,
fewer have the heart to dress them, and we pity them
in civility or with a transient prayer, but we do not
feel their sorrows by the mercies of a religious pity :
and therefore as we leave their sorrows in many degrees unrelieved and uneased, so we contract, by our
unmercifulness, a guilt by which ourselves become
liable to the same calamities.   Those many that need
pity,

pity, and those infinities of people that refuse to pity, are miserable upon a several charge, but yet they almost make up all mankind.

4. All wicked men are in love with that which entangles them in huge varieties of troubles; they are slaves to the worst of masters, to sin and to the devil, to a passion, and to an imperious woman. Good men are for ever persecuted, and God chastises every son whom he receives; and whatsoever is easy is trifling and worth nothing; and whatsoever is excellent is not to be obtained without labour and sorrow; and the conditions and states of men that are free from great cares are such as have in them nothing rich and orderly; and those that have are stuck full of thorns and trouble. Kings are full of care; and learned men*, in all ages, have been observed to be very poor, *et honestas miserias accusant,* they complain of their honest miseries.

5. But these evils are notorious and confessed; even they also whose felicity men stare at and admire, besides their splendour and the sharpness of their light, will, with their appendant sorrows, wring a tear from the most resolved eye: for not only the winter quarter is full of storms and cold and darkness, but the beauteous spring hath blasts and sharp frosts, the fruitful teeming summer is melted with heat, and burnt with the kisses of the sun, her friend, and choked with dust, and the rich autumn is full of sickness; and we are weary of that which we enjoy, because sorrow is its bigger portion: and when we remember, that upon the fairest face is placed one of the worst sinks of the body, *the nose;* we may use it not only

---

* Vilis adulator picto jacet ebrius ostro,
  Et qui sollicitat nuptas ad præmia peccat.
  Sola pruinosis horret facundia pannis,
  Atque inopi linguâ desertas invocat artes.   *Petron.*
  Hinc et jocus apud *Aristŏph.* in Avibus; v. 934.
  Σὺ μέν τοι σπολάδα καὶ χιτῶν ἔχεις,
  Ἀπόδυθι καὶ δὸς τῷ ποιητῇ τῷ σοφῷ.

D

as a mortification to the pride of beauty, but as an
allay to the fairest outside of condition, which any
of the sons and daughters of *Adam* do possess. For
look upon kings and conquerors *: I will not tell that
many of them fall into the condition of servants, and
their subjects rule over them, and stand upon the ruins
of their families, and that to such persons the sorrow
is bigger than usually happens in smaller fortunes:
but let us suppose them still conquerors, and see what
a goodly purchase they get by all their pains, and
amazing fears, and continual dangers. They carry
their arms beyond *Ister*, and pass the *Euphrates*,
and bind the *Germans* with the bounds of the river
Rhine: I speak in the style of the *Roman* greatness;
for now-a-days the biggest fortune swells not beyond
the limits of a petty province or two, and a hill confines the progress of their prosperity, or a river checks
it. But whatsoever tempts the pride and vanity of
ambitious persons, is not so big as the smallest star
which we see scattered in disorder and unregarded
upon the pavement and floor of heaven. And if we
would suppose the pismires had but our understanding,
they also would have the method of a man's greatness,
and divide their little mole-hills into provinces and
exarchates; and if they also grew as vicious and as
miserable, one of their princes would lead an army
out, and kill his neighbour-ants, that he might reign
over the next handful of a turf. But then if we consider at what price and with what felicity all this is
purchased, the sting of the painted snake will quickly
appear, and the fairest of their fortunes will properly
enter into this account of human infelicities.

We may guess at it by the constitution of *Augustus's*
fortune, who struggled for his power, first with the
Roman citizens, then with *Brutus* and *Cassius*, and

---

* Vilis servus habet regni bona, cellâque capti;
   Deridet festam Romuleamque casam. *Petron.*
  Omnia, crede mihi, etiam felicibus dubia sunt. *Seneca.*

all

all the fortune of the republic, then with his colleague *Mark Antony*, then with his kindred and nearest relatives: and after he was wearied with slaughter of the *Romans*, before he could sit down and rest in his imperial chair, he was forced to carry armies into *Macedonia*, *Galatia*, beyond *Euphrates*, *Rhine*, and *Danubius;* and when he dwelt at home in greatness, and within the circles of a mighty power, he hardly escaped the sword of the *Egnatii*, of *Lepidus*, *Cepio*, and *Murœna:* and after he had entirely reduced the felicity and grandeur into his own family, his daughter, his only child, conspired with many of the young nobility, and being joined with adulterous complications as with an impious sacrament*, they affrighted and destroyed the fortune of the old man, and wrought him more sorrow than all the troubles that were hatched in the baths and beds of *Egypt*, between *Antony* and *Cleopatra*.† This was the greatest fortune that the world had then or ever since; and therefore we cannot expect it to be better in a less prosperity.

6. The prosperity of this world is so infinitely soured with the overflowing of evils, that he is counted the most happy who hath the fewest; all conditions being evil and miserable, they are only distinguished by the number of calamities. The collector of the *Roman* and foreign examples, when he had reckoned two-and-twenty instances of great fortunes, every one of which had been allayed with great variety of evils; in all his reading or experience, he could tell but of two who had been famed for an entire prosperity, *Quintus Metellus*, and *Gyges* the king of *Lydia*. And yet concerning the one of them, he tells, that his felicity was so inconsiderable, (and yet it was the bigger of the two,) that the oracle said, that *Aglaus Sophidius*, the poor *Arcadian* shepherd, was more happy than he, that is, he had fewer troubles ‡: for so in-

---

* Et adulterio velut sacramento adacti. *Tacit.*
† Plusque et iterum timenda cum *Antonio* mulier.
‡ Ὅςϼ τᾶ μεγέϑϛς τῶν ἡδονῶν, ἡ παντὸς τᾶ ἀλγεινᾶ ὑπεξαίρεσις.

deed

deed we are to reckon the pleasures of this life; *the limit of our joy is the absence of some degrees of sorrow*, and he that hath the least of this is the most prosperous person. But then we must look for prosperity, not in palaces or courts of princes, not in the tents of conquerors, or in the gaieties of fortunate and prevailing sinners; but something rather in the cottages of honest, innocent, and contented persons, whose mind is no bigger than their fortune, nor their virtue less than their security. As for others, whose fortune looks bigger, and allures fools to follow it, like the wandering fires of the night, till they run into rivers, or are broken upon rocks with staring and running after them, they are all in the condition of *Marius*, than whose condition *nothing was more constant, and nothing more mutable. If we reckon them amongst the happy, they are the most happy men: if we reckon them amongst the miserable, they are the most miserable.* For just as is a man's contrition, great or little, so is the state of his misery. All have their share; but kings and princes, great generals and consuls, rich men and mighty, as they have the biggest business and the biggest charge, and are answerable to God for the greatest accounts, so they have the biggest trouble; that the uneasiness of their appendage may divide the good and evil of the world, making the poor man's fortune as eligible as the greatest; and also restraining the vanity of man's spirit, which a great fortune is apt to swell from a vapour to a bubble: but God in mercy hath mingled wormwood with their wine, and so restrained the drunkenness and follies of prosperity.

7. Man never hath one day to himself of entire peace from the things of the world, but either something troubles him, or nothing satisfies him, or his very fulness swells him, and makes him breathe short

* Quem si inter miseros posueris, miserrimus; inter felices, felicissimus reperiebatur.

upon his bed.   Men's joys are troublesome; and besides that, the fear of losing them takes away the present pleasure (and a man hath need of another felicity to preserve this); they are also wavering and full of trepidation, not only from their inconstant nature, but from their weak foundation; they rise from vanity, and they dwell upon ice, and they converse with the wind, and they have the wings of a bird, and are serious but as the resolutions of a child, commenced by chance, and managed by folly, and proceed by inadvertency, and end in vanity and forgetfulness.   So that, as *Livius Drusius* said of himself, *he never had any play-days, or days of quiet, when he was a boy *; for he was troublesome and busy, a restless and unquiet man:* the same may every man observe to be true of himself; he is always restless and uneasy, he dwells upon the waters, and leans upon thorns, and lays his head upon a sharp stone.

SECT. V.

This Consideration reduced to Practice.

1. THE effect of this consideration is this; that the sadnesses of this life help to sweeten the bitter cup of death.   For let our life be never so long, if our strength were great as that of oxen and camels, if our sinews were strong as the cordage at the foot of an oak, if we were as fighting and prosperous people as *Siccius Dentatus*, who was on the prevailing side in an hundred and twenty battles, who had three hundred and twelve public rewards assigned him by his generals and princes for his valour and conduct in sieges

---

* Uni sibi nec puero unquam ferias contigisse. Seditiosus et foro gravis.

and

and short encounters, and, besides all this, had his
share in nine triumphs; yet still the period shall be,
that all this shall end in death, and the people shall
talk of us a while, good or bad, according as we deserve, or as they please; and once it shall come to
pass, that concerning every one of us, it shall be told
in the neighbourhood that we are dead. This we are
apt to think a sad story; but therefore let us help it
with a sadder. For we therefore need not be much
troubled that we shall die, because we are not here in
ease, nor do we dwell in a fair condition : but our days
are full of sorrow and anguish, dishonoured and made
unhappy with many sins, with a frail and a foolish
spirit, entangled with difficult cases of conscience,
ensnared with passions, amazed with fears, full of
cares, divided with curiosities and contradictory interests, made airy and impertinent with vanities, abused
with ignorance and prodigious errors, made ridiculous
with a thousand wickednesses, worn away with labours,
loaden with diseases, daily vexed with dangers and
temptations, and in love with misery; we are weakened
with delights, afflicted with want, with the evils of
myself and of all my family, and with the sadnesses
of all my friends, and of all good men, even of the
whole church : and therefore methinks we need not be
troubled that God is pleased to put an end to all these
troubles, and to let them sit down in a natural period,
which, if we please, may be to us the beginning of a
better life. When the prince of *Persia* wept because
his army should all die in the revolution of an age,
Artabanus told him, that they should all meet with
evils so many, and so great, that every man of them
should wish himself dead long before that. Indeed,
it were a sad thing to be cut of the stone, and we that
are in health tremble to think of it; but the man that
is wearied with the disease, looks upon that sharpness
as upon his cure and remedy: and as none need to
have a tooth drawn, so none could well endure it, but

1

he that hath felt the pain of it in his head. So is our life
so full of evils, that therefore death is no evil to them
that have felt the smart of this, or hope for the joys of
a better.

2. But as it helps to ease a certain sorrow, as a fire
draws out a fire, and a nail drives forth a nail; so it
instructs us in a present duty, that is, that we should
not be so fond of a perpetual storm, or doat upon the
transient gauds and gilded thorns of this world. They
are not worth a passion, nor worth a sigh or a groan,
not of the price of one night's watching : and therefore they are mistaken and miserable persons, who,
since *Adam* planted thorns round about paradise, are
more in love with that hedge than all the fruits of the
garden — sottish admirers of things that hurt them, of
sweet poisons, gilded daggers, and silken halters.
Tell them they have lost a bounteous friend, a rich
purchase, a fair farm, a wealthy donative, and you
dissolve their patience ; it is an evil bigger than their
spirit can bear ; it brings sickness and death ; they can
neither eat nor sleep with such a sorrow. But if you
represent to them the evils of a vicious habit, and the
dangers of a state of sin ; if you tell them they have
displeased God, and interrupted their hopes of
heaven ; it may be they will be so civil as to hear it
patiently, and to treat you kindly, and first to commend, and then forget your story ; because they prefer
this world, with all its sorrows, before the pure unmingled felicities of heaven. But it is strange that
any man should be so passionately in love with the
thorns that grow on his own ground, that he should
wear them for armlets, and knit them in his shirt, and
prefer them before a kingdom and immortality. No
man loves this world the better for his being poor ;
but men that love it because they have great possessions, love it because it is troublesome and chargeable,
full of noise and temptation, because it is unsafe and
ungoverned, flattered and abused : and he that con-

siders

siders the troubles of an over long garment, and of a crammed stomach, a trailing gown, and a loaden table, may justly understand that all that for which men are so passionate is their hurt, and their objection, that which a temperate man would avoid, and a wise man cannot love.

He that is no fool, but can consider wisely, if he be in love with this world, we need not despair but that a witty man might reconcile him with tortures, and make him think charitably of the rack, and be brought to dwell with vipers and dragons, and entertain his guests with the shrieks of mandrakes, cats, and screech-owls, with the filing of iron, and the harshness of rending silk, or to admire the harmony that is made by an herd of evening wolves, when they miss their draught of blood in their midnight revels. The groans of a man in a fit of the stone are worse than all these; and the distractions of a troubled conscience are worse than those groans: and yet a merry careless sinner is worse than all that. But if we could from one of the battlements of heaven espy how many men and women at this time lie fainting and dying for want of bread, how many young men are hewn down by the sword of war, how many poor orphans are now weeping over the graves of their father, by whose life they were enabled to eat; if we could but hear how mariners and passengers are at this present in a storm, and shriek out because their keel dashes against a rock, or bulges under them, how many people there are that weep with want, and are mad with oppression, or are desperate by too quick a sense of a constant infelicity; in all reason we should be glad to be out of the noise and participation of so many evils. This is a place of sorrows and tears, of so great evils and a constant calamity: let us remove from hence, at least in affections and preparation of mind.

CHAP. II.

A GENERAL PREPARATION TOWARDS AN HOLY AND BLESSED DEATH, BY WAY OF EXERCISE.

───────

SECT. I.

Three Precepts preparatory to an Holy Death, to be practised in our whole Life.

HE *that would die well must always look for death, every day knocking at the gates of the grave,* and then the gates of the grave shall never prevail upon him to do him mischief. *   This was the advice of all the wise and good men of the world, who, especially in the days and periods of their joy and festival egressions, chose to throw some ashes into their chalices, some sober remembrances of their fatal period. †   Such was the black shirt of *Saladine ;* the tombstone presented to the emperor of *Constantinople* on his coronation-day ; the bishop of *Rome's* two reeds with flax and a wax-taper ; the *Egyptian* skeleton served up at feasts ; and *Trimalcion's* banquet in *Petronius,* in which was brought in the image of a dead man's bones of silver, with spondyles exactly turning to every of the guests, and saying to every one, that you and you must die,

---

* Propera vivere, et singulos dies singulas vitas puta.   Nihil interest inter diem et seculum.

 † Si sapis, utaris totis, Coline, diebus :
  Extremumque tibi semper adesse putes.   *Martial.*

           and

and look not one upon another, for every one is
equally concerned in this sad representment. * These
in fantastic semblances declare a severe counsel and
useful meditation : and it is not easy for a man to
be gay in his imagination, or to be drunk with joy or
wine, pride or revenge, who considers sadly that he must
ere long dwell in a house of darkness and dishonour,
and his body must be the inheritance of worms, and
his soul must be what he pleases, even as a man makes
it here by his living good or bad. I have read of a
young eremite, who, being passionately in love with
a young lady, could not, by all the arts of religion
and mortification, suppress the trouble of that fancy ;
till at last being told that she was dead, and had been
buried about fourteen days, he went secretly to her
vault, and with the skirt of his mantle wiped the
moisture from the carcase, and, still at the return of
his temptation, laid it before him, saying, *Behold,
this is the beauty of the woman thou didst so much
desire :* and so the man found his cure. And if we
make death as present to us, our own death, dwelling
and dressed in all its pomp of fancy and proper circumstances ; if any thing will quench the heats of
lust, or the desires of money, or the greedy passionate
affections of this world, this must do it. But withal,
the frequent use of this meditation, by curing our
present inordinations, will make death safe and
friendly ; and, by its very custom, will make that the
king of terrors shall come to us, without his affrighting
dresses ; and that we shall sit down in the grave as we
compose ourselves to sleep, and do the duties of nature
and choice. The old people that lived near the *Ri-
phæan* mountains, were taught to converse with death,
and to handle it on all sides, and to discourse of it

---

* Heu, heu, nos miseros ! quam totus homuncio nil est !
   Sic erimus cuncti postquam nos auferet Orcus,
      Ergo vivamus, dum licet esse bene.

as of a thing that will certainly come, and ought so
to do. * Thence their minds and resolutions became
capable of death, and they thought it a dishonourable
thing with greediness to keep a life that must go from
us, to lay aside its thorns, and to return again circled
with a glory and a diadem.

2. *He that would die well, must all the days of his
life lay up against the day of death* † ; not only by the
general provisions of holiness, and a pious life inde-
finitely, but provisions proper to the necessities of
that great day of expense, in which a man is to throw
his last cast for an eternity of joys or sorrows ; ever
remembering, that this alone, well performed, is not
enough to pass us into paradise, but that alone, done
foolishly, is enough to send us into hell ; and the want
of either a holy life or death, makes a man to fall
short of the mighty price of our high calling. ‡ In
order to this rule, we are to consider what special
graces we shall then need to exercise, and by the
proper arts of the spirit, by a heap of proportioned
arguments, by prayers, and a great treasure of devotion
laid up in heaven, provide before hand a reserve of
strength and mercy. Men, in the course of their
lives, walk lazily and incuriously, as if they had both
their feet in one shoe ; and when they are passively
revolved to the time of their dissolution, they have no
mercies in store, no patience, no faith, no charity to
God, or despite of the world, being without gust or
appetite for the land of their inheritance, which Christ
with so much pain and blood hath purchased for them.
When we come to die indeed, we shall be very much

* —— Certè populi quos despicit Arctos
Felices errore suo, quos ille timorum
Maximus haud urget, Lethi metus ——
Inde ruendi
In ferrum mens prona viris, animæque capaces
Mortis, et ignavum reditura parcere vitæ.
† Qui quotidie vitæ suæ manum imposuit non indiget tempore.
Seneca.

‡ Insere nunc, *Meliboee*, pyros, pone ordine vites.

put to it, to stand firm upon the two feet of a Christian, *Faith* and *Patience*. When we ourselves are to use the articles, to turn our former discourses into present practice, and to feel what we never felt before, we shall find it to be quite another thing, to be willing presently to quit this life and all our present possessions, for the hopes of a thing which we were never suffered to see, and such a thing of which we may fail so many ways, and of which if we fail any way we are miserable for ever. Then we shall find how much we have need to have secured the spirit of God, and the grace of faith, by an habitual, perfect, immoveable resolution. The same is also the case of patience, which will be assaulted with sharp pains, disturbed fancies, great fears, want of a present mind, natural weaknesses, frauds of the devil, and a thousand accidents and imperfections. It concerns us therefore highly, in the whole course of our lives, not only to accustom ourselves to a patient suffering of injuries and affronts, of persecutions and losses, of cross accidents and unnecessary circumstances; but also, by representing death as present to us, to consider with what argument then to fortify our patience, and by assiduous and fervent prayer to God all our life long, to call upon him to give us patience and great assistances, a strong faith, and a confirmed hope, the spirit of God and his holy angels assistants at that time, to resist and to subdue the devil's temptations and assaults; and so to fortify our heart, that it break not into intolerable sorrows and impatience, and end in wretchedness and infidelity. But this is to be the work of our life, and not to be done at once; but as God gives us time, by succession, by parts and little periods. For it is very remarkable, that God who giveth plenteously to all creatures, he hath scattered the firmament with stars as a man sows corn in his fields, in a multitude bigger than the capacities of human order; he hath made so much variety of creatures

tures, and gives us great choice of meats and drinks, although any one of both kinds would have served our needs ; and so in all instances of nature : yet in the distribution of our time, God seems to be strait-handed ; and gives it to us, not as nature gives us rivers, enough to drown us, but drop by drop, minute after minute ; so that we never can have two minutes together, but he takes away one when he gives us another. This should teach us to value our time, since God so values it, and by his so small distribution of it, tells us it is the most precious thing we have. Since therefore in the day of our death we can have still but the same little portion of this precious time, let us in every minute of our life, I mean in every discernible portion, lay up such a stock of reason and good works, that they may convey a value to the imperfect and shorter actions of our death-bed : while God rewards the piety of our lives by his gracious acceptation and benediction upon the actions preparatory to our death-bed.

3. *He that desires to die well and happily, above all things must be careful that he do not live a soft, a delicate, and a voluptuous life ;* but a life severe, holy, and under the discipline of the cross, under the conduct of prudence and observation, a life of warfare and sober counsels, labour and watchfulness. No man wants cause of tears, and a daily sorrow. Let every man consider what he feels, and acknowledge his misery ; let him confess his sin and chastise it ; let him bear his cross patiently, and his persecutions nobly, and his repentances willingly and constantly ; let him pity the evils of all the world, and bear his share in the calamities of his brother ; let him long and sigh for the joys of heaven ; let him tremble and fear, because he hath deserved the pains of hell ; let him commute his eternal fear with a temporal suffering, preventing God's judgment by passing one of his own ; let him groan for the labours of his pilgrimage, and

and the dangers of his warfare: and by that time he hath summed up all these labours, and, duties, and contingencies, all the proper causes, instruments, and acts of sorrow, he will find, that for a secular joy and wantonness of spirit, there are not left many void spaces of his life. It was St. *James's* advice, *Be afflicted, and mourn, and weep; let your laughter be turned into mourning, and your joy into weeping* * : and *Bonadventure,* in the Life of Christ, reports, that the holy virgin-mother said to St. *Elizabeth, That grace does not descend into the soul of a man, but by prayer and affliction.* Certain it is, that a mourning spirit and an afflicted body are great instruments of reconciling God to a sinner, and they always dwell at the gates of atonement and restitution. But besides this, a delicate and prosperous life is hugely contrary to the hopes of a blessed eternity. *Woe be to them that are at ease in Sion* †, so it was said of old: and our blessed Lord said, *Woe be to you that laugh, for ye shall weep* ‡ ; but, *Blessed are they that mourn, for they shall be comforted.* § Here or hereafter we must have our portion of sorrows. *He that now goeth on his way weeping, and beareth forth good seed with him, will doubtless come again with joy, and bring his sheaves with him.* ‖ And certainly, he that sadly considers the portion of *Dives,* and remembers that the account which *Abraham* gave him for the unavoidableness to his torment, was, because he had *his good things in this life,* must in all reason with trembling run from a course of banquets, and *faring deliciously every day,* as being a dangerous estate, and a consignation to an evil greater than all danger, the pains and torments of unhappy souls. If either by patience or repentance, by compassion or persecution, by

---

* *Chap.* iv. 9.   Neque enim Deus ullâ re perinde atque corporis ærumnâ conciliatur. *Naz.* Orat. 18.

† *Amos,* vi. 1.   ‡ *Luke,* vi. 25.   § Matth. v. 4.   ‖ Psal. cxxvi. 6.

choice

choice or by conformity, by severity or discipline, we
allay the festival-follies of a soft life, and profess
under the cross of Christ, we shall more willingly and
more safely enter into our grave; but the death-bed
of a voluptuous man upbraids his little and cozening
prosperities, and exacts pains made * sharper by the
passing from soft beds and a softer mind. *He that
would die holily and happily, must in this world love
tears, humility, solitude, and repentance.*

SECT. II.

*Of Daily Examination of our Actions in the whole
Course of our Health, preparatory to our Death-
bed.*

HE that will die well and happily, must dress his
soul by a diligent and frequent scrutiny: he must perfectly understand and watch the state of his soul; he
must set his house in order before he be fit to die.
And for this there is great reason, and great necessity.

Reasons for a Daily Examination.

1. For, if we consider the disorders of every day,
the multitude of impertinent words, the great portions
of time spent in vanity, the daily omissions of duty,
the coldness of our prayers, the indifferences of our
spirit in holy things, the uncertainty of our secret
purposes, our infinite deceptions and hypocrisies,
sometimes not known, very often not observed by

* ———— Sed longi pœnas fortuna favoris
Exigit à misero, quæ tanto pondere famæ
Res premit adversas, fatisque prioribus urget.
                              Lucan. l. 8. v. 21.

ourselves,

ourselves, our want of charity, our not knowing in
how many degrees of action and purpose every virtue
is to be exercised, the secret adherences of pride, and
too forward complacency in our best actions, our
failings in all our relations, the niceties of difference
between some virtues and some vices, the secret un-
discernible passages from lawful to unlawful in the
first instances of change, the perpetual mistakings of
permissions for duty, and licentious practices for permissions, our daily abusing the liberty that God gives
us, our unsuspected sins in the managing a course of
life certainly lawful, our little greedinesses in eating,
our surprises in the proportions of our drinkings, our
too great freedoms and fondnesses in lawful loves,
our aptness for things sensual, and our deadness and
tediousness of spirit in spiritual employments; besides
infinite variety of cases of conscience that do occur in
the life of every man, and in all intercourses of every
life, and that the productions of sin are numerous and
encreasing, like the families of the northern people,
or the genealogies of the first patriarchs of the world;
from all this we shall find, that the computations of a
man's life are busy as the tables of sines and tangents,
and intricate as the accounts of eastern merchants:
and therefore it were but reason we should sum up
our accounts at the foot of every page; I mean, that
we call ourselves to scrutiny every night when we compose ourselves to the little images of death.

2. For, if we make but one general account, and
never reckon till we die, either we shall only reckon
by great sums, and remember nothing but clamorous
and crying sins, and never consider concerning particulars, or forget very many : or if we could consider
all that we ought, we must needs be confounded with
the multitude and variety. But if we observe all the
little passages of our life, and reduce them into the
order of accounts and accusations, we shall find them
multiply so fast, that it will not only appear to be an
                                              ease

ease to the accounts of our death-bed, but by the instrument of shame will restrain the inundation of evils; it being a thing intolerable to human modesty, to see sins increase so fast, and virtues grow up so slow; to see every day stained with the spots of leprosy, or sprinkled with the marks of a lesser evil.

3. It is not intended we should take accounts of our lives only to be thought religious, but that we may see our evil and amend it, that we dash our sins against the stones, that we may go to God, and to a spiritual guide, and search for remedies, and apply them. And, indeed, no man can well observe his own growth in grace, but by accounting seldomer returns of sin, and a more frequent victory over temptations; concerning which, every man makes his observations according as he makes his enquiries and search after himself. In order to this it was that St. *Paul* wrote, before the receiving the holy sacrament, *Let a man examine himself, and so let him eat.* This precept was given in those days when they communicated every day, and therefore *a daily examination* also was intended.

4. And it will appear highly fitting, if we remember, that at the day of judgment, not only the greatest lines of life, but every branch and circumstance of every action, every word and thought shall be called to scrutiny and severe judgment: insomuch that it was a great truth which one said, *Woe be to the most innocent life, if God should search into it without mixtures of mercy.* And therefore we are here to follow St. *Paul's* advice, *Judge yourselves, and ye shall not be judged of the Lord.* The way to prevent God's anger, is to be angry with ourselves; and by examining our actions, and condemning the criminal, by being assessors in God's tribunal, at least we shall obtain the favour of the court. *As therefore every night we must make our bed the memorial of our grave, so let our evening thoughts be an image of the day of judgment.*

E

5. This

5. This advice was so reasonable and proper an instrument of virtue, that it was taught even to the scholars of *Pythagoras*, by their master; " *Let not* " *sleep seize upon the regions of your senses, before* " *you have three times recalled the conversation and* " *accidents of the day.*" * Examine what you have committed against the divine law, what you have omitted of your duty, and in what you have made use of the divine grace to the purposes of virtue and religion; *joining the judge reason to the legislative mind or conscience,* that God may reign there as a lawgiver and a judge. Then Christ's kingdom is set up in our hearts; then we always live in the eye of our judge, and live by the measures of reason, religion, and sober counsels.

The benefits we shall receive by practising this advice, in order to a blessed death, will also add to the account of reason and fair inducements.

The Benefits of this Exercise.

1. By a daily examination of our actions, we shall the easier cure a great sin, and prevent its arrival to become habitual : for [*to examine*] we suppose to be a relative duty, and instrumental to something else. We examine ourselves, that we may find out our failings and cure them; and therefore if we use our remedy when the wound is fresh and bleeding, we shall find the cure more certain and less painful. For so a taper, when its crown of flame is newly blown off, retains a nature so symbolical to light, that it will with greediness re-inkindle and snatch a ray from the neighbour fire. So is the soul of man, when it is newly fallen into sin; although God be angry with it, and the state of God's favour and its own graciousness is interrupted, yet the habit is not naturally changed; and still God leaves some roots of virtue standing,

---

* χρύσ. ἔπη.

and

and the man is modest, or apt to be made ashamed,
and he is not grown a bold sinner : but if he sleeps
on it, and returns again to the same sin, and by degrees grows in love with it, and gets the custom, and
the strangeness of it taken away, then it is his master,
and is swelled into an heap, and is abetted by use,
and corroborated by newly entertained principles, and
is insinuated into his nature, and hath possessed his
affections, and tainted the will and understanding :
and by this time a man is in the state of a decaying
merchant, his accounts are so great, and so intricate,
and so much in arrear, that to examine it will be but
to represent the particulars of his calamity ; therefore they think it better to pull the napkin before
their eyes, than to stare upon the circumstances of
their death.

2. A daily or frequent examination of the parts of
our life will interrupt the proceeding, and hinder the
journey of little sins into an heap. For many days
do not pass the best persons, in which they have not
many idle words or vainer thoughts to sully the fair
whiteness of their souls, some indiscreet passions or
trifling purposes, some impertinent discontents or
unhandsome usages to their own persons, or their
dearest relatives. And though God *is not extreme to
mark what is done amiss,* and therefore puts these
upon the accounts of his mercy, and the title of the
cross ; yet in two cases, these little sins combine and
cluster ; (and we know, that grapes were once in so
great a bunch, that one cluster was the load of two
men :) that is, 1. When either we are in love with
small sins ; or, 2. When they proceed from a careless
and incurious spirit into frequency and continuance.
For so the smallest atoms that dance in all the little
cells of the world, are so trifling and immaterial, that
they cannot trouble an eye, nor vex the tenderest part
of a wound, where a barbed arrow dwelt : yet when
by their infinite numbers (as *Melissa* and *Parmenides*
affirm)

affirm) they danced first into order, then into little bodies, at last they made the matter of the world. So are the little indiscretions of our life; *they are always inconsiderable, if they be considered; and contemptible, if they be not despised; and God does not regard them, if we do.* We may easily keep them asunder by our daily or nightly thoughts, and prayers, and severe sentences: but even the least sand can check the tumultuous pride, and become a limit to the sea, when it is in an heap, and in united multitudes; but if the wind scatter and divide them, the little drops and the vainer froth of the water begins to invade the strand. Our sighs can scatter such little offences: but then be sure to breathe such accents frequently, lest they knot and combine, and grow big as the shore, and *we perish in sand*, in trifling instances. * *He that despiseth little things shall perish by little and little;* so said the son of *Sirach.*

3. A frequent examination of our actions will intenerate and soften our consciences, so that they shall be impatient of any rudeness or heavier load: and he that is used to shrink when he is pressed with a branch of twining osier, will not willingly stand in the ruins of a house, when the beam dashes upon the pavement.† And provided that our nice and tender spirit be not vexed into scruple, nor the scruple turned into unreasonable fears, nor the fears into superstition; he that by any arts can make his spirit tender and apt for religious impressions, hath made the fairest seat for religion, and the unaptest and uneasiest entertainment for sin and eternal death, in the whole world.

4. A frequent examination of the smallest parts of our lives, is the best instrument to make our repentance particular, and a fit remedy to all the

---

* Ecclus. xix. 1.

† Qui levi comminatione pellitur, non opus est ut fortitudine et armis invadatur. *Seneca.*

members

members of the whole body of sin.   For our examination put off to our death-bed, of necessity
brings us into this condition, that very many thousands of our sins must be (or not be at all) washed
off with a general repentance, which the more general and indefinite it is, it is ever so much the worse.
And if he that repents the longest and the oftenest,
and upon the most instances, is still, during his whole
life, but an imperfect penitent, and there are very
many reserves left to be wiped off by God's mercies,
and to be eased by collateral assistances, or to be
groaned for at the terrible day of judgment; it will
be but a sad story to consider, that the sins of a
whole life, or of very great portions of it, shall be
put upon the remedy of one examination, and the
advices of one discourse, and the activities of a decayed body, and a weak and an amazed spirit.   Let
us do the best we can, we shall find that the mere
sins of ignorance and unavoidable forgetfulness, will
be enough to be intrusted to such a bank; and that
if a general repentance will serve toward their expi-
ation it will be an infinite mercy: but we have
nothing to warrant our confidence, if we shall think
it to be enough on our death-bed to confess the notorious actions of our lives, and to say, [*The Lord be
merciful to me, for the infinite transgressions of my
life, which I have wilfully or carelessly forgot;*] for
very many of which, the repentance, the distinct, particular, circumstantiate repentance of a whole life
would have been too little, if we could have done
more.

5. After the enumeration of these advantages, I
shall not need to add, that if we decline or refuse to
call ourselves frequently to account, and to use daily
advices concerning the state of our souls, it is a very
ill sign that our souls are not right with God, or that
they do not dwell in religion.   But this I shall say,
that they who do use this exercise frequently, will

make their conscience much at ease, by casting out a daily load of humour and surfeit, the matter of diseases, and instruments of death. *He that does not frequently search his conscience is a house without a window*, and like a wild untutored son of a fond and undiscerning widow.

But if this exercise seem too great a trouble, and that by such advices religion will seem a burthen; I have two things to oppose against it.

One is, that we had better bear the burden of the Lord, than the burden of a base and polluted conscience. Religion cannot be so great a trouble as a guilty soul; and whatsoever trouble can be fancied in this or any other action of religion, it is only to unexperienced persons.* It may be a trouble at first, just as is every change and every new accident: but if you do it frequently, and accustom your spirit to it, as the custom will make it easy, so the advantages will make it delectable; *That* will make it facile as nature, *These* will make it as pleasant and eligible as reward.

2dly, The other thing I have to say is this: That to examine our lives will be no trouble, if we do not intricate it with businesses of the world, and the labyrinths of care and impertinent affairs.† A man had need of a quiet and disentangled life, who comes to search into all his actions, and to make judgment concerning his errors and his needs, his remedies and his hopes. *They that have great intrigues of the world, have a yoke upon their necks, and cannot look back.* And he that covets many things greedily, and snatches at high things ambitiously, that despises his neighbour proudly, and bears his crosses peevishly, or his prosperity impotently and passionately; he that is prodigal of his precious time, and is tenacious and

* Elige vitam optimam; consuetudo faciet jucundissimam. *Seneca.*
† Securæ et quietæ mentis est in omnes vitæ partes discurrere; occupatorum animi velut sub jugo sunt, respicere non possunt. *Seneca.*

retentive

retentive of evil purposes, is not a man disposed to this exercise: He hath reason to be afraid of his own memory, and to dash his glass in pieces, because it must needs represent to his own eyes an intolerable deformity. He therefore that resolves to live well whatsoever it costs him, he that will go to Heaven at any rate, shall best tend this duty, by neglecting the affairs of the world in all things where prudently he may. But if we do otherwise, we shall find that the accounts of our death-bed, and the examination made by a disturbed understanding, will be very empty of comfort, and full of inconveniences.

6. For hence it comes that men die so timorously and uncomfortably, as if they were forced out of their lives by the violences of an executioner. Then, without much examination, they remember how wickedly they had lived, without religion, against the laws of the covenant of grace, *without God in the world :* then they see sin goes off like an amazed, wounded, affrighted person from a lost battle, without honour, without a veil, with nothing but shame and sad remembrances: then they can consider, that if they had lived virtuously, all the trouble and objection of that would now be passed, and all that had remained should be peace and joy, and all that good which dwells within the House of God, and eternal life. But now they find they have done amiss and dealt wickedly, they have no bank of good works, but a huge treasure of wrath, and they are going to a strange place, and what shall be their lot is uncertain ; (so they say, when they would comfort and flatter themselves :) but in truth of religion their portion is sad and intolerable, without hope, and without refreshment, and they must use little silly arts to make them go off from their stage of sins with some handsome circumstances of opinion: they will in civility be abused, that they may die quietly, and go decently to their execution, and leave their friends indifferently contented, and

E 4   apt

apt to be comforted : and by that time they are gone awhile, they see that they deceived themselves all their days, and were by others deceived at last.

Let us make it our own case : We shall come to that state and period of condition, in which we shall be infinitely comforted, if we have lived well ; or else be amazed and go off trembling, because we are guilty of heaps of unrepented and unforsaken sins. It may happen we shall not then understand it so, because most men of late ages have been abused with false principles : and they are taught (or they are willing to believe) that a little thing is enough to save them, and that Heaven is so cheap a purchase, that it will fall upon them whether they will or no. The misery of it is, they will not suffer themselves to be confuted, till it be too late to recant their error. In the *interim*, they are impatient to be examined, as a leper is of a comb, and are greedy of the world, as children of raw fruit ; and they hate a severe reproof, as they do thorns in their bed ; and they love to lay aside religion, as a drunken person does to forget his sorrow ; and all the way they dream of fine things, and their dreams prove contrary, and become the hieroglyphics of an eternal sorrow. The daughter of *Polycrates* dreamed that her father was lifted up, and that *Jupiter* washed him, and the sun anointed him ; but it proved to him but a sad prosperity : for after a long life of constant prosperous successes he was surprised by his enemies, and hanged up till the dew of Heaven wet his cheeks, and the sun melted his grease. Such is the condition of those persons who, living either in the despite or in the neglect of religion, lie wallowing in the drunkenness of prosperity or worldly cares : they think themselves to be exalted till the evil day overtakes them ; and then they can expound their dream of life to end in a sad and hopeless death. I remember that *Cleomenes* was called a God by the *Egyptians*, because when he was

was hanged, a serpent grew out of his body, and wrapped itself about his head ; till the philosophers of *Egypt* said it was natural that from the marrow of some bodies such productions should arise. And indeed it represents the condition of some men, who being dead are esteemed saints and beatified persons, when their head is encircled with dragons, and is entered into the possession of devils, *that old serpent and deceiver.* For indeed their life was secretly so corrupted, that such serpents fed upon the ruins of the spirit, and the decays of grace and reason. To be cozened in making judgments concerning our final condition is extremely easy ; but if we be cozened, we are infinitely miserable.

SECT. III.

Of exercising Charity during our whole Life.

He that would die well and happily, must in his lifetime, according to all his capacities, exercise charity* ; and because religion is the life of the soul, and charity is the life of religion, the same which gives life to the better part of man which never dies, may obtain of God a mercy to the inferior part of man in the day of its dissolution.

1. Charity is the great channel through which God passes all his mercy upon mankind. For we receive absolution of our sins in proportion to our forgiving our brother. This is the rule of our hopes, and the measure of our desire of this world ; and in the day of death and judgment the great sentence upon mankind shall be transacted according to our alms, which

* Respice quid prodest præsentis temporis ævum
  Omne quod est nihil est, præter amare Deum.

is

is the other part of charity. Certain it is, that God cannot, will not, never did reject a charitable man in his greatest needs, and in his most passionate prayers * ; for *God* himself *is love*, and every degree of charity that dwells in us is the participation of the divine nature : and therefore, when upon our death-bed, a cloud covers our head, and we are enwrapped with sorrow ; when we feel the weight of a sickness, and do not feel the refreshing visitations of God's loving kindness ; when we have many things to trouble us, and looking round about us we see no comforter ; then call to mind what injuries you have forgiven, how apt you were to pardon all affronts and real persecutions, how you embraced peace when it was offered you, how you *followed after peace* when it ran from you : and when you are weary of one side, turn upon the other, and remember the *alms* that by the grace of God, and his assistances, you have done, and look up to God, and with the eye of faith behold his coming in the cloud, and pronouncing the sentence of doomsday according to his mercies, and thy charity.

2. Charity, with its twin-daughters alms and forgiveness, is especially effectual for the procuring God's mercies in the day and the manner of our death. *Alms deliver from death* †, saith old *Tobias ;* and *alms make an atonement for sins* ‡, said the son of *Sirach ;* and so said *Daniel* §, and so say all the wise men of the world. And in this sense also is that of St. *Peter, Love covers a multitude of sins* ‖ ; and St. *Clement* ¶ in his Constitutions gives this counsel, *If you have any thing in your hands, give it, that it may*

---

* Quod expendi habui
Quod donavi habeo ;
Quod negavi punior,
Quod servavi perdidi.

† Tob. iv. 10. et xii. 9.　　　‡ Ecclus. iii. 30.　　　§ Dan. iv. 27.

‖ 1 Pet. iv. 8. Isa. i. 17.

¶ Lib. vii. 13. Ἐὰν ἔχεις διὰ τῶν χειρῶν ϲȣ, δός, ἵνα ἐργάσῃ, εἰς λύτρωσιν ἁμαρτιῶν ϲȣ, ἐλεημοσύναις, γὰρ καὶ πίϛεσιν ἀποκαθαίρονται ἁμαρτίαι.

work

work to the remission of thy sins. For by faith and alms sins are purged. The same also is the counsel of *Salvian,* who wonders that men who are guilty of great and many sins will not work out their pardon by alms and mercy. But this also must be added out of the words of *Lactantius,* who makes this rule complete and useful ; *But think not, because sins are taken away by alms, that by thy money thou mayest purchase a licence to sin. For sins are abolished, if because thou hast sinned thou givest to God,* that is, to God's poor servants, and his indigent necessitous creatures * ; but if thou sinnest upon confidence *of giving,* thy sins, are not abolished. For God desires infinitely that men should be purged from their sins, and therefore commands us to repent : but to repent is nothing else but to profess and affirm (that is, to purpose, and to make good that purpose) that they will sin no more.

Now alms are therefore effective to the abolition and pardon of our sins, because they are preparatory *to,* and impetratory *of* the grace of repentance, and are fruits of repentance ; and therefore St. *Chrysostome* † affirms, that repentance without alms is dead, and without wings, and can never soar upwards to the element of love. But because they are a part of repentance, and hugely pleasing to Almighty God, therefore they deliver us from the evils of an unhappy and accursed death : for so Christ delivered his disciples from the sea, when he appeased the storm, though they still sailed in the channel. And this St. *Hierome* verifies with all his reading and experience, saying, *I do not remember to have read, that ever any charitable person died an evil death.* ‡ And although a long experience hath observed God's mercies to de-

* Agere autem pœnitentiam nihil aliud est quàm profiteri et affirmare se non ulteriùs peccaturum.

† Orat. 2. de pœnitentia.

‡ Nunquam memini me legisse malâ morte mortuum, qui libenter opera charitatis exercuit, *ad* Nepot.

scend

scend upon charitable people, like the dew upon *Gi-deon's* fleece when all the world was dry; yet for this also we have a promise, which is not only an argument of a certain number of years (as experience is), but a security for eternal ages. *Make ye friends of the mammon of unrighteousness, that when ye fail, they may receive you into everlasting habitations.** When faith fails, and chastity is useless, and temperance shall be no more, then charity shall bear you upon wings of cherubims, to the eternal mountain of the Lord. *I have been a lover of mankind, and a friend, and merciful; and now I expect to communicate in that great kindness which he shews that is the great God and father of men and mercies†*, said *Cyrus* the *Persian* on his death-bed.

I do not mean this should only be a death-bed charity, any more than a death-bed repentance; but it ought to be the charity of our life and healthful years, a parting with portions of our goods then when we can keep them.‡ We must not first kindle our lights when we are to descend into our houses of darkness, or bring a glaring torch suddenly to a dark room, that will amaze the eye, and not delight it, or instruct the body; but if our tapers have in their constant course descended into their grave, crowned all the way with light, then let the death-bed charity be doubled, and the light burn brightest when it is to deck our hearse. But concerning this I shall afterwards give account.

---

* Luke, xvi. 9.   † Ἐγὼ φιλάνθρωπ⊙ ἐγενόμην, καὶ νῦν ἡδέως ἄν μοι δοκῶ κοινωνῆσαι τῷ εὐεργητῦντ⊙ ἀνθρώπυς.

‡ Da dum tempus habes, tibi propria sit manus hæres.
    Aufert hoc nemo quod dabis ipse Deo.

SECT. IV.

General Considerations to enforce the former Practices.

THESE are the general instruments of preparation in order to a holy death : it will concern us all to use them *diligently* and *speedily ; for we must be long in doing that which must be done but once* * : and therefore we must begin betimes, and lose no time ; especially since it is so great a venture, and upon it depends so great a state. *Seneca* said well, *There is no science or art in the world so hard as to live and die well: the professors of other arts are vulgar and many* † : but he that knows how to do this business is certainly instructed to eternity. ‡   But then let me remember this, that a wise person will also put most upon the greatest interest. Common prudence will teach us this. No man will hire a general to cut wood, or shake hay with a sceptre, or spend his soul and all his faculties upon the purchase of a cockleshell ; but he will fit instruments to the dignity and exigence of the design. And therefore since heaven is so glorious a state, and so certainly designed for us, if we please let us spend all that we have, all our passions and affections, all our study and industry, all our desires and stratagems, all our witty and ingenious faculties, toward the arriving thither, whither if we do come, every minute will infinitely pay for all the troubles of our whole life ; if we do not, we shall have the reward of fools, an unpitied and an upbraided misery.

* Quod sæpe fieri non potest fiat diu. *Seneca.*
† Nullius rei quàm vivere difficilior est scientia : Professores aliarum artium vulgò multique sunt. *Seneca.*
‡ Nunc ratio nulla est, restandi nulla facultas,
Æternas quoniam pœnas in morte timendum. *Lucret.*
Virtutem videant, intabescántque relicta.

To

To this purpose I shall represent the state of dying and dead men in the devout words of some of the fathers of the church, whose sense I shall exactly keep, but change their order; that by placing some of their dispersed meditations into a chain or sequel of discourse, I may with their precious stones make an *union*, and compose them into a jewel; for though the meditation is plain and easy, yet it is affectionate, and material, and true, and necessary.

The circumstances of a dying Man's Sorrow and Danger.

When the sentence of death is decreed, and begins to be put in execution, it is sorrow enough to see or feel respectively the sad accents of the agony and last contentions of the soul, and the reluctances and unwillingnesses of the body: the forehead washed with a new and stranger baptism, besmeared with a cold sweat, tenacious and clammy, apt to make it cleave to the roof of his coffin *; the nose cold and undiscerning, not pleased with perfumes, nor suffering violence with a cloud of unwholesome smoke; the eyes dim as a sullied mirror, or the face of heaven when God shews his anger in a prodigious storm; the feet cold, the hands stiff †; the physicians despairing, our friends weeping, the rooms dressed with darkness and sorrow; and the exterior parts betraying what are the violences which the soul and spirit suffer: the nobler part, like the lord of the house, being assaulted by exterior rudenesses, and driven from all the outworks, at last faint and weary with short and frequent breathings, interrupted with the longer accents of sighs, without moisture, but the excrescences of a spilt humour, when the pitcher is broken at the cistern, it retires to its last fort, *the heart*, whither it is pursued, and

* *Nilus.*   † *S. Basil.*

stormed,

stormed, and beaten out, as when the barbarous *Thracian* sacked the glory of the *Grecian* empire. Then calamity is great, and sorrow rules in all the capacities of man ; then the mourners weep, because it is civil, or because they need thee, or because they fear : but who suffers for thee with a compassion sharp as is thy pain ? Then the noise is like the faint echo of a distant valley, and few hear, and they will not regard thee, who seemest like a person void of understanding, and of a departing interest. *Verè tremendum est mortis sacramentum.* But these accidents are common to all that die ; and when a special providence shall distinguish them, they shall die with easy circumstances : but as no piety can secure it, so must no confidence except it, but wait for the time, and accept the manner of the dissolution. But that which distinguishes them is this :

He that hath lived a wicked life, if his conscience be alarmed, and that he does not die like a wolf or a tiger, without sense or remorse of all his wildness and his injury, his beastly nature, and desart and untilled manners, if he have but sense of what he is going to suffer, or what he may expect to be his portion ; then we may imagine the terror of their abused fancies, how they see affrighting shapes, and because they fear them, they feel the gripes of devils, urging the unwilling souls from the kinder and fast embraces of the body, calling to the grave, and hastening to judgment, exhibiting great bills of uncancelled crimes, awakening and amazing the conscience, breaking all their hope in pieces, and making faith useless and terrible, because the malice was great, and the charity was none at all. Then *they look for some to have pity on them, but there is no man.* * No man dares be their pledge ; *no man can redeem their soul,* which now feels what it never feared. Then the tremblings and the sorrow, the memory of the past sin, and the fear of

* *S. Chrysostomus.*

future

future pains, and the sense of an angry God, and the presence of some devils, consign him to the eternal company of all the damned and accursed spirits.* Then they want an angel for their guide, and the holy spirit for their comforter, and a good conscience for their testimony, and Christ for their advocate, and they die and are left in prisons of earth or air, in secret and undiscerned regions, to weep and tremble, and infinitely to fear the coming of the day of Christ; at which time they shall be brought forth to change their condition into a worse, where they shall for ever feel more than we can believe or understand.

But when a good man dies, one that hath lived innocently, or made *joy in heaven* at his timely and effective repentance, and in whose behalf the holy *Jesus* hath interceded prosperously, and for whose interest *the spirit makes interpellations with groans and sighs unutterable,* and in whose defence the angels drive away the devils on his death-bed, because his sins are pardoned, and because he resisted the devil in his lifetime, and fought successfully, and persevered unto the end; then the joys break forth through the clouds of sickness, and the conscience stands upright, and confesses the glory of God, and owns so much integrity that it can hope for pardon, and obtain it too: then the sorrows of the sickness, and the flames of the fever, or the faintness of the consumption, do but untie the soul from its chain, and let it go forth, first into liberty, and then to glory. For it is but for a little while that the face of the sky was black, like the preparations of the night, but quickly the cloud was torn and rent, the violence of thunder parted it into little portions, that the sun might look forth with a watery eye, and then shine without a tear. But it is an infinite refreshment to remember all the comforts of his prayers, the frequent victory over his temptations, the mortification of his lust, the

* *Ephrem Syrus.*

noblest

noblest sacrifice to God, in which he most delights, that we have given him our wills, and killed our appetites for the interests of his services: then all the trouble of that is gone, and what remains is a portion in the inheritance of *Jesus,* of which he now talks no more as a thing at a distance, but is entering into the possession.* When the veil is rent, and the prison-doors are open at the presence of God's angel, the soul goes forth full of hope, sometimes with evidence, but always with certainty in the thing, and instantly it passes into the throngs of spirits, where angels meet it singing, and the devils flock with malicious and vile purposes, desiring to lead it away with them into their houses of sorrow : there they see things which they never saw, and hear voices which they never heard. There the devils charge them with many sins, and the angels remember that themselves rejoiced when they were repented of. Then the devils aggravate and describe all the circumstances of the sin, and add calumnies ; and the angels bear the sword forward still, because their lord doth answer for them. Then the devils rage and gnash their teeth † ; they see the soul chaste and pure, and they are ashamed ; they see it penitent, and they despair ; they perceive that the tongue was refrained and sanctified, and then hold their peace. Then the soul passes forth and rejoices, passing by the devils in scorn and triumph, being securely carried into the bosom of the Lord, where they shall rest till their crowns are finished, and their mansions are prepared ; and then they shall feast and sing, rejoice and worship for ‡ ever and ever. Fearful and formidable to unholy persons is the first meeting with spirits in their separation. But the victory which holy souls receive by the mercies of *Jesus*

---

* *S. Martyrius, S. Eustratius* Martyr.   † *S. Chrysostomus.*
‡ Μεγίϛη των αἱϱετῶν θεοσέβεια δἰ ἧς ἀθανατίζεϊαι ἡ ψυχή.   Philo.

F   Christ,

Christ, and the conduct of angels, is a joy that we must not understand till we feel it; and yet such which, by an early and a persevering piety, we may secure: but let us enquire after it no farther, because it is secret.

CHAP. III.

OF THE STATE OF SICKNESS, AND THE TEMPTATIONS
INCIDENT TO IT, WITH THEIR PROPER REMEDIES.

———

SECT. I.

Of the State of Sickness.

Adam's sin brought death into the world, and
man did *die the same day in which he sinned,* according as God had threatened. He did not die, as
death is taken for a separation of soul and body;
that is not death properly, but the ending of the last
act of death; just as a man is said to be born, when
he ceases any longer to be born in his mother's womb:
but whereas to man was intended a life long and
happy, without sickness, sorrow, or infelicity, and
this life should be lived here or in a better place, and
the passage from one to the other should have been
easy, safe, and pleasant, now that man sinned, he fell
from that state to a contrary.

If *Adam* had stood, he should not always have
lived in this world; for this world was not a place capable of giving a dwelling to all those myriads of men
and women which should have been born in all the
generations of infinite and eternal ages; for so it
must have been if man had not died at all, nor yet

F 2   have

have removed hence at all. Neither is it likely that man's innocence should have lost to him all possibility of going thither where the duration is better, measured by a better time, subject to fewer changes, and which is now the reward of a returning virtue, which in all natural senses is less than innocence, save that it is heightened by Christ to an equality of acceptation with the state of innocence: but so it must have been, that his innocence should have been punished with an eternal confinement to this state, which in all reason is the less perfect, the state of a traveller, not of one possessed of his inheritance. It is therefore certain, man should have changed his abode; for so did *Enoch*, and so did *Elias*, and so shall all the world that shall be alive at the day of judgment; *They shall not die, but they shall change* their place and their abode, their duration and their state, and all this without death.

That death therefore which God threatened to *Adam*, and which passed upon his posterity, is not the going out of this world, but *the manner of going*. If he had staid in innocence, he should have gone from hence placidly and fairly, without vexatious and afflictive circumstances; he should not have died by sickness, misfortune, defect, or unwillingness *: but when he fell, then he began to die; *the same day* (so said God): and that must needs be true, and therefore it must mean, that upon that very day he fell into an evil and dangerous condition, a state of change and affliction †: then death began, that is, the man began to die by a natural diminution and aptness to disease and misery. His first state was and should have been (so long as it lasted) a happy duration; his second was a daily and miserable change: and this was the dying properly.

---

* Prima quæ vitam dedit hora carpsit. *Hercul. Fur.*
† Nascentes morimur, finisque ab origine pendet. *Manil.*

This

This appears in the great instance of *damnation,* which in the style of scripture is called *eternal death ;* not because it kills or ends the duration, it hath not so much good in it, but because it is a perpetual infelicity. Change or separation of soul and body is but accidental to death, death may be with or without either: but the formality, the curse and the sting of death, that is, misery, sorrow, fear, diminution, defect, anguish, dishonour, and whatsoever is miserable and afflictive in nature, that is death. Death is not an action, but a whole state and condition; and this was first brought in upon us by the offence of one man.

But this went no farther than thus to subject us to temporal infelicity. If it had proceeded so as was supposed, man had been much more miserable ; for man had more than one original sin in this sense : and though this death entered first upon us by *Adam's* fault, yet it came nearer unto us and increased upon us by the sins of more of our forefathers. For *Adam's* sin left us in strength enough to contend with human calamities for almost a thousand years together : but the sins of his children, our forefathers, took off from us half the strength about the time of the flood ; and then from five hundred to two hundred and fifty, and from thence to one hundred and twenty, and from thence to threescore and ten ; so often halfing it, till it is almost come to nothing. But by the sins of men in the several generations of the world, *death,* that is, misery and disease, is hastened so upon us, that we are of a contemptible age : and because we are to die by suffering evils, and by the daily lessening of our strength and health, this death is so long a doing, that it makes so great a part of our short life useless and unserviceable, that we have not time enough to get the perfection of a single manufacture, but ten or twelve generations of the world must go to the making up of one wise man, or one excellent art : and in the

F 3　　　　　　　　　succession

succession of those ages there happen so many changes
and interruptions, so many wars and violences, that
seven years fighting sets a whole kingdom back in
learning and virtue, to which they were creeping it
may be a whole age.

And thus also we do evil to our posterity, as *Adam*
did to his, and *Cham* did to his, and *Eli* to his, and
all they to theirs, who by sins caused God to shorten
the life and multiply the evils of mankind. And for
this reason it is the world grows worse and worse,
because so many original sins are multiplied, and so
many evils from parents descend upon the succeeding
generations of men, that they derive nothing from us
but original misery.

But he who restored the law of nature did also
restore us to the condition of nature; which, being
violated by the introduction of death, Christ then re-
paired when he suffered and overcame death for us:
that is, he hath taken away the unhappiness of sickness, and the sting of death, and the dishonours of
the grave, of dissolution and weakness, of decay and
change, and hath turned them into acts of favour,
into instances of comfort, into opportunities of virtue.
Christ hath now knit them into rosaries and coronets,
he hath put them into promises and rewards, he hath
made them part of the portion of his elect: they are
instruments, and earnests, and securities, and passages
to the greatest perfection of human nature, and the
divine promises: so that it is possible for us now to be
reconciled to sickness; *It came in by sin, and therefore is cured when it is turned into virtue:* and
although it may have in it the uneasiness of labour;
yet it will not be uneasy as sin, or the restlessness of a
discomposed conscience. If therefore we can well
manage our state of sickness, *that we may not fall
by pain, as we usually do by pleasure,* we need not
fear; for no evil shall happen to us.

SECT. II.

*Of the first Temptation proper to the State of Sickness,
Impatience.*

MEN that are in health are severe exactors of *patience* at the hands of them that are sick; and they usually judge it not by terms of relation between God and the suffering man, but between him and the friends that stand by the bed-side. It will be therefore necessary that we truly understand to what duties and actions the patience of a sick man ought to extend.

1. Sighs and groans, sorrow and prayers, humble complaints and dolorous expressions, are the sad accents of a sick man's language. * For it is not to be expected that a sick man should act a part of patience with a countenance like an orator, or grave like a dramatic person: it were well if all men could bear an exterior decency in their sickness, and regulate their voice, their face, their discourse, and all their circumstances, by the measures and proportions of comeliness and satisfaction to all the standers-by. But this would better please them than assist them; the sick man would do more good to others than he would receive to himself.

2. Therefore silence, and still composures, and not complaining, are no parts of a sick man's duty, they are not necessary parts of patience. † We find that *David roared for the very disquietness of his sickness;* and he lay *chattering like a swallow,* and *his throat was dry* with calling for help upon his God.

* Ejulatu, questu, gemitu, fremitibus, resonando multùm flebiles voces refert. *Cic.* Tusc.
† Concedendum est gementi.

That's

That's the proper voice of sickness : and certain it is that the proper voices of sickness are expressly *vocal* and *petitory* in the ears of God, and call for pity in the same accent as the cries and oppressions of widows and orphans do for vengeance upon their persecutors, though they say no collect against them. For there is *the voice of a man,* and there is *the voice of the disease,* and God hears both ; and the louder the disease speaks, there is the greater need of mercy and pity, and therefore God will the sooner hear it. *Abel's blood had a voice,* and cried to God; and *humility hath a voice,* and cries so loud to God that *it pierces the clouds ;* and so hath every sorrow and every sickness : and when a man cries out, and complains * but according to the sorrows of his pain, it cannot be any part of a culpable impatience, but an argument for pity.

3. Some men's senses are so subtle, and their perceptions so quick and full of relish, and their spirits so active, that the same load is double upon them to what it is to another person : and therefore comparing the expressions of the one to the silence of the other, a different judgment cannot be made concerning their patience. Some natures are querulous, and melancholic, and soft, and nice, and tender, and weeping, and expressive ; others are sullen, dull, without apprehension, apt to tolerate and carry burdens : and the crucifixion of our blessed Saviour, falling upon a delicate and virgin body, of curious temper, and strict, equal composition, was naturally more full of torment than that of the ruder thieves, whose proportions were coarser and uneven.

4. In this case it was no imprudent advice which *Cicero* gave† : nothing in the world is more amiable

---

* ————Flagrantior æquo
　　Non debet dolor esse viri, nec vulnere major. *Juven.* Sat. 12.
　† Omnino si quicquam est decorum ; nihil est profectò magis quàm æquabilitas universæ vitæ, tum singularum actionum : quam autem conservare non possis, si aliorum naturam imitans omittas tuam.

than

than an even temper in our whole life, and in every action : but this evenness cannot be kept unless every man follows his own nature, without striving to imitate the circumstances of another. And what is so in the thing itself, ought to be so in our judgments concerning the things. We must not call any one impatient if he be not silent in a fever, as if he were asleep, as if he were dull, as *Herod's* son of *Athens*.

5. Nature in some cases hath made cryings-out and exclamations to be an entertainment of the spirit, and an abatement or diversion of the pain. For so did the old champions, when they threw their fatal nets that they might load their enemy with the snares and weights of death*, they groaned aloud, and sent forth the anguish of their spirit into the eyes and heart of the man that stood against them. So it is in the endurance of some sharp pains, the complaints and shriekings, the sharp groans and the tender accents send forth the afflicted spirits, and force away, that they may ease their oppression and their load, that when they have spent some of their sorrows by a sally forth, they may return better able to fortify the heart. Nothing of this is a certain sign, much less an action or part of impatience; and when our blessed Saviour suffered his last and sharpest pang of sorrow, *he cried out with a loud voice*, and resolved to die, and did so.

SECT. III.

Constituent or Integral Parts of Patience.

1. THAT we may secure our patience, we must take care that *our complaints be without despair*. De-

---

* Quia profundendâ voce omne corpus intenditur, venitque plaga vehementior. *Cic.* Tusc.

spair

spair sins against the reputation of God's goodness, and the efficacy of all our old experience. By despair we destroy the greatest comfort of our sorrows, and turn our sickness into the state of devils and perishing souls. No affliction is greater than despair: for that it is which makes hell-fire, and turns a natural evil into an intolerable; it hinders prayers, and fills up the intervals of sickness with a worse torture; it makes all spiritual arts useless, and the office of spiritual comforters and guides to be impertinent.

Against this, *Hope* is to be opposed: and its proper acts as it relates to the virtue and exercise of patience are, 1. Praying to God for help and remedy: 2. Sending for the guides of souls: 3. Using all holy exercises and acts of grace proper to that state: which whoso does hath not the impatience of despair; every man that is patient hath hope in God in the day of his sorrows.

2. Our complaints in sickness must be *without murmur*. Murmur sins against God's providence and government: by it we grow rude, and, like the falling angels, displeased at God's supremacy; and nothing is more unreasonable: it talks against God, for whose glory all speech was made; it is proud and phantastic, hath better opinions of a sinner than of the Divine justice, and would rather accuse God than himself.

Against this is opposed that part of patience which resigns the man into the hands of God, saying with old *Eli, It is the Lord, let him do what he will;* and [*Thy will be done in earth, as it is in heaven:*] and so the admiring God's justice and wisdom does also dispose the sick person for receiving God's mercy, and secure him the rather in the grace of God. The proper acts of this part of patience: 1. To confess our sins and our own demerits. 2. It encreases and exercises humility. 3. It loves to sing praises to God, even from the lowest abyss of human misery.

3. Our

3. Our complaints in sickness must be *without peevishness*. This sins against civility, and that necessary decency which must be used towards the ministers and assistants. By peevishness we encrease our own sorrows, and are troublesome to them that stand there to ease ours. It hath in it harshness of nature and ungentleness, wilfulness and phantastic opinions, morosity and incivility.

Against it are opposed obedience, tractability, easiness of persuasion, aptness to take counsel. The acts of this part of patience are, 1. To obey our physicians: 2. To treat our persons with respect to our present necessities*: 3. Not to be ungentle and uneasy to the ministers and nurses that attend us; but to take their diligent and kind offices as sweetly as we can, and to bear their indiscretions or unhandsome accidents contentedly and without disquietness within, or evil language or angry words without: 4. Not to use unlawful means for our recovery.

If we secure these particulars, we are not lightly to be judged of by noises and posture, by colours and images of things, by paleness, or tossing from side to side. For it were a hard thing that those persons who are loaden with the greatest of human calamities should be strictly tied to ceremonies and forms of things. He is patient that calls upon God, that hopes for health or heaven, that believes God is wise and just in sending him afflictions, that confesses his sins, and accuses himself, and justifies God, that expects God will turn this into good, that is civil to his physicians and his servants, that converses with the guides of souls, the ministers of religion, and in all things submits to God's will, and would use no indirect means for his recovery, but had rather be sick and die, than enter at all into God's displeasure.

---

* *Vid.* Chap. iv. Sect. 1.

7

SECT. IV.

Remedies against Impatience, by Way of Consideration.

As it happens concerning death, so it is in sickness, which is death's hand-maid. It hath the fate
to suffer calumny and reproach, and hath a name
worse than its nature.

1. For there is no sickness so great but children
endure it, and have natural strengths to bear them
out quite through the calamity, what period soever
nature hath allotted it. Indeed, they make no reflections upon their sufferings, and complain of sickness with an uneasy sigh or a natural groan, but
consider not what the sorrows of sickness mean; and
so bear it by a direct sufferance, and as a pillar bears
the weight of a roof. But then why cannot we bear
it so too. For this which we call a reflection upon,
or considering of our sickness, is nothing but a perfect instrument of trouble, and consequently a temptation to impatience. It serves no end of nature; it
may be avoided, and we may consider it only as an
expression of God's anger, and an emissary or pro-
curator of repentance.* But all other considering it,
except where it serves the purposes of medicine and
art, is nothing but, under the colour of reason, an
unreasonable device to heighten the sickness and increase the torment. But then, as children want this
act of reflex perception or reasonable sense, whereby
their sickness becomes less pungent and dolorous; so
also do they want the helps of reason, whereby they
should be able to support it. For certain it is, reason
was as well given us to harden our spirits, and stiffen

---

* Prætulerim ——— delirus inérsque videri,
Dum mea delectent mala me, vel denique fallant,
Quàm sapere et ringi.   *Hor.* lib. ii. ep. 2.

them

them in passions and sad accidents, as to make us
bending and apt for action : and if in men God hath
heightened the faculties of apprehension, he hath increased the auxiliaries of reasonable strengths that
God's rod and God's staff might go together, and the
beam of God's countenance may as well refresh us
with its light as scorch us with its heat.   But poor
children, that endure so much, have not inward supports and refreshments, to bear them through it ;
they never heard the sayings of old men, nor have
been taught the principles of severe philosophy, nor
are assisted with the results of a long experience,
nor know they how to turn a sickness into virtue, and
a fever into a reward ; nor have they any sense of
favours, the remembrance of which may alleviate their
burden ; and yet nature hath in them teeth and nails
enough to scratch, and fight against their sickness ;
and by such aids as God is pleased to give them, they
wade through the storm, and murmur not.   And besides this, yet, although infants have not such brisk
perceptions upon the stock of reason, they have a
more tender feeling upon the accounts of sense, and
their flesh is as uneasy by their unnatural softness
and weak shoulders, as ours by our too forward apprehensions.*   Therefore bear up ; either you or I,
or some man wiser, and many a woman weaker than
us both, or the very children, have endured worse evil
than this that is upon thee now.

That sorrow is hugely tolerable, which gives its
smart but by instants and smallest proportions of time.
No man at once feels the sickness of a week, or of a
whole day ; but the smart of an instant : and still
every portion of a minute feels but its proper share,
and the last groan ended all the sorrow of its peculiar
burden.   And what minute can that be which can
pretend to be intolerable ? and the next minute is but

* Στῆθ͞Θ͏ δε πλήξας κραδίην, ἠνίπαπε μύθῳ,

Τίτλαϑι δὴ κραδίη, καὶ κύντερον ἄλλο ποτ᾽ ἔτλης.   Ulysses *apud* Hom. *Od. v.*

the

the same as the last, and the pain flows like the drops
of a river, or the little shreds of time: and if we do
but take care of the present minute, it cannot seem a
great charge or a great burthen; but that care will
secure our duty, if we still but secure the present
minute.

3. If we consider how much men can suffer if they
list, and how much they do suffer for great and little
causes, and that no causes are greater than the proper
causes of patience and sickness, (that is, necessity and
religion,) we cannot, without huge shame to our nature, to our persons, and to our manners, complain
of this tax and impost of nature. This experience
added something to the old philosophy. When the
Gladiators were exposed naked to each others short
swords, and were to cut each others souls away in
portions of flesh, as if their forms had been as divi-
sible as the life of worms, they did not sigh or groan,
it was a shame to decline the blow, but according to
the just measures of art. The * women that saw the
wound shriek out, and he that receives it holds his
peace.† He did not only stand bravely, but would
also fall so; and when he was down, scorned to
shrink his head, when the insolent conqueror came to
lift it from his shoulders: and yet this man in his
first design only aimed at liberty, and the reputation
of a good fencer; and when he sunk down, he saw
he could only receive the honour of a bold man, the
noise of which he shall never hear when his ashes are
crammed in his narrow urn. And what can we complain of the weakness of our strengths, or the pressures of diseases, when we see a poor soldier stand in
a breach almost starved with cold and hunger, and
his cold apt to be relieved only by the heats of anger,

---

* Spectatores vociferantur, ictus tacet.
† Quis mediocris gladiator ingemuit?
  Quis vultum mutavit unquam ?
  Quis non modò stetit, verùm etiam decubuit turpiter ?

Tusc. Q. lib. ii.

a fever,

a fever, or a fired musket, and his hunger slacked by a greater pain, and a huge fear? This man shall stand in his arms and wounds, *patiens luminis atque solis*, pale and faint, weary and watchful; and at night shall have a bullet pulled out of his flesh, and shivers from his bones, and endure his mouth to be sewed up for a violent rent to its own dimension; and all this for a man whom he never saw, or, if he did, was not noted by him, but one that shall condemn him to the gallows if he runs from all this misery. It is seldom that God sends such calamities upon men as men bring upon themselves, and suffer willingly. But that which is most considerable is, that any passion and violence upon the spirit of man, makes him able to suffer huge calamities with a certain constancy and an unwearied patience. *Scipio Africanus* was wont to commend that saying in *Xenophon*, That the same labours of warfare were easier far to a general than to a common soldier, because he was supported by the huge appetites of honour, which made his hard marches nothing but stepping forward and reaching at a triumph. Did not the lady of *Sabinus* for others interest, bear twins privately, and without groaning? Are not the labours and cares, the spare diet and the waking nights of covetous and adulterous, of ambitious and revengeful persons, greater sorrows and of more smart than a fever, or the short pains of childbirth? What will not tender women suffer to hide their shame? And if vice and passion, lust and inferior appetites can supply to the tenderest persons strengths more than enough for the sufferance of the greatest natural violences, can we suppose that honesty and religion, and the grace of God, are more nice, tender, and effeminate?

4. Sickness is the more tolerable, because it cures very many evils, and takes away the sense of all the cross fortunes which amaze the spirits of some men, and transport them certainly beyond all the limits of patience.

patience.   Here all losses and disgraces, domestic
cares and public evils, the apprehensions of pity and
a sociable calamity, the fears of want and the troubles
of ambition, lie down and rest upon the sick man's
pillow.   One fit of the stone takes away from the
fancies of men all relations to the world and secular
interests : at least they are made dull and flat, without
sharpness and an edge.

And he that shall observe the infinite variety of
troubles which afflict some busy persons, and almost
all men in very busy times, will think it not much
amiss that those huge numbers were reduced to certainty, to method, and an order; and there is no
better *compendium* for this, than that they be reduced
to one.   And a sick man seems so unconcerned in the
things of the world, that although this separation be
done with violence, yet it is no otherwise than all
noble contentions are, and all honours are purchased,
and all virtues are acquired, and all vices mortified,
and all appetites chastised, and all rewards obtained :
there is infallibly to all these a difficulty and a sharpness annexed, without which there could be no proportion between a work and a reward.   To this add,
that sickness does not take off the sense of secular
troubles and worldly cares from us, by employing all
the perceptions and apprehensions of men ; by filling
all faculties with sorrow, and leaving no room for the
lesser instances of troubles, as little rivers are swal-
lowed up in the sea : but sickness is a messenger of
God, sent with purposes of abstraction and separation
with a secret power and a proper efficacy to draw
us from unprofitable and useless sorrows.   And this is
effected partly, by reason that it represents the use-
lessness of the things of this world, and that there is a
proportion of this life in which honours and things
of the world cannot serve us to many purposes;
partly, by preparing us to death, and telling us that
a man shall descend thither whence this world cannot
                                            redeem

redeem us, and where the goods of this world cannot serve us.

5. And yet after all this, sickness leaves in us appetites so strong, and apprehensions so sensible, and delights so many, and good things in so great a degree, that a healthless body and a sad disease do seldom make men weary of this world, but still they would fain find an excuse to live.* The gout, the stone, and the tooth-ache, the sciatica, sore-eyes, and an aching head, are evils indeed; but such, which rather than die, most men are willing to suffer; and *Mæcenas* added also a wish, rather to be crucified than to die: and though his wish was low, timorous and base, yet we find the same desires in most men, dressed up with better circumstances. It was a cruel mercy in *Tamerlane,* who commanded all the leprous persons to be put to death, as we knock some beasts quickly on their head, to put them out of pain, and lest they should live miserably: the poor men would rather have endured another leprosy, and have more willingly taken two diseases than one death. Therefore *Cæsar* wondered that the old crazed soldier begged leave he might kill himself, and asked him, *Dost thou think then to be more alive than now thou art?* We do not die suddenly, but we descend to death by steps and slow passages: and therefore men (so long as they are sick) are unwilling to proceed and go forward in the finishing that sad employment. Between a disease and death there are many degrees, and all those are like the reserves of evil things, the declining of every one of which is justly reckoned among those good things which alleviate the sickness, and make it tolerable. Never account that sickness intolerable, in which thou hadst rather remain than die: and yet if thou hadst rather die than suffer it,

---

* Debilem facito manu, debilem pede, coxâ, lubricos quate dentes; vita dum superest bene est. Hanc mihi, vel acutam, si das, sustineo crucem. *Sen.* Ep. 101.

the

the worst of it that can be said is this, that the sickness is worse than death ; that is, it is worse than
that which is the best of all evils, and the end of all
troubles ; and then you have said no great harm
against it.

6. Remember that thou art under a supervening
necessity. *Nothing is intolerable that is necessary ;*
and therefore when men are to suffer a sharp incision,
or what they are pleased to call *intolerable*, tie the
man down to it, and he endures it.* Now God hath
bound the sickness upon thee by the condition of
nature : (for every flower must wither and drop :) it
is also bound upon thee by special Providence, and
with a design to try thee, and with purposes to reward and to crown thee. These cords thou canst
not break ; and therefore lie thou down gently, and
suffer the hand of God to do what he pleases, that at
least thou mayest swallow an advantage, which the
care and severe mercies of God force down thy
throat.

7. Remember that all men have passed this way †,
the bravest, the wisest, and the best men have been
subject to sickness and sad diseases ; and it is esteemed a prodigy, that a man should live to a long age
and not be sick : and it is recorded for a wonder concerning *Xenophilus* the musician, that he lived to 106
years of age, in a perfect and continual health. No
story tells the like of a prince ‡, or a great or a wise
person : unless we have a mind to believe the tales
concerning *Nestor* and the *Eubœan Sibyl*, or reckon
Cyrus of *Persia*, or *Masinissa* the *Mauritanian* to
be rivals of old age, or that *Argentonius* the *Tar-
tesian* king did really out-strip that age, according as
his story tells, reporting him to have § reigned 80

---

* Improbæque Tigres indulgent patientiam flagello : Impiger et fortis
virtute coactus.
    † Cerno equidem geminâ constratos morte Philippos,
      Thessaliæque rogos, et funera gentis Iberæ.
    ‡ Rara est in nobilitate senectus.   § *Cicero* de Senect.

years,

years, and to have lived 120. Old age and healthful
bodies are seldom made the appendages to great fortunes : and under so great and so * universal precedents, so common fate of men, he that will not suffer
his portion deserves to be something else than a man,
but nothing that is better.

8. We find in story that many Gentiles, who
walked by no light but that of reason, opinion, and
humane examples, did bear their sickness nobly, and
with great contempt of pain, and with huge interests
of virtue. When *Pompey* came from *Syria,* and
called at *Rhodes* to see *Possidonius* the philosopher,
he found him hugely afflicted with the gout, and expressed his sorrow that he could not hear his lectures,
from which, by this pain, he must needs be hindered.
Possidonius told him, *But you may hear me for all
this :* and he discoursed excellently in the midst of
his tortures, even then *when the torches were put to
his feet*†, that *nothing was good but what was honest ;*
and therefore *nothing could be an evil if it were not
criminal :* and summed up his lectures with this saying, *O pain, in vain dost thou attempt me ; for I
will never confess thee to be an evil as long as I can
honestly bear thee.* And when *Pompey* himself was
desperately sick at *Naples,* the *Neapolitans* wore
crowns and triumphed, and the men of *Puteoli* came
to congratulate his sickness, not because they loved
him not, but because it was the custom of their country
to have better opinions of sickness than we have. The
boys of *Sparta* would at their altars endure whip-
ping till their very entrails saw the light through their
torn flesh, and some of them to death, without crying
or complaint. *Cæsar* would drink his potions of
rhubarb rudely mixt, and unfitly allayed, with little
suppings, and tasted the horror of the medicine,
spreading the loathsomeness of his physic so, that all

* Ferre quam sortem patiuntur omnes, nemo recusat.
† Tusc. l. 2. Cùm faces doloris admoverentur.

　　　　　　　the

the parts of his tongue and palate might have an entire share. And when *C. Marius* suffered the veins of his leg to be cut out for the curing of his gout, and yet shrunk not, he declared not only the rudeness of their physic, but the strength of a man's spirit, if it be contracted and united by the aids of reason or religion, by resolution or any accidental harshness, against a violent disease.

9. All impatience, howsoever expressed, is perfectly useless to all purposes of ease, but hugely effective to the multiplying the trouble; and the impatience and vexation is another, but the sharper disease of the two; it does mischief *by itself*, and mischief *by the disease*. For *men grieve themselves as much as they please* *; and when, by impatience, they put themselves into the retinue of sorrows, they become solemn mourners. For so have I seen the rays of the sun or moon dash upon a brazen vessel, whose lips kissed the face of those waters that lodged within its bosom †; but being turned back and sent off with its smooth pretences or rougher waftings, it wandered about the room and beat upon the roof, and still doubled its heat and motion. So is a sickness and a sorrow, entertained by an unquiet and a discontented man, turned back either with anger or with excuses; but then the pain passes from the stomach to the liver, and from the liver to the heart, and from the heart to the head, and from feeling to consideration, from thence to sorrow, and at last ends in impatience and useless murmur; and all the way the man was impotent and weak, but the sickness

---

* Tantum doluerunt quantum doloribus inservierunt. S. *August. Virg.* l. 8. v. 2.

     † Ceu rore seges viret,
Sic crescunt riguis tristia fletibus;
     Urget lacryma lacrymam,
Fœcundúsque sui se numerat dolor.
     Quem fortuna semel virum
Udo degenerem lumine viderit,
     Illum sæpe ferit ――――

was

was doubled, and grew imperious and tyrannical over the soul and body. *Masurius Sabinus* tells, that the image of the Goddess *Angerona* was with a muffler upon her mouth placed upon the altar of *Volupia*, to represent, that those persons who bear their sicknesses and sorrows without murmurs*, shall certainly pass from sorrow to pleasure, and the ease and honours of felicity; but they that with spite and indignation bite the burning coal, or shake the yoke upon their necks, gall their spirits, and fret the skin, and hurt nothing but themselves.

10. Remember that this sickness is but for a short time: if it be sharp, it will not last long; if it be long, it will be easy and very tolerable. And although *S. Eadsine*, archbishop of *Canterbury*, had twelve years of sickness, yet all that while he ruled his church prudently, gave example of many virtues, and after his death was enrolled in the calendar of Saints, who had finished their course prosperously. Nothing is more unreasonable than to entangle our spirits in wildness and amazement, like a partridge fluttering in a net, which she breaks not, though she breaks her wings.

SECT. V.

Remedies against Impatience, by way of Exercise.

1. THE fittest instrument of esteeming sickness easily tolerable is, to remember that which indeed makes it so; and that is, that God doth minister proper aids and supports to every of his servants whom he visits with his rod. He knows our needs,

---

* ———— Levius fit patientiâ
Quicquid corrigere est nefas. *Horat.*

he

he pities our sorrows, he relieves our miseries, he supports our weakness, he bids us ask for help, and he promises to give us all that, and he usually gives us more. And indeed it is observable, that no story tells of any godly man, who, living in the fear of God, fell into a violent and unpardoned impatience in his natural sickness, if he used those means which God and his Holy Church have appointed. We see almost all men bear their last sickness *with sorrows* indeed, but *without violent passions;* and unless they fear death violently, they suffer the sickness with some indifferency: and it is a rare thing to see a man who enjoys his reason in his sickness, to express the proper signs of a direct and solemn impatience. For when God lays a sickness upon us, he seizes commonly on a man's spirits; which are the instruments of action and business; and when they are secured from being tumultuous, the sufferance is much the easier: and therefore sickness secures all that which can do the man mischief; it makes him tame and passive, apt for suffering, and confines him to an active condition. To which if we add, that God then commonly produces fear, and all those passions which naturally tend to humility and poverty of spirit, we shall soon perceive by what instruments God verifies his promise to us, (which is the great security for our patience, and the easiness of our condition,) that * *God will lay no more upon us than he will make us able to bear, but together with the affliction he will find a way to escape.* Nay, if any thing can be more than this †, we have two or three promises in which we may safely lodge ourselves, and roll from off our thorns, and find ease and rest. God hath promised *to be with us in our trouble,* and *to be with us in our*

* 1 Cor. x. 13.
† Psal. ix. 9. Matth. vii. 7. Jam. v. 13. Psal. xxxi. 19. 24. Psal. xxxiv. 22.

prayers,

prayers, and *to be with us in our hope* and *confidence*.

2. Prevent the violence and trouble of thy spirit by an act of thanksgiving: for which in the worst of sicknesses thou canst not want cause, especially if thou rememberest that this pain is not an eternal pain. *Bless God for that:* but take heed also, lest you so order your affairs, that you pass from hence to an eternal sorrow. If that be hard, this will be intolerable. But as for the present evil, a few days will end it.

3. Remember that thou art a man, and a Christian: as the *covenant of nature* hath made it *necessary*, so the *covenant of grace* hath made it to be *chosen* by thee, to be a suffering person: either you must renounce your religion, or submit to the impositions of God, and thy portion of sufferings. So that here we see our advantages, and let us use them accordingly. The barbarous and warlike nations of old could fight well and willingly, but could not bear sickness manfully. The *Greeks* were cowardly in their fights, as most wise men are; but because they were learned and well taught, they bore their sickness with patience and severity. The *Cimbrians* and *Celtiberians* rejoice in battle like giants, but in their diseases they weep like women. These, according to their institutions and designs, had unequal courages, and accidental fortitude. But since our religion hath made *a covenant of sufferings*, and the great business of our lives is *sufferings*, and most of the virtues of a Christian are *passive graces*, and all the promises of the gospel are passed upon us through *Christ's cross*, we have a necessity upon us to have an equal courage in all the variety of our sufferings: for without an universal fortitude we can do nothing of our duty.

4. Resolve to do as much as you can: for certain it is, we can suffer very much, if we list: and many

men

men have afflicted themselves unreasonably by not being skilful to consider how much their strength and estate could permit; and how flesh is nice and imperious, crafty to persuade reason that she hath more necessities than indeed belong to her, and that she demands nothing superfluous. Suffer as much in obedience to God as you can suffer for necessity or passion, fear or desire. And if you can for one thing, you can for another, and there is nothing wanting but the mind. Never say *I can do no more, I cannot endure this :* for God would not have sent it, if he had not known thee strong enough to abide it; only he that knows thee well already, would also take this occasion to make thee to know thyself. But it will be fit that you pray to God to give you a discerning spirit, that you may rightly distinguish *just necessity* from the *flattery* and fondnesses of flesh and blood.

5. Propound to your eyes and heart the example of the Holy *Jesus* upon the cross: he endured more for thee than thou canst either for thyself or him. And remember that if we be put to suffer, and do suffer *in a good cause*, or *in a good manner*, so that in any sense your sufferings be conformable to his sufferings, or can be capable of being united to his, we shall reign together with him. *The high way of the cross*, which the king of sufferings hath trodden before us, is the way to *ease*, to a *kingdom*, and to *felicity*.

6. The very suffering is a title to an excellent inheritance: for *God chastens every son whom he receives*, and if we be not chastised, *we are bastards, and not sons*. And be confident, that although God *often* sends pardon without correction, yet he never sends correction without pardon, unless it be thy fault; and therefore take every or any affliction as an earnest penny of thy pardon; and upon condition there may be peace with God, let any thing be welcome
that

that he can send as its instrument or condition. Suffer therefore God to choose his own circumstances of adopting thee, and be content to be under discipline, when the reward of that is *to become the son of God :* and by such inflictions he hews and breaks thy body, first dressing it to funeral, and then preparing it for immortality. And if this be the effect or the design of God's love to thee, let it be occasion of thy love to him : and remember that the truth of love is hardly known but by somewhat that puts us to pain.

7. Use this as a punishment for thy sins; and so God intends it most commonly, that is certain : if therefore thou submittest to it, thou approvest of the Divine judgment: and no man can have cause to complain of any thing but of himself, if either he believes God to be just, or himself to be a sinner ; if he either thinks he hath deserved hell, or that this little may be a means to prevent the greater, and bring him to heaven.

8. It may be that this may be the last instance and the last opportunity that ever God will give thee to exercise any virtue, to do him any service, or thyself any advantage: be careful that thou losest not this ; for to eternal ages this never shall return again.

9. Or if thou, peradventure, shalt be restored to health, be careful that in the day of thy thanksgiving thou mayest not be ashamed of thyself, for having behaved thyself poorly and weakly upon thy bed. It will be a sensible and excellent comfort to thee, and double upon thy spirit, if when thou shalt worship God for restoring thee, thou shalt also remember that thou didst do him service in thy suffering, and tell that God was hugely gracious to thee in giving thee the opportunity of a virtue at so easy a rate, as a sickness from which thou didst recover.

10. Few men are so sick, but they believe that they may recover ; and we shall seldom see a man lie
down

down with a perfect persuasion that it is his last hour; for many men have been sicker, and yet have recovered. But whether thou dost or no, thou hast a virtue to exercise, which may be a hand-maid to thy patience. *Epaphroditus* was sick, *sick unto death, and* yet *God had mercy upon him:* and he hath done so to thousands, to whom he found it useful in the great order of things, and the events of universal Providence: if therefore thou desirest to recover, here is cause enough of hope, and hope is designed in the arts of God and of the spirit to support patience. But if thou recoverest not, yet there is something that is matter of joy naturally, and very much spiritually, if thou belongest to God; and *joy* is as certain a support of patience as *hope:* and it is no small cause of being pleased, when we remember that, if we recover not, our sickness shall the sooner set down in rest and joy. For recovery by death, as it is easier and better than the recovery by a sickly health, so it is not so long in doing: it suffers not the tediousness of a creeping restitution, nor the inconvenience of surgeons and physicians, watchfulness and care, keepings in and suffering trouble, fears of relapse, and the little reliques of a storm.

11. While we hear, or use, or think of these remedies, part of the sickness is gone away, and all of it is passing. And if by such instruments we stand armed, and ready dressed before-hand, we shall avoid the mischiefs of amazements and surprise *; while the accidents of sickness are such as were expected, and against which we stood in readiness with our spirits contracted, instructed, and put upon the defensive.

12. But our patience will be the better secured, if we consider that it is not violently tempted by the

* Nulla mihi nova nunc facies inopináque surgit:
Omnia præcepi atque animo mecum antè revolvi.
Virgil, lib. 6.

usual

usual arrests of sickness : for patience is with reason
demanded while the sickness is tolerable, that is, so
long as the evil is not too great ; but if it be also eligible, and have in it some degrees of good, our patience
will have in it the less difficulty and the greater necessity.   This therefore will be a new stock of consideration : *sickness is in many degrees eligible to many men,
and to many purposes.*

SECT. VI.

Advantages of Sickness.

1. I CONSIDER one of the great felicities of heaven
consists in an immunity from sin : then we shall love
God without mixtures of malice, then we shall enjoy
without envy ; then we shall see fuller vessels running
over with glory, and crowned with bigger circles ; and
this we shall behold without spilling from our eyes
(those vessels of joy and grief) any sign of anger,
trouble, or any repining spirit : our passions shall be
pure, our charity without fear, our desire without lust,
our possessions all our own ; and all in the inheritance
of Jesus, in the richest soil of God's eternal kingdom.   Now half of this reason which makes heaven
so happy by being innocent, is also in the state of
sickness, making the sorrows of old age smooth, and
the groans of a sick heart apt to be joined to the music
of angels : and though they sound harsh to our untuned
ears and discomposed organs ; yet those accents must
needs be in themselves excellent which God loves to
hear, and esteems them as *prayers* and *arguments of
pity*, instruments of mercy and grace, and preparatives
to glory.
In sickness the soul begins to dress herself for immortality.

mortality. And first, *she unties the strings of vanity,
that made her upper garment cleave to the world, and
sit uneasy.* First, *she puts off the light and phantastic
summer robe of lust and wanton appetite :* and as soon
as that *Cestus,* that lascivious girdle is thrown away,
then the *reins chasten us, and give us warning in the
night ;* then that which called us formerly to serve
the manliness of the body, and *the childishness of the
soul,* keeps us waking, to divide the hours with the
intervals of prayer, and to number the minutes with
our penitential groans ; then the flesh sits uneasily,
and dwells in sorrow ; and then the spirit feels itself
at ease, freed from the petulant solicitations of those
passions which in health were as busy and as restless
as atoms in the sun, always dancing, and always busy,
and never sitting down, till a sad night of grief and
uneasiness draws the veil, and lets them die alone in
secret dishonour.

2. Next to this, *the soul by the help of sickness
knocks off the fetters of pride and vainer complacen-
cies.* Then she draws the curtains, and stops the
light from coming in *, and takes the pictures down,
those fantastic images of self-love, and gay remembrances of vain opinion, and popular noises. Then
the spirit stoops into the sobrieties of humble thoughts,
and feels corruption chiding the forwardness of fancy,
and allaying the vapours of conceit and factious opinions. For humility is the soul's grave, into which she
enters, not to die, but to meditate and inter some of
its troublesome appendages. There she sees the
dust, and feels the dishonour of the body, and reads
the register of all its sad adherences ; and then she
lays by all her vain reflections, beating upon her
crystal and pure mirror from the fancies of strength
and beauty, and little decayed prettinesses of the

---

* Nunc festinatos nimiùm sibi sentit honores,
Actaque lauriferæ damnat Syllana juventæ.
                                        Lucan. lib. viii.

body·

body. And when in sickness we forget all our knotty
discourses of Philosophy, and a syllogism makes our
head ache, and we feel our many and loud talkings
serving no lasting end of the soul, no purpose that
now we must abide by, and that the body is like to
descend to the land where all things are forgotten ;
then she lays aside all her remembrances of applauses,
all her ignorant confidences, and cares only to *know
Christ Jesus and him crucified*, to know him plainly,
and with much heartiness and simplicity. And I cannot think this to be a contemptible advantage. For
ever since man tempted himself by his impatient desires of knowing, and being as God, man thinks it
the finest thing in the world to know much, and therefore is hugely apt to esteem himself better than his
brethren, if he knows some little impertinences, and
them imperfectly, and that with infinite uncertainty.
But God hath been pleased with a rare heart to prevent the inconveniences apt to arise by this passionate
longing after knowledge ; even by giving to every
man a sufficient opinion of his own understanding :
and who is there in the world that thinks himself to
be a fool, or indeed not fit to govern his brother ?
There are but few men but they think they are wise
enough, and every man believes his own opinion the
soundest ; and if it were otherwise, men would burst
themselves with envy, or else become irrecoverable
slaves to the talking and disputing man. But when
God intended this permission to be an antidote of
envy, and a satisfaction and allay to the troublesome
appetites of knowing, and made that this universal
opinion, by making men in some proportions equal,
should be a keeper out, or a great restraint to slavery,
and tyranny respectively ; man (for so he uses to do)
hath turned this into bitterness : for when nature
had made so just a distribution of understanding,
that every man might think he had enough, he is not
content with that, but will think he hath more than
his

his brother: and whereas it might be well employed
n restraining slavery, he hath used it to break off the
bands of all obedience, and it ends in pride and
schisms, in heresies and tyrannies; and it being a
spiritual evil, it grows upon the soul with old age and
flattery, with health and the supports of a prosperous
fortune. Now besides the direct operations of the
spirit, and a powerful grace, there is in nature left to
us no remedy for this evil, but a sharp sickness, or
an equal sorrow, and allay of fortune: and then we
are humble enough to ask counsel of a despised priest,
and to think that even a common sentence from the
mouth of an appointed comforter *, streams forth
more refreshment than all our own wiser and more
reputed discourses: then our understandings and our
bodies, peeping through their own breaches, see their
shame and their dishonour, their dangerous follies and
their huge deceptions, and they go into the clefts of
the rock, and every little hand may cover them.

3. Next to these, *as the soul is still undressing,
she takes off the roughness of her great and little
angers and animosities,* and receives the oil of mercies and smooth forgiveness, fair interpretations and
gentle answers, designs of reconcilement and christian
atonement in their places. For so did the wrestlers
in *Olympus,* they stripped themselves of all their garments, and then anointed their naked bodies with oil,
smooth and vigorous; with contracted nerves and
enlarged voice they contended vehemently, till they
obtained their victory, or their ease; and a crown
of olive, or a huge pity, was the reward of their fierce
contentions. Some wise men have said, that anger
sticks to a man's nature † as inseparably as other vices

----

* ———— Ubi jam validis quassatum est viribus ævi
Corpus, et obtusis ceciderunt viribus artus,
Claudicat ingenium, delirat linguaque mensque.
　　　　　　　　　　　　　　　　　Lucr. l. iii.

† ———— Quatenus excidit penitùs vitium iræ,
Cætera item nequeunt stulti hærentia.
　　　　　　　　　　　　　　　Hor. lib. i. Sat. 3.

do

do to the manners of fools, and that anger is never quite cured : but God, that hath found out remedies for all diseases, hath so ordered the circumstances of man, that, in the worser sort of men, anger and great indignation consume and shrivel into little peevish-nesses and uneasy accents of sickness, and spend themselves in trifling instances ; and in the better and more sanctified, it goes off in prayers, and alms, and solemn reconcilement. And however the temptations of this state, such I mean which are proper to it, are little and inconsiderable ; the man is apt to chide a servant too bitterly, and to be discontented with his nurse, or not satisfied with his physician, and he rests uneasily, and (poor man !) nothing can please him : and indeed these little indecencies must be cured and stopped, lest they run into an inconvenience. But sickness is in this particular a little image of the state of blessed souls, or of *Adam's* early morning in Para-dise, free from the troubles of lust, and violences of anger, and the intricacies of ambition, or the rest-lessness of covetousness. For though a man may carry all these along with him into his sickness, yet there he will not find them ; and in despite of all his own malice, his soul shall find some rest from labour-ing in the galleys and baser captivity of sin : and if we value those moments of being in the love of God and in the kingdom of grace, which certainly are the beginnings of felicity ; we may also remember that the not sinning actually is one step of innocency ; and therefore this state is not intolerable, which by a sen-sible trouble makes it, in most instances, impossible to commit those great sins which make death, hell, and horrid damnations. And then let us but add this to it, that God sends sicknesses, but he never causes sin ; that God is angry with a sinning person, but never with a man for being sick ; that sin causes God to hate us, and sickness causes him to pity us ; that all wise men in the world choose trouble rather than dishonour,

dishonour, affliction rather than baseness ; and that
sickness stops the torrent of sin, and interrupts its
violence, and even to the worst men makes it to
retreat many degrees. We may reckon sickness
amongst good things, as we reckon rhubarb, and aloes,
and child-birth, and labour and obedience, and discipline : these are unpleasant, and yet safe ; they are
troubles in order to blessings, or they are securities
from danger, or the hard choices of a less and a more
tolerable evil.

4. Sickness is in some sense eligible, because it is
the opportunity and the proper scene of exercising
some virtues * : it is that agony in which men are
tried for a crown. And if we remember what glorious things are spoken of *the grace of faith,* that it
is the life of just men, the restitution of *the dead in
trespasses and sins,* the justification of sinners, the
support of the weak, the confidence of the strong, the
magazine of promises, and the title to very glorious
rewards ; we may easily imagine that it must have in
it a work and a difficulty in some proportion answerable to so great effects. But when we are bidden to
believe strange propositions, we are put upon it when
we cannot judge, and those propositions have possessed our discerning faculties, and have made a party
there, and are become domestic, before they come to
be disputed ; and then the articles of faith are so few,
and are made so credible, and in their event, and in
their object, are so useful and gaining upon the affections, that he were a prodigy of man, and would
be so esteemed, that should in all our present circumstances disbelieve any point of faith : and all is well
as long as the sun shines, and the fair breath of heaven
gently wafts us to our own purposes. But if you will
try the excellency, and feel the work of faith, place

* Nolo quod cupio statim tenere,
Nec victoria mî placet parata.
Petron.

the

the man in a persecution, let him ride in a storm, let
his bones be broken with sorrow, and his eye-lids
loosed with sickness, let his bread be dipped with
tears, and all the daughters of music be brought low;
let God commence a quarrel against him, and be
bitter in the accents of his anger or his discipline:
then God tries your faith. Can you then trust his
goodness, and believe him to be a father, when you
groan under his rod? Can you rely upon all the
strange propositions of scripture, and be content to
perish if they be not true? Can you receive comfort
in the discourses of death and heaven, of immortality
and the resurrection, of the death of Christ, and con-
forming to his sufferings? Truth is, there are but
two great periods in which faith demonstrates itself to
be a powerful and mighty grace : and they are *persecution* and *the approaches of death,* for *the passive
part;* and *a temptation* for *the active.* In the days
of pleasure, and the night of pain, faith is to fight
her *agonisticon,* to contend for mastery ; and faith
overcomes all alluring and fond temptations to sin,
and faith overcomes all our weaknesses and faintings
in our troubles. By the faith of the promises we
learn to despise the world, choosing those objects which
faith discovers ; and by expectation of the same promises we are comforted in all our sorrows, and enabled to look through and see beyond the cloud : but
the vigour of it is pressed and called forth, when all
our fine discourses come to be reduced to practice.
For * in our health, and clearer days, it is easy to talk
of putting trust in God ; we readily trust him for life
when we are in health, for provisions when we have
fair revenues, and for deliverance when we are newly
escaped : but let us come to sit upon the margent of

---

* Mors ipsa beatior indè est,
Quod per cruciamina lethi
Vir panditur ardua justis,
Et ad astra doloribus itur.
              Prud. hymn. in Exeq. defunct.

our grave, and let a tyrant lean hard upon our fortunes, and dwell upon our wrong, let the storm arise, and the keels toss till the cordage crack, or that all our hopes bulge under us, and descend into the hollowness of sad misfortunes: then can you believe, when you neither hear, nor see, nor feel any thing but objections?   This is the proper work of sickness: faith is then brought into the theatre, and so exercised, that if it abides but to the end of the contention, we may see that work of faith, which God will hugely crown.   The same I say of *hope*, and of *charity*, or *the love of God*, and of *patience* *, which is a grace produced from the mixtures of all these: they are *virtues which are greedy of danger*.   And no man was ever honoured by any wise or discerning person for dining upon *Persian* carpets, nor rewarded with a crown for being at ease.   It was the fire that did honour to *Mutius Scævola*, poverty made *Fabritius* famous, *Rutilius* was made excellent by banishment †, *Regulus* by torments, *Socrates* by prison, *Cato* by his death: and God hath crowned the memory of *Job* with a wreath of glory, because he sat upon his dunghill wisely and temperately; and his potsheard and his groans, mingled with praises and justifications of God, pleased him like an anthem sung by angels in the morning of the resurrection. God could not choose but be pleased with the delicious accents of martyrs, when in their tortures they cried out nothing but [*Holy Jesus*] and [*Blessed be God*], and they also themselves, who, with a hearty designation to the Divine pleasure, can delight in God's severe dispensation, will have the transportations of cherubims when they enter into the joys of God.   If God be delicious to his servants when he smites them,

---

* Virtutes avidæ periculi monstrant quàm non pœniteat tanto pretio æstimâsse virtutem. *Senec.*

† Non enim hilaritate, nec lasciviâ, nec risu, aut joco comite levitatis, sed sæpe etiam tristes firmitate et constantiâ sunt beati.

Cic. de Fin. l. xxii.

he

he will be nothing but ravishments and ecstasies to their spirits, when he refreshes them with the over-flowings of joy in the day of recompences. *No man is more miserable than he that hath no adversity; that man is not tried* whether he be good or bad: and God never crowns those virtues which are only *faculties* and *dispositions;* but *every act* of virtue is an ingredient into reward. And we see many children fairly planted, whose parts of nature were never dressed by art, nor called from the furrows of their first possibilities by discipline and institution, and they dwell for ever in ignorance, and converse with beasts; and yet if they had been dressed and exercised, might have stood at the chairs of princes, or spoken parables amongst the rulers of cities. Our virtues are but in the seed when the grace of God comes upon us first: but this grace must be thrown into broken furrows, and must † *twice feel the cold, and twice feel the heat,* and be softened with storms and showers, and then it will arise into fruitfulness and harvests. And what is there in the world to distinguish virtues from dishonours, or the valour of *Cæsar* from the softness of the *Egyptian* eunuchs, or that can make any thing rewardable, but the labour and the danger, the pain and the difficulty? Virtue could not be any thing but sensuality, if it were the entertainment of our senses and fond desires; and *Apicius* had been the noblest of all the *Romans,* if feeding a great appetite, and despising the severities of temperance had been the work and proper employment of a wise man. But otherwise do fathers, and otherwise do mothers handle their children. These soften them with kisses and imperfect noises, with the pap and breast-milk of soft endearments, they rescue them

---

* Nihil infelicius eo cui nihil unquam contigit adversi. Non licuit illi se experiri. *Seneca.*

† ———— Illa seges votis respondet avari
Agricolæ, bis quæ solem, bis frigora sensit.
                          Virg. Georg. 1.

from

from tutors, and snatch them from discipline, they
desire to keep them fat and warm *, and their feet dry,
and their bellies full : and then the children govern,
and cry, and prove fools and troublesome, so long as
the feminine republic does endure. But fathers, because they design to have their children wise and
valiant †, apt for counsel or for arms, send them to
severe governments, and tie them to study, to hard
labour, and afflictive contingencies. They rejoice
when the bold boy strikes a lion with his hunting-
spear, and shrinks not when the beast comes to affright his early courage. ‡ Softness is for slaves and
beasts, for minstrels and useless persons, for such who
cannot ascend higher than the state of a fair ox, or a
servant entertained for vainer offices : but the man
that designs his son for nobler employments, to honours
and to triumphs, to consular dignities and presiden-
cies of councils, loves to see him pale with study, or
panting with labour, hardened with sufferance, or
eminent by dangers. And so God dresses us for
heaven. He loves to see us struggling with a disease, and resisting the devil, and contesting against
the weaknesses of nature, and *against hope* to *believe
in hope*, resigning ourselves to God's will, praying him
to choose for us, and dying in all things but *faith* and
*its blessed consequents ; ut ad officium cum periculo
simus prompti ;* and the *danger* and the *resistance*
shall endear the *office*. § For so have I known the
boisterous north-wind pass through the yielding air,
which opened its bosom ‖, and appeased its violence by
entertaining it with easy compliance in all the regions

* Languent per inertiam saginata, nec labore tantum, sed mole et ipso
sui onere deficiunt. *Seneca.*
† Callum per injurias ducunt,
    Ut sit luminis atque aquæ cœlestis patiens latus.
‡ Modestiâ filiorum delectantur ; vernularum licentia et canum, non
puerorum.
    § Ventus ut amittit vires, nisi robore densæ
        Occurrant sylvæ, spatio diffusus inani. *Luc.*
‖ Marcet sine adversario virtus.

                                                      of

of its reception: but when the same breath of heaven hath been checked with the stiffness of a tower, or the united strength of a wood, it grew mighty and dwelt there, and made the highest branches stoop, and make a smooth part for it on the top of all its glories. So is sickness, and so is the grace of God: when sickness hath made the difficulty, then God's grace hath made a triumph, and by doubling its power hath created new proportions of a reward: and then shews its biggest glory when it hath the greatest difficulty to master, the greatest weaknesses to support, the most busy temptations to contest with: for so God loves that *his strength should be seen in our weakness* and our danger.* Happy is that state of life in which our services to God are the dearest and the most expensive.

5. Sickness hath some degrees of eligibility, at least by an after-choice; because to all persons which are within the possibilities and state of pardon, it becomes a great instrument of pardon of sins. For as God seldom rewards here and hereafter too, so it is not very often that he punishes in both states. In great and final sins he doth so; but we find it expressed only in the case of the sin against the Holy Ghost, *which shall never be forgiven in this world, nor in the world to come;* that is, it shall be punished in both worlds, and the infelicities of this world shall but usher in the intolerable calamities of the next. But this is in a case of extremity, and in sins of an unpardonable malice: in those lesser stages of death which are deviations from the rule, and not a destruction and perfect antinomy to the whole institution, God very often smites with the rod of sickness, that he may not for ever be slaying the soul with eternal death. † *I will visit their offences with the rod, and their sin with scourges: nevertheless my loving kindness will I not utterly take from him, nor suffer my truth to fail.*‡

* Lætius est quoties magno tibi constat honestum.
† Psal. lxxxix. 32, 33.   ‡ 1 Cor. v. 5. 1 Tim. i. 20.

And

And there is in the New Testament *a delivering over to Satan*, and a consequent *buffeting*, for the mortification of the flesh indeed, but *that the soul may be saved in the day of the Lord.* And to some persons the utmost process of God's anger reaches but to a sharp sickness, or at most but to a temporal death; and then the *little moment any anger* is spent, and expires in rest and a quiet grave. *Origen*, S. *Augustin*, and *Cassian* say concerning *Ananias* and *Sapphira* *, that they were slain with a sudden death, that by such a judgment their sin might be punished, and their guilt expiated, and their persons reserved for mercy in the day of judgment.† And God cuts off many of his children from the land of the living; and yet when they are numbered amongst our dead, he finds them in the book of life, written amongst those that shall live to him for ever. And thus it happened to many new Christians in the church of *Corinth*, for their little indecencies and disorders in the circumstances of receiving the holy sacrament. S. *Paul* says [that *many amongst them were sick, many were weak, and some were fallen asleep.*] ‡ He expresses the Divine anger against those persons in no louder accents; which is according to the style of the New Testament, where all the great transactions of duty and reproof are generally made upon the stock of *heaven*, and *hell* is plainly a *reserve*, and a *period* set to the declaration of God's wrath. For God knows that the torments of hell are so horrid, so insupportable a calamity, that he is not easy and apt to cast those souls which he hath taken so much care, and hath been at so much expense to save, into the eternal, never-dying flames of hell, lightly, for smaller

---

* Digni erant in hoc seculo recipere peccatum suum, ut mundiores exeant ab hac vitâ, mundati castigatione sibi illatâ per mortem communem, quoniam credentes erant in Christum.

† *Origen*, S. *Aug.* l. iii. c. 1. contr. *Parmen. et Cassian.* collat. 6. c. 11.

‡ 1 Cor. xi. 30.

sins,

sins, or after a fairly begun repentance, and in the midst of holy desires to finish it: but God takes such penalties, and exacts such fines of us, which we may pay *salvo contenemento*, saving the main stake of all, even *our precious souls*. And therefore S. *Augustin* prayed to God in his penitential sorrows. *Here, O Lord, burn and cut my flesh, that thou mayest spare me for ever.* For so said our blessed Saviour, *Every sacrifice must be seasoned with salt, and every sacrifice must be burnt with fire;* that is, we must abide in the state of grace, and if we have committed sins, we must expect to be put into the state of affliction; and yet the sacrifice will send up a right and untroubled cloud, and a sweet smell to join with the incense of the altar, where the eternal Priest offers a never-ceasing sacrifice. And now I have said a thing against which there can be no exceptions, and of which no just reason can make abatement. For when sickness, which is the condition of our nature, is called for with purposes of redemption; when we are sent to death to secure eternal life; when God strikes us that he may spare us, it shows that we have done things which he essentially hates, and therefore we must be smitten with the rod of God: but *in the midst of judgment God remembers mercy*, and makes the rod to be medicinal, and, like the rod of God in the hand of *Aaron*, to shoot forth buds, and leaves, and almonds, hopes and mercies and eternal recompences in the day of restitution. This is so great a good to us, if it be well conducted in all the channels of its intention and design, that if we had put off the objections of the flesh, with abstractions, contempts, and separations, so as we ought to do, it were as earnestly to be prayed for as any gay blessing that crowns our cups with joy, and our heads with garlands and forgetfulness. But this was it which I said, that this may, nay, that it ought to be chosen, at least by an *after-election:* for so said S. *Paul, If we judge ourselves, we shall not be*

condemned

condemned of the Lord; that is, if we judge ourselves worthy of the sickness, if we acknowledge and confess God's justice in smiting us, if we take the rod of God in our own hands, and are willing to imprint it in the flesh, *we are workers together with God* in the infliction; and then the sickness, beginning and being managed in the virtue of repentance, and patience, and resignation, and charity, will end in peace, and pardon, and justification, and consignation to glory. That I have spoken truth, I have brought God's spirit speaking in scripture for a witness. But if this be true, there are not many states of life that have advantages which can outweigh this great instrument of security to our final condition. *Moses died at the mouth of the Lord, said the story; he died with the kisses of the Lord's mouth (so the Chaldee paraphrase): it was the greatest act of kindness that God did to his servant Moses; he kissed him, and he died. But I have some things to observe for the better finishing this consideration.

1. All these advantages and lessenings of evils in the state of sickness are only upon the stock of virtue and religion. †There is nothing can make sickness in any sense eligible, or in many senses tolerable, but only the grace of God: that only turns sickness into easiness and felicity, which also turns it into virtue. For whosoever goes about to comfort a vicious person when he lies sick upon his bed, can only discourse of the necessities of nature, of the unavoidableness of the suffering, of the accidental vexations and increase of torments by impatience, of the fellowship of all the sons of *Adam,* and such other little considerations;

---

* Deut. xxxiv. 5.
† Hæc clementia non paratur arte:
　　Sed nôrunt cui serviunt leones.
　　Si latus aut renes morbo tententur acuto,
　　Quære fugam morbi. Vis rectè vivere? quis non?
　　Si virtus hoc una potest dare, fortis omissis
　　Hoc age deliciis ————　　　　　　　*Horat. l. i. ep. 6.*

which

which indeed, if sadly reflected upon, and found to
stánd alone, teach him nothing but the degree of his
calamity, and the evil of his condition, and teach him
such a patience, and minister to him such a comfort,
which can only make him to observe decent gestures
in his sickness, and to converse with his friends and
standers-by so as may do them comfort, and ease their
funeral and civil complaints; but do him no true
advantages.   For all that may be spoken to a beast
when he is crowned with hair laces, and bound with
fillets to the altar, to bleed to death to appease the
anger of the Deity, and to ease the burthen of his
relatives.   And indeed what comfort can he receive,
whose sickness, as it looks back, is an effect of God's
indignation and fierce vengeance, and if it goes
forward, and enters into the gates of the grave, is a
beginning of a sorrow that shall never have an ending?
But when the sickness is a messenger sent from a chas-
tising Father; when it first turns into degrees of innocence, and then into virtues, and thence into pardon;
this is no misery, but such a method of the Divine
economy and dispensation, as resolves to bring us to
heaven without any new impositions, but merely upon
the stock and charges of nature.

2. Let it be observed, that these advantages which
spring from sickness are not in all instances of virtue,
nor to all persons.   Sickness is the proper scene of
patience and resignation, for all the passive graces of
a Christian, for faith and hope, and for some single acts
of the love of God.   But *sickness is not a fit station
for a penitent;* and it can serve the ends of the grace
of *repentance* but *accidentally.*   Sickness may * begin
a repentance, if God continues life, and if we co-ope-
rate with the Divine grace; or sickness may help to
alleviate the wrath of God, and to facilitate the pardon,
if all the other parts of this duty be performed in our

* Nec tamen putaverant ad rem pertinere, ubi inciperent quod placuerat
ut fieret.

                                              healthful

healthful state, so that it may serve at the entrance in, or at the going out.   But sickness at no hand is a good stage to represent all the substantial parts of this duty. 1. It invites to it; 2. It makes it appear necessary; 3. It takes off the fancies of vanity ; 4. It attempers the spirit; 5. It cures hypocrisy ; 6. It tames the fumes of pride ; 7. It is the school of patience ; 8. And by taking us from off the brisker relishes of the world, it makes us with more gust to taste the things of the Spirit : And all this, only when God fits the circumstances of the sickness so as to consist with acts of reason, consideration, choice, and a present and reflecting mind; which then God sends when he means that the sickness of the body should be the cure of the soul.   But let no man so rely upon it as by design, to trust the beginning, the progress, and the consummation of our piety to such an estate which for ever leaves it imperfect.   And though to some persons it adds degrees, and ministers opportunities, and exercises single acts with great advantage, *in passive graces*; yet it is never an entire or sufficient instrument for the change of our condition from the state of death *to the liberty* and life *of the sons of God.*

3. It were good if we would transact the affairs of our souls with nobleness and ingenuity, and that we would by an early and forward religion prevent the necessary arts of the Divine Providence.   It is true that God cures some by incision, by fire and torments ; but these are ever the more obstinate and more unrelenting natures.   God's Providence is not so afflictive and full of trouble, as that it hath placed sickness and infirmity amongst things simply necessary ;   and in most persons it is but a sickly and an effeminate virtue which is imprinted upon our spirits with fears, and the sorrows of a fever, or a peevish consumption. *   It is but a miserable remedy to be beholden to a sickness

* Neque tam aversa unquam videbitur ab opere suo providentia, ut debilitas inter optima inventa sit.

for

for our health, and though it be better to suffer the
loss of a finger, than that the arm and the whole body
should putrefy ; yet even then also it is a trouble and
an evil to lose a finger. He that mends with sickness
pares the nails of the beast when they have already
torn off some of the flesh : but he that would have a
sickness become a clear and an entire blessing, a thing
indeed to be reckoned among the good things of God,
and the evil things of the world, must lead an holy
life, and judge himself with an early sentence, and so
order the affairs of his soul, that in the usual method
of God's saving us, there may be nothing left to be
done, but that such virtues should be exercised which
God intends to crown.   And then, as when the *Athe-
nians,* upon a day of battle, with longing and uncertain souls, sitting in their common-hall, expecting what
would be the sentence of the day, at last received a
messenger who only had breath enough left him to
say, [*We are conquerors,*] and so died ; so shall the
sick person, who hath *fought a good fight, and kept
the faith,* and only waits for his dissolution and his
sentence, breathe forth his spirit with the accents of a
conqueror, and his sickness and his death shall only
make the mercy and the virtue more illustrious.

But for the sickness itself; if all the calumnies
were true concerning it with which it is aspersed,
yet it is far to be preferred before the most pleasant
sin, and before a great secular business and a temporal care. And some men wake as much in the
foldings of the softest beds, as others on the cross :
and sometimes the very weight of sorrow, and the
weariness of a sickness presses the spirit into slumbers
and the images of rest, when the intemperate or the
lustful person rolls upon his uneasy thorns, and sleep
is departed from his eyes. Certain it is, *some sickness is a blessing.* Indeed, blindness were a most
cursed thing, if no man were ever blind but he
whose eyes were pulled out with tortures or burning

ing basins * : and if sickness were always a testimony
of God's anger, and a violence to a man's whole condition, then it were a huge calamity. But because
God sends it to his servants, to his children, to little
infants, to apostles and saints, with designs of mercy,
to preserve their innocence, to overcome temptation,
to try their virtue, to fit them for rewards; it is certain that sickness never is an evil but by our own
faults; and if we will do our duty, we shall be sure to
turn it into a blessing. If the sickness be great, it may
end in death †, and the greater it is the sooner; and
if it be very little, it hath great intervals of rest: if it
be between both, we may be masters of it, and by
serving the ends of Providence, serve also the perfective end of human nature, and enter into the possession of everlasting mercies.

The sum is this: he that is afraid of pain, is afraid
of his own nature; and if his fear be violent, it is a
sign his patience is none at all, and an impatient person is not ready dressed for heaven. None but suffering, humble, and patient persons can go to heaven;
and when God hath given us the whole stage of our
life to exercise all the active virtues of religion, it is
necessary in the state of virtues that some portion and
period of our lives be assigned to passive graces; for
patience, for Christian fortitude, for resignation or
conformity to the divine will. But as the violent fear
of sickness makes us impatient, so it will make our
death without comfort and without religion: and we
shall go off from our stage of actions and sufferings
with an unhandsome *exit*, because we were willing to
receive the kindness of God when he expressed it as
we listed; but we would not suffer him to be kind and
gracious to us in his own method, nor were willing to

---

* Detestabilis erit cæcitas, si nemo oculos perdiderit nisi cui eruendi
sunt.

† Memineris ergò maximos dolores morte finiri, parvos habere multa
intervalla requietis, mediocrium nos esse dominos. *Cicero.*

exercise

exercise and improve our virtues at the charge of a sharp fever, or a lingering consumption. *Woe be to the man that hath lost patience ; for what will he do when the Lord shall visit him?* *

SECT. VII.

The second Temptation proper to the State of Sickness, Fear of Death, with its Remedies.

THERE is nothing which can make sickness un-sanctified, but the same also will give us cause to fear death. If therefore we so order our affairs and spirits, that we do not fear death, our sickness may easily become our advantage, and we can then receive counsel, and consider, and do those acts of virtue which are in that state the proper services of God; and such which men in bondage and fear are not capable of doing, or of advices how they should, when they come to the appointed days of mourning. And indeed if men would but place their design of being happy in the nobleness, courage, and perfect resolutions of doing handsome things, and passing through our unavoidable necessities, in the contempt and despite of the things of this world, and in holy living, and the perfective desires of our natures, the longings, and pursuances after heaven, it is certain they could not be made miserable by chance and change, by sickness and death. But we are so softened and made effeminate with delicate thoughts and meditations of ease and brutish satisfactions, that if our death comes before we have seized upon a great fortune, or enjoy the promises of the fortune-tellers, we esteem ourselves to be robbed of our goods, to be mocked, and miserable. Hence it comes that men are impatient of the thoughts

* Ecclus. ii. 14.

of

of death; hence come those arts of protraction and
delaying the significations of old age : thinking to
deceive the world, men cozen themselves, and by representing themselves youthful, they certainly continue
their vanity, till *Proserpina* pulls the peruke from
their heads.* We cannot deceive God and nature,
for a coffin is a coffin, though it be covered with a
pompous veil ; and the minutes of our times strike on,
and are counted by angels, till the period comes which
must cause the passing-bell to give warning to all the
neighbours that thou art dead, and they must be so;
and nothing can excuse or retard this. And if our
death could be put off a little longer, what advantage
can it be in thy accounts of nature or felicity?
They that three thousand years agone died unwillingly,
and stopped death two days, or staid it a week, what
is their gain? where is that week? And poor-spirited
men use arts of protraction, and make their persons
pitiable, but their condition contemptible ‡, being like
the poor sinners at *Noah's* flood : the waters drove
them out of their lower rooms §, then they crept up to
the roof, having lasted half a day longer, and then
they knew not how to get down : some crept up on
the top branch of a tree, and some climbed up to a
mountain, and staid it may be three days longer : but
all that while they endured a worse torment than
death ; they lived with amazement, and were distracted
with the ruins of mankind, and the horror of an universal deluge.

---

* Mentiris juvenem tinctis, Lentine, capillis,
    Tam subitò corvus, qui modò cygnus eras.
Non omnes fallis, scit te Proserpina canum :
    Personam capiti detrahet illa tuo.
                       Mart. lib. iii. ep. 43.

† Audet iter, numerátque dies, spatióque viarum
    Metitur vitam, torquetur morte futurâ.   *Horat.*

‡ Τί γαρ βρστῶν ἂν ἦ κακοῖς μεμιγμένον;
   Θνήσκειν ὁ μέλλων τῶ χρόνω κέρδ۞ φέρει.   Soph.

§ Nihil est miserius dubitatione volutantium quorsum evadant, quantum
sit illud quod restat, aut quale. *Seneca,* l. xvii. ep. 102.

                                              Remedies

Remedies against the Fear of Death, by Way of Consideration.

1. God having in this world placed us in a sea, and troubled the sea with a continual storm, hath appointed the *church* for a *ship*, and *religion* to be the *stern :* but there is no *haven* or *port* but *death.* Death is that harbour whither God hath designed every one, that there he may find rest from the troubles of the world. How many of the noblest *Romans* have taken death for sanctuary, and have esteemed it less than shame or a mean dishonour! And *Cæsar* was cruel to *Domitius,* captain of *Corfinium,* when he had taken the town from him *, that he refused to sign his petition of death. Death would have hid his head with honour, but that cruel mercy reserved him to the shame of surviving his disgrace. The holy scripture, giving an account of the reasons of the Divine Providence taking godly men from this world, and shutting them up in a hasty grave, says, that they *are taken from the evils to come :* and concerning ourselves it is certain, if we had ten years agone taken seizure of our portion of dust, death had not taken us from good things, but from infinite evils, such which the sun hath seldom seen. † Did not *Priamus* weep oftener than *Troilus?* and happy had he been if he had died when his sons were living, and his kingdom safe, and houses full, and his city unburnt. It was a long life that made him miserable, and an early death only could have secured his fortune. ‡ And it hath happened many times, that

---

* ———— Heu, quantò meliùs vel câde peractæ
Parcere Romano potuit fortuna pudori !   *Lucanus.*
† Hæc omnia vidit inflammari, Jovis aram sanguine turpari.
‡ ———— Sic longius ævum
Destruit ingentes animos, et vita superstes
Imperio : nisi summa dies cum fine bonorum
Affluit, et celeri prævertit tristia leto,
Dedecori est fortuna prior.   *Lucan.* lib. viii.

persons

persons of a fair life and a clear reputation, of a good fortune and an honourable name, have been tempted in their age to folly and vanity, have fallen under the disgrace of dotage, or into an unfortunate marriage, or have besotted themselves with drinking, or out-lived their fortunes, or become tedious to their friends, or are afflicted with lingering and vexatious diseases, or lived to see their excellent parts buried, and cannot understand the wise discourses and productions of their younger years.* In all these cases, and infinite more, do not all the world say that it had been better this man had died sooner? but so have I known passionate women to shriek aloud when their nearest relatives were dying, and that horrid shriek hath stayed the spirit of the man a while to wonder at the folly, and represent the inconvenience; and the dying person hath lived one day longer full of pain, amazed with an undeterminate spirit, distorted with convulsions, and only come again to act one scene more of a new calamity, and to die with less decency. So also do very many men, with passion and a troubled interest they strive to continue their life longer; and it may be they escape this sickness, and live to fall into a disgrace; they escape the storm, and fall into the hands of pirates, and instead of dying with liberty, they live like slaves, miserable and despised; servants to a little time, and sottish admirers of the breath of their own lungs. *Paulus Æmilius* did handsomely reprove the cowardice of the king of *Macedon,* who begged of him for pity's sake and humanity, that having conquered him, and taken his kingdom from him, he would be content with that, and not lead him in triumph a prisoner to *Rome.* *Æmilius* told him, he need not be beholden to him for that; himself might prevent that in despite of him. But the timorous king durst not die. But certainly every wise man will easily believe that it had been

---

* Mors illi meliùs quàm tu consuluit quidem
———— Quisquamne secundis
Tradere se fatis audet nisi morte paratâ?   *Luc.* l. viii.

better

better the *Macedonian* kings should have died in battle, than protract their life so long, till some of them
came to be scriveners and joiners at *Rome :* or that the
tyrant of *Sicily* better had perished in the *Adriatic,*
than to be wafted to *Corinth* safely, and there turn
schoolmaster. It is a sad calamity, that the fear of
death shall so imbecile man's courage and understanding, that he dares not suffer the remedy of all his
calamities ; but that he lives to say as *Liberius* did, *I
have lived this one day longer than I should.* * Either
therefore let us be willing to die when God calls, or
let us never more complain of the calamities of our
life which we feel so sharp and numerous. And when
God sends his angel to us with a scroll of death, let us
look on it as an act of mercy, to prevent many sins,
and many calamities of a longer life, and lay our heads
down softly, and go to sleep without wrangling like
babies and froward children. *For a man (at least)
gets this by death, that his calamities are not immortal.* †

But I do not only consider death by the advantages
of comparison ; but if we look on it in itself, it is no
such formidable thing, if we view it on both sides, and
handle it, and consider all its appendages.

2. *It is necessary,* and therefore *not intolerable :*
and nothing is to be esteemed evil which God and
nature hath fixed with eternal sanctions. It is *a law of
God,* it is *a punishment of our sins,* and it is *the constitution of our nature.* ‡ Two differing substances
were joined together with the breath of God, and
when that breath is taken away they part asunder,
and return to their several principles : the § soul

---

* Nimirum hàc die unà plus vixi mihi quàm vivendum fuit.
† Hoc homo morte lucratur, nè malum esset immortale. *Naz.*
‡ Nihil in malis ducamus, quod sit à Diis immortalibus vel à Natura
parente omnium constitutum.
§ Concretum fuit, discretum est, rediítque unde venerat, terra deorsum,
spiritus sursum. Quid ex his omnibus iniquum est? nihil. *Epichar.*

to

to God our Father, the body to the earth our mother:
and what in all this is evil? Surely nothing, but
that we are men; nothing but that we are not born
immortal: but by declining this change with great
passion, or receiving it with a huge natural fear, we
accuse the Divine Providence of tyranny, and exclaim
against our natural constitution, and are discontent
that we are men.

3. *It is a thing that is no great matter in itself;*
if we consider that we die daily, that it meets us in
every accident, that every creature carries a dart along
with it, and can kill us. And therefore when *Lysima-
chus* threatened *Theodorus* to kill him, he told him that
was no great matter to do, and he could do no more
than the *Cantharides* could; a little fly could do as
much.

4. It is a thing that every one suffers, even persons
of the lowest resolution, of the meanest virtue, of no
breeding, of no discourse.* Take away but the pomps
of death, the disguises, and solemn bug-bears, the
tinsel, and the actings by candle-light, and proper and
fantastic ceremonies, the minstrels, and the noise-
makers, the women and the weepers, the swoonings
and the shriekings, the nurses and the physicians, the
dark room and the ministers, the kindred and the
watches; and then to die is easy, ready, and quitted
from its troublesome circumstances. It is the same
harmless thing that a poor shepherd suffered yesterday,
or a maid-servant to-day; and at the same time in
which you die †, in that very night a thousand creatures
die with you, some wise men and many fools; and the
wisdom of the first will not quit him, and the folly of
the latter does not make him unable to die.

5. Of all the evils of the world which are reproached with an evil character, death is the most

---

* Natura dedit usuram vitæ tanquam pecuniæ, quid est ergò quòd que-
rare si repetat cùm vult? eâdem enim lege acceperas. *Seneca.*

† Vitæ est avidus quisquis non vult mundo secum pereunte mori. *Seneca.*

innocent

innocent of its accusation. * For when it is present, it hurts nobody †; and when it is absent, it is indeed troublesome, but the trouble is owing to our fears, not to the affrighting and mistaken object. And besides this if it were an evil‡, it is so transient, that it passes like the instant or undiscerned portion of the present time: *and either it is past, or it is not yet;* for just when it is, no man hath reason to complain of so insensible, so sudden, so undiscerned a change.

6. It is so harmless a thing, that no good man was ever thought the more miserable for dying, but much the happier. When men saw the graves of *Calatinus,* of the *Servilii,* the *Scipios,* the *Metelli,* did ever any man amongst the wisest *Romans* think them unhappy? And when St. *Paul* fell under the sword of *Nero,* and St. *Peter* died upon the cross, and St. *Stephen* from an heap of stones was carried into an easier grave, they that made great lamentation over them wept for their own interest, and after the manner of men; but the martyrs were accounted happy, and their days kept solemnly, and their memories preserved in never-dying honours. When St. *Hilary,* bishop of *Poictiers* in *France,* went into the East to reprove the *Arian* heresy, he heard that a young noble gentleman treated with his daughter *Abra* for marriage. The bishop wrote to his daughter that she should not engage her promise, nor do countenance to that request, because he had provided for her a husband, fair, rich, wise, and noble, far beyond her present offer. The event of which was this: She obeyed, and when her father returned from his eastern triumph to his western charge, he prayed to God that his daughter might die quickly: and God heard his prayers, and Christ took her into his bosom, entertaining her with antepasts and caresses

---

* Τὲς γὰρ θανόντας ἐχ ὁρῶ λυπυμένυς.

† Par est moriri : neque est melius morte in malis rebus miseris.

Plaut. Rud.

‡ Aut fuit, aut veniet; nihil est præsentis in illa :
  Mórsque minus pœnæ, quàm mora mortis habet.

of

of holy love, till the day of the marriage supper of the Lamb shall come. But when the bishop's wife observed this event, and understood of the good man her husband what was done, and why, she never let him alone till he obtained the same favour for her; and she also at the prayers of St. *Hilary* went into a more early grave and a bed of joys.

7. It is a sottish and an unlearned thing to reckon the time of our life, as it is short or long, to be good or evil fortune; life in itself being neither good nor bad, but just as we make it, and therefore so is death.

8. But when we consider, death is not only better than a miserable life, not only an easy and an innocent thing in itself, but also that it is a state of advantage, we shall have reason not to double the sharpness of our sickness by our fear of death. Certain it is, death hath some good upon its proper stock; *praise*, and *a fair memory, a reverence* and * *religion* toward them so great, that it is counted dishonest to speak evil of the dead †; then they rest in peace, and are quiet from their labours, and are designed to immortality. *Cleobis* and *Biton, Trophonius* and *Agamedes* had an early death sent them as a reward: to the former for their piety to their mother, to the latter for building of a temple. To this all those arguments will minister which relate the advantages of the state of separation and resurrection.

SECT. VIII.

Remedies against Fear of Death, by way of Exercise.

1. *He that would willingly be fearless of death must learn to despise the world;* he must neither love any thing passionately, nor be proud of any circum-

---

＊ Virtutem incolumem odimus,
　　Sublatam ex oculis quærimus invidi.　　*Horat.*
† Et laudas nullos nisi mortuos poetas.　　*Mart.*

stance

stance of his life. *O death, how bitter is the re-*
membrance of thee to a man that liveth at rest in his
possessions, to a man that hath nothing to vex him,
and that hath prosperity in all things, yea, unto him
that is yet able to receive meat? * said the son of *Sirach.*
But the parts of this exercise help each other.
If a man be not incorporated in all his passions to the
things of the world, he will less fear to be divorced
from them by a supervening death ; and yet because
he must part with them all in death, it is but reasonable he should not be passionate for so fugitive and
transient interest. But if any man thinks well of himself for being a handsome person †, or if he be stronger
and wiser than his neighbours, he must remember
that what he boasts of, will decline into weakness and
dishonour ; but that very boasting and complacency
will make death keener and more unwelcome, because it comes to take him from his confidences and
pleasures, making his beauty equal to those ladies
that have slept some years in charnel-houses, and
their strength not so stubborn as the breath of an
infant, and their wisdom such which can be looked
for in the land where all things are forgotten.

2. *He that would not fear death, must strengthen*
his spirit with the proper instruments of Christian
fortitude. All men are resolved upon this, that to
bear grief honestly and temperately, and to die willingly and nobly, is the duty of a good and of a valiant man ‡ : and they that are not so are *vicious,* and
fools, and *cowards.* All men praise the *valiant* and
honest ; and that which the very heathens admired in

---

* Ecclus. xli. 1.
† Εἰ δέ τις ὄλβον ἔχων Μορφᾶ παραμεύσεται ἄλλων,
   Ἔν᾽ ἀέθλοισιν ἄμι ——— ϛεύων ἐπέδειξεν βίαν,
   Θνατὰ μεμνήσθω περιϛέλλων μέλη
   Καὶ τελευτὰν ἁπάντων γᾶν ἐτιεσσόμιν⊙. *Pind.*
   Dic homo, vas cinerum quid confert flos facierum ?
   Copia quid rerum ? mors ultima meta dierum.
‡ Amittenda fortitudo est aut sepeliendus dolor. *Cicero.*
   Fortem posce animum mortis terrore carentem,
   Quit spatium vitæ extremum inter munera ponat.

their

their noblest examples is especially *patience* and *con-tempt of death*. *Zeno Eleates* endured torments rather than discover his friends, or betray them to the danger of the tyrant: and *Calanus*, the barbarous and unlearned *Indian*, willingly suffered himself to be burnt alive; and all the women did so, to do honour to their husbands' funerals, and to represent and prove their affections great to their lords. The religion of a Christian does more command fortitude than ever did any institution; for we are commanded to be willing to die for Christ, to die for the brethren, to die rather than to give offence or scandal. The effect of which is this, that he that is instructed to do the necessary parts of his duty, is by the same instrument fortified against death: as he that does his duty needs not fear death, so neither shall he; the parts of his duty are parts of his security. It is certainly a great baseness and pusillanimity of spirit that makes death terrible, and extremely to be avoided.

3. *Christian prudence* is a great security against the fear of death. For if we be afraid of death, it is but reasonable to use all spiritual arts to take off the apprehension of the evil; but therefore we ought to remove our fear, because fear gives to death wings, and spurs, and darts. Death hastens to a fearful man : if therefore you would make death harmless and slow, to throw off fear is the way to do it; and prayer is the way to do that. If therefore you be afraid of death, consider you will have less need to fear it, by how much the less you do fear it: and so cure your direct fear by a reflex act of prudence and consideration. *Fannius* had not died so soon, if he had not feared * death: and when *Cneius Carbo* begged the respite of a little time for a base employment of the soldiers of *Pompey*, he got nothing but that the baseness of his fear dishonoured the dignity of his third consulship; and he chose to die in a place where none of his meanest servants should have seen him. I remember a story

---

* Hostem cùm fugeret, se Fannius ipse premit. *Mart.*

of

of the wrestler *Polydamas*, that running into a cave
to avoid the storm, the water at last swelled so high,
that it began to press that hollowness to a ruin :
which, when his fellows espied, they chose to enter
into the common fate of all men, and went abroad :
but *Polydamas* thought by his strength to support the
earth, till its intolerable weight crushed him into flatness and a grave.   Many men run for shelter to a
place, and they only find a remedy for their fears by
feeling the worst of evils.   Fear itself finds no sanctuary but the worst of sufferance : and they that fly
from a battle are exposed to the mercy and fury of
the pursuers, who, if they faced about, were as well
disposed to give laws of life and death as to take them,
and at worst can but die nobly ; but now even at the
very best they live shamefully, or die timorously.
Courage is the greatest security; for it does most
commonly safeguard the man, but always rescues the
condition from an intolerable evil.

4. If thou wilt be fearless of death, endeavour to be
in love with the felicities of saints and angels, and
be once persuaded to believe that there is a condition
of living better than this ; that there are creatures
more noble than we; that above there is a country
better than ours ; that the inhabitants know more and
know better, and are in places of rest and desire :
and first learn to value it, and then learn to purchase
it ; and death cannot be a formidable thing, which
lets us into so much joy and so much felicity.   And
indeed who would not think his condition mended, if
he passed from conversing with dull mortals, with
ignorant and foolish persons, with tyrants and enemies
of learning, to converse with *Homer* and *Plato*, with
Socrates and *Cicero*, with *Plutarch* and *Fabricius?*
So the heathens speculated, but we consider higher.
The *dead that die in the Lord* shall converse with
St. *Paul* and all the college of the apostles, and all
the saints and martyrs, with all the good men, whose

memory

memory we preserve in honour, with excellent kings
and holy bishops, and with *the great Shepherd and
Bishop of our souls Jesus Christ,* and with God himself. For *Christ died for us, that whether we wake or
sleep, we may live together with him.* Then we shall
be free from lust and envy, from fear and rage, from
covetousness and sorrow, from tears and cowardice:
and these indeed properly are the only evils that are
contrary to felicity and wisdom.* Then we shall see
strange things, and know new propositions, and all
things in another manner, and to higher purposes.
Cleombrotus was so taken with this speculation, that
having learned from *Plato's Phædon* the soul's abode,
he had not patience to stay nature's dull leisure, but
leapt from a wall to his portion of immortality. And
when *Pomponius Atticus* resolved to die by famine, to
ease the great pains of his gout, in the abstinence of
two days he found his foot at ease: but when he began to feel the pleasures of an approaching death, and
the delicacies of that ease he was to inherit below, he
would not withdraw his foot, but went on and finished
his death; and so did *Cleanthes.* And every wise
man will despise those little evils of that state which
indeed is *the daughter of fear,* but the *mother of rest,*
and *peace,* and *felicity.*

5. If God should say to us, Cast thyself into the
sea, (as Christ did to St. *Peter,* or as God concerning
Jonas,) I have provided for thee a dolphin, or a whale,
or a port, a safety or a deliverance, security or a
reward, were we not incredulous and pusillanimous
persons if we should tremble to put such a felicity into
act, and ourselves into possession? The very duty of
resignation and the love of our own interest are good
antidotes against fear. In forty or fifty years we find
evils enough, and arguments enough to make us weary

* Beati erimus cùm, corporibus relictis, et cupiditatum et æmulationum
erimus expertes, quódque nunc facimus, cum laxati curis sumus, ut spectare
aliquid velimus et visere. *Tuscul.* Q.

of

of this life: and to a good man there are very many more reasons to be afraid of life than death, this having in it less of evil, and more of advantage. And it was a rare wish of that *Roman*, that death might come only to wise and excellent persons, and not to fools and cowards * ; that it might not be a sanctuary for the timorous, but the reward of the virtuous: and indeed they only make advantage of it.

6. Make no excuses to make thy desires of life seem reasonable, neither cover thy fear with pretences, but suppress it rather with arts of severity and ingenuity. Some are not willing to submit to God's sentence and arrest of death, till they have finished such a design, or made an end of the last paragraph of their book, or raised such portions for their children, or preached so many sermons, or built their house, or planted their orchard, or ordered their estate with such advantages.† It is well for the modesty of these men, that the excuse is ready; but if it were not, it is certain they would search one out: for an idle man is never ready to die, and is glad of any excuse: and a busied man hath always something unfinished, and he is ready for every thing but death. And I remember, that *Petronius* brings in *Eumolpus* composing verses in a desperate storm, and being called upon to shift for himself when the ship dashed upon the rock, crying out to let him alone till he had finished and trimmed his verse, which was lame in the hinder leg: the man either had too strong a desire to end his verse, or too great a desire not to end his life. But we must know God's times are not to be measured by our circumstances; and what I value, God regards not: or if it be valuable in the accounts of men, yet God will supply it with other contingencies of his providence. And if *Epaphroditus* had died when he

* Mors, utinam pavidos vitâ subducere nolles,
  Sed virtus te sola daret.   *Lucret.*
† Maneant opera interrupta minæque Murorum ingentes.
                                      Virg. Æn. 4. v. 88.

had

had his great sickness St. *Paul* speaks of, God would have secured the work of the Gospel without him; and he could have spared *Epaphroditus* as well as St. *Stephen*, and St. *Peter* as well as St. *James*. Say no more; but, when God calls, lay aside thy papers, and first dress thy soul, and then dress thy hearse.

Blindness is odious, and widowhood is sad, and destitution is without comfort, and persecution is full of trouble, and famine is intolerable, and tears are the sad ease of a sadder heart: but these are evils of our life, not of our death. For *the dead that die in the Lord* are so far from wanting the commodities of this life, that they do not want life itself.

After all this, I do not say it is a sin to be afraid of death: we find the boldest spirit, that discourses of it with confidence, and dares undertake a danger as big as death, yet doth shrink at the horror of it, when it comes dressed in its proper circumstances. And *Brutus*, who was as bold a *Roman* to undertake a noble action as any was since they first reckoned by consuls; yet when *Furius* came to cut his throat, after his defeat by *Anthony*, he ran from it like a girl; and being admonished to die constantly, *he swore by his life*, that he would shortly *endure death*. But what do I speak of such imperfect persons? Our Blessed Lord was pleased to legitimate fear to us, by his agony and prayers in the garden. It is not a sin to be afraid, but it is a great felicity to be without fear; which felicity our dearest Saviour refused to have, because it was agreeable to his purposes to suffer any thing that was contrary to felicity, every thing but sin. But * when men will *by all means avoid death*, they are like those who at *any hand* resolve to be *rich*: the case may happen in which they will blaspheme, and dishonour providence, or do a base action, or *curse God and die*: but in all cases they die miserable and ensnared, and in no case do they die the less for it.

* Ἀλλ' οἱ ἐξ ἅπαντ᾽ ᾧ φεύγοντες τὸν θάνατον.

Nature

Nature hath left us the key of the church-yard, and custom hath brought cemeteries and charnel-houses into cities and churches, places most frequented, that we might not carry ourselves strangely in so certain, so expected, so ordinary, so unavoidable an * accident. All reluctancy or unwillingness to obey the divine de- cree, is but a snare to ourselves, and a load to our spirits, and is either an entire cause, or a great aggra- vation of the calamity.† Who did not scorn to look upon *Xerxes* when he caused three hundred stripes to be given to the sea, and sent a chartel of defiance against the mountain *Athos?* Who did not scorn the proud vanity of *Cyrus,* when he took so goodly a re- venge upon the river *Cydnus,* for his hard passage over it? Or did not deride or pity the *Thracians,* for shooting arrows against heaven when it ‡ thunders? To be angry with God, to quarrel with the Divine Providence, by repining against an unalterable, a na- tural, an easy sentence, is an argument of a huge folly, and the parent of a great trouble; a man is base and foolish to no purpose, he throws away a vice to his own misery, and to no advantages of ease and pleasure.§ *Fear keeps men in bondage all their life,* saith St. *Paul;* and patience makes him his own man, and lord of his own interest and person. There- fore *possess yourselves in patience,* with reason and religion, and you shall die with ease.

If all the parts of this discourse be true, if they be better than dreams, and unless *Virtue be nothing but words, as a grove is a heap of trees* ¶ ; if they be not the phantasms of hypochondriacal persons, and de- signs upon the interests of men and their persuasions

---

* Quam pellunt lacrymæ fovent sortem:
   Dura negant cedere mollibus.
† Siccas si videat genas, Duræ cedet hebes sors patientiæ.
‡ Νήπιοι οἱ Ζηνὶ μενεαίνομεν ἀφρονέοντες.   Iliad. *ὑ.* v. 104.
§ Et cum nihil imminuat dolores,
   Cur frustrà turpes esse volumus?   *Seneca.*
   Non levat miseros dolor.
¶ Virtutem verba putas ut lucum ligna.

to evil purposes; then there is no reason but that we should really desire death, and account it among the good things of God, and the sour and laborious felicities of man. St. *Paul* understood it well, when he *desired to be dissolved :* he well enough knew his own advantages, and pursued them accordingly. But it is certain, that he that is afraid of death, I mean, with a violent and transporting fear, with a fear apt to discompose his duty or his patience, that man either loves this world too much, or dares not trust God for the next.

SECT. IX.

General Rules and Exercises, whereby our Sickness may become safe and sanctified.

1. *Take care that the cause of thy sickness be such as may not sour it in the principal and original causes of it.* It is a sad calamity to pass into the house of mourning, through the gates of intemperance, by a drunken meeting, or the surfeits of a loathed and luxurious table: for then a man suffers the pain of his own folly, and he is like a fool smarting under the whip which his own viciousness twisted for his back ; then a man pays the price of his sin, and hath a pure and an unmingled sorrow in his suffering; and it cannot be alleviated by any circumstances, for the whole affair is a mere process of death and sorrow. Sin is in the head, sickness is in the body, and death and an eternity of pains in the tail; and nothing can make this condition tolerable, unless the miracles of the Divine Mercy will be pleased to exchange the eternal anger for the temporal. True it is, that in all sufferings, the cause of it makes it noble or ignoble, honour

or

or shame, tolerable or intolerable. For when patience is assaulted by a ruder violence, by a blow from heaven or earth, from a gracious God or an unjust man, patience looks forth to the doors which way she may escape * ; and if innocence or a cause of religion keep the first entrance, then, whether she escapes at the gates of life or death, there is a good to be received, greater than the evils of a sickness : but if sin thrust in that sickness, and that hell stands at the door, then patience turns into fury † ; and seeing it impossible to go forth with safety, rolls up and down with a circular and infinite revolution, making its motion not from, but upon its own centre ; it doubles the pain, and increases the sorrow, till by its weight it breaks the spirit, and bursts into the agonies of infinite and eternal ages. If we had seen St. *Polycarp* burning to death, or St. *Laurence* roasted upon his gridiron, or St. *Ignatius* exposed to lions, or St. *Sebastian* pierced with arrows, or St. *Attalus* carried about the theatre with scorn unto his death, for the cause of *Jesus,* for religion, for God, and a holy conscience ; we should have been in love with flames, and have thought the gridiron fairer than the *spondæ,* the *ribs of a marital bed,* and we should have chosen to converse with those beasts rather than those men that brought those beasts forth, and estimated the arrows to be the rays of light brighter than the moon, and that disgrace and mistaken pageantry were a solemnity richer and more magnificent than *Mordecai's* procession upon the king's horse, and in the robes of majesty: for so did these holy men account them; they kissed their stakes, and hugged their deaths, and ran violently to torments, and counted whippings and secular disgraces to be the enamel of their persons, and the ointment of their heads, and the embalming their

* Solatium est pro honesto dura tolerare, et ad causam patientia respicit. 1 Pet. ii. 19. Heb. xi. 36. Matth. v. 11.
† Magis his quæ patitur vexat causa patiendi.

names,

names, and securing them for immortality. But to see *Sejanus* torn in pieces by the people, or *Nero* crying or creeping timorously to his death, when he was condemned to die *more majorum ;* to see *Judas* pale and trembling, full of anguish, sorrow and despair; to observe the groanings and intolerable agonies of *Herod* and *Antiochus,* will tell and demonstrate the causes of patience and impatience to proceed from the causes of the suffering : and it is sin only that makes the cup bitter and deadly. When men, by vomiting, measure up the drink they took in, and sick and sad do again taste their meat turned into choler by intemperance, the * sin and its punishment are mingled so, that shame covers the face, and sorrow puts a veil of darkness upon the heart : and we scarce pity a vile person that is haled to execution for murder or for treason, but we say he deserves it, and that every man is concerned in it that he should die. If lust brought the sickness or the shame, if we truly suffer the rewards of our evil deeds, we must thank ourselves; that is, we are fallen into an evil condition, and are the sacrifice of the divine justice. But if we live holy lives, and if we enter well in, we are sure to pass on safe, and to go forth with advantage, *if we list ourselves.*

2. To this relates, that *we should not counterfeit sickness :* for he that is to be careful of his passage into a sickness, will think himself concerned that he fall not into it through a trap-door; for so it hath sometimes happened, that such counterfeiting to light and evil purposes, hath ended in a real sufferance. — *Appian* tells of a *Roman* gentleman, who, to escape the proscription of the *Triumvirate,* fled, and to secure his privacy, counterfeited himself blind on one eye, and wore a plaster upon it, till beginning to be free from the malice of the three prevailing princes, he opened his hood, but could not open his eye, but

* Hi quicquid biberint vomitu remetientur tristes, et bilem suam regustantes. *Seneca.*

for

for ever lost the use of it, and with his eye paid for his liberty and hypocrisy. And *Cœlius* counterfeited the gout, and all its circumstances and pains, its dressings and arts of remedy and complaint, till at last the gout really entered, and spoiled the * pageantry. His arts of dissimulation were so witty, that they put life and motion into the very image of the disease; he made the very picture to sigh and groan.

It is easy to tell upon the interest of what virtue such counterfeiting is to be reproved. But it will be harder to snatch the politics of the world from following that which they call a canonized and authentic precedent. And *David's* counterfeiting himself mad before the *King of Gath*, to save his life and liberty, will be sufficient to entice men to serve an end upon the stock and charges of so small an irregularity; not in the matter of manners, but in the rules and decencies of natural or civil deportment. I cannot certainly tell what degrees of excuse David's action might put on. This only, besides his present necessity, the laws, whose coercive or directive power *David* lived under, had less of severity, and more of liberty, and towards enemies had so little of restraint, and so great a power, that what amongst them was a direct sin, if used to their brethren the sons of *Jacob*, was lawful and permitted to be acted against enemies. To which also I add this general caution; that the actions of holy persons, in scripture, are not always good precedents to us Christians, who are to walk by a rule and a greater strictness, with more simplicity and heartiness of pursuit. And amongst them, sanctity and holy living did in very many of its instances increase in new particulars of duty; and the prophets reproved many things which the law forbade not, and taught many duties which *Moses* prescribed not: and as the time of *Christ's* approach came, so the sermons and

---

* Tantum cura potest et ars doloris,
  Desiit fingere Cœlius podagram. *Mart.* l. vii. ep. 38.

revelations

revelations too were more evangelical, and like the
patterns which were fully to be exhibited by the Son
of God. Amongst which, it is certain that *Christian
simplicity*, and *godly sincerity* is to be accounted:
and * counterfeiting of sickness is a huge enemy to
this: * it is an upbraiding the Divine Providence,
* a jesting with fire, * a playing with a thunderbolt,
* a making decrees of God to serve the vicious or
secular ends of men; * it is a tempting of a judgment, * a false accusation of God, * a forestalling and
antedating his anger; it is a cozening of men, by
making God a party in the fraud: and therefore if
the cozenage returns upon the man's own head, he
enters like a fox into his sickness, and perceives himself catched in a trap, or earthed in the intolerable
dangers of the grave.

3. Although we must be infinitely careful to prevent it, that sin does not thrust us into a sickness;
yet when we are in the House of Sorrow, we should
do well to take physic against sin, and suppose that it
is the cause of the evil; if not by way of natural
casuality and proper effect, yet by a moral influence,
and by a just demerit. We can easily see when a
man hath got a surfeit; intemperance is as plain as
the hand-writing upon the wall, and easier to be read:
but covetousness may cause a fever as well as drunkenness, and pride can produce a falling sickness as
well as long washings and dilutions of the brain, and
intemperate lust. And we find it recorded in scripture, that the contemptuous and unprepared manner
of receiving of the holy sacraments caused sickness
and death; and *sacrilege* and *vow-breach* in *Ananias* and *Sapphira* made them to descend quick into
their graves. Therefore when sickness is upon us,
let us cast about, and, if we can, let us find out the
cause of God's displeasure, that it being removed, we
may return into the health and securities of God's
loving kindness. Thus in the three years famine,
                                                    David

David enquired of the Lord, what was the matter ? And God answered, *It is for Saul and his bloody house :* and then *David* expiated the guilt, and the people were full again of food and blessing. And when *Israel* was smitten by the *Amorites, Joshua* cast about, and found out the accursed thing, and cast it out : and the people, after that, fought prosperously. And what God in that case said to *Joshua* *, he will also verify to us ; *I will not be with you any more, unless ye destroy the accursed thing from among you.* But in pursuance of this, we are to observe, that although in case of loud and clamorous sins, the discovery is easy, and the remedy not difficult ; yet because Christianity is a nice thing, and religion is as pure as the sun, and the soul of man is apt to be troubled from more principles than the intricate and curiously composed body in its innumerable parts, it will often happen, that if we go to enquire into the particular, we shall never find it out ; and we may suspect drunkenness, when it may be also a morose delectation in unclean thoughts, or covetousness, or oppression, or a crafty invasion of my neighbour's rights, or my want of charity, or my judging unjustly in my own cause, or my censuring my neighbours, or a secret pride, or a base hypocrisy, or the pursuance of little ends with violence and passion, that may have procured the present messenger of death. Therefore ask no more after any one, but heartily endeavour to reform all : *sin no more, lest a worse thing happen.†* For a single search or accusation may be the design of an imperfect repentance ; but no man does heartily return to God, but he that decrees against every irregularity : and then only we can be restored to health or life, when we have taken away the causes of sickness and accursed death.

* Josh. vii. 12.

† Ὅρα κακῶς πράσσοντες, μὴ ἐμείζω, κακὰ κτησώμεθ. Soph.

K   4. He

4. He that means to have his sickness turn into safety and life, into health and virtue, must *make religion the employment of his sickness, and prayer the employment of his religion.* For there are certain *compendiums* or *abbreviatures*, and shortenings of religion, fitted to several states. They that first gave up their names to *Christ*, and that turned from Paganism to Christianity, had an abbreviature fitted for them; that were to renounce their false worshippings, and give up their belief, and vow their obedience unto Christ; and in the very profession of this they were forgiven in baptism. For God hastens to snatch them from the power of the devil, and therefore shortens the passage, and secures the estate. In the case of poverty, God hath reduced this duty of man to an abbreviature of those few graces which they can exercise; such as are patience, contentedness, truth, and diligence; and the rest he accepts in good-will, and the charities of the soul, in prayers, and the actions of a cheap religion. And to most men *charity* is also an *abbreviature :* and as the love of God shortens the way to the purchase of all virtues; so the expression of this to the poor, goes a huge way in the requisites, and towards the consummation of an excellent religion. And *martyrdom* is another abbreviature : and so is every act of an excellent and heroical virtue. But when we are fallen into the state of sickness, and that our understanding is weak and troubled, our bodies sick and useless, our passions turned into fear, and the whole state into suffering, God, in compliance with man's infirmity, hath also turned our religion into such a duty which a sick man can do most passionately, and a sad man and a timorous can perform effectually, and a dying man can do to many purposes of pardon and mercy; and that is *prayer.* For although a sick man is bound to do many acts of virtue of several kinds, yet the most of them are to be done *in the way of prayer.*

Prayer

Prayer is not only the religion that is proper to a sick man's condition, but it is the manner of doing other graces which is then left, and in his power. For thus the sick man is to do his repentance and his mortifications, his temperance and his chastity, by a fiction of imagination bringing the offers of the virtue to the spirit, and making an action of election : and so our prayers are a direct act of chastity, when they are made in the matter of that grace ; just as repentance for our cruelty is an act of the grace of *mercy ;* and repentance for uncleanness is an act of *chastity,* is a means of its purchase, an act in order to the habit. And though such acts of virtue, which are only *in the way of prayer,* are ineffective to the entire purchase, and of themselves cannot change the vice into virtue ; yet they are good renewings of the grace, and proper exercise of a habit already gotten.

The purpose of this discourse is, to represent the excellency of prayer, and its proper advantages, which it hath in the time of sickness. For besides that it moves God to pity, piercing the clouds, and making the heavens like a pricked eye, to weep over us, and refresh us with showers of pity ; it also doth the work of the soul, and expresses the virtue of his whole life *in effigie,* in pictures and lively representments ; so preparing it for a never-ceasing crown, by renewing the actions in the continuation of a never-ceasing, a never-hindered affection. Prayer speaks to God, when the tongue is stiffened with the approachings of death. Prayer can dwell in the heart, and be signified by the hand or the eye, by a thought or a groan. Prayer, of all the actions of religion, is the last alive, and it serves God without circumstances, and exercises material graces by abstraction from matter, and separation, and makes them to be spiritual : and therefore best dresses our bodies for *funeral* or *recovery,* for *the mercies of restitution,* or *the mercies of the grave.*

K 2   5. In

5. In every sickness, whether it will or will not be so in nature and in the event, yet in thy spirit, and preparations resolve upon it, and treat thyself accordingly as if it were a *sickness unto death*. For many men support their unequal courages by flattery and false hopes, and because sicker men have recovered, believe that they shall do so; but therefore they neglect to adorn their souls, or set their house in order. Besides the temporal inconveniences that often happen by such persuasions, and putting off the evil day, such as are *dying intestate, leaving estates entangled*, and *some relatives unprovided for*, they suffer infinitely in the interest and affairs of their soul, they die carelessly and surprised, their burthens on, and their scruples unremoved, and their cases of conscience not determined, and, like a sheep, without any care taken concerning their precious souls. Some men will never believe that a villain will betray them, though they receive often advices from suspicious persons and likely accidents, till they are entered into the snare; and then they believe it when they feel it, and when they cannot return: but so the treason entered, and the man was betrayed by his own folly, placing the snare in the regions and advantages of opportunity. This evil looks like *boldness*, and a *confident spirit*, but it is the greatest timorousness and cowardice in the world. They are so fearful to die, that they dare not look upon it as possible; and think that the making of a will is a mortal sign, and sending for a spiritual man an irrecoverable disease; and they are so afraid lest they should think and believe *now they must die*, that they will not take care that it may not be evil *in case they should*. So did the eastern slaves drink wine, and wrap their heads in a veil, that they might die without sense or sorrow, and wink hard that they might sleep the easier. In pursuance of this rule let a man consider, that whatsoever must be done in sickness, ought to be done in health: only

5   let

let him observe, that his sickness, as a good monitor, chastises his neglect of duty, and forces him to live as he always should : and then all *these solemnities and dressings for death* are nothing else but the part of a *religious life*, which he ought to have exercised in all his days ; and if those circumstances can affright him, let him please his fancy by this truth, that then he does but begin to live. But it will be a huge folly, if he shall think that confession of his sins will kill him, or receiving the holy sacrament will hasten his agony, or the priest shall undo all the hopeful language and promises of his physician. *Assure thyself, thou canst not die the sooner ; but by such addresses thou mayest die much the better.*

6. *Let the sick person be infinitely careful that he do not fall into a state of death upon a new account ;* that is, at no hand commit a deliberate sin, or retain any affection to the old : for in both cases he falls into the evils of a surprise, and the horrors of a sudden death. For a sudden death is but a sudden joy, if it takes a man in the state and exercises of virtue : and it is only then an evil, when it finds a man unready. They were sad departures, when *Tigillinus, Cornelius Gallus* the Prætor, *Lewis* the son of *Gonzaga,* duke of *Mantua, Ladislaus* king of *Naples, Speusippus, Giachettus* of *Geneva,* and one of the popes, died in the forbidden embraces of abused women : or if *Job* had cursed God, and so died ; or when a man sits down in despair, and in the accusation and calumny of the Divine Mercy ; they make their night sad, and stormy, and eternal. When *Herod* began to sink with the shameful torment of his bowels, and felt the grave open under him, he imprisoned the nobles of his kingdom, and commanded his sister that they should be a sacrifice to his departing ghost. This was an egress fit only for such persons who meant to dwell with devils to eternal ages : and that man is hugely in love with sin, who cannot

forbear

forbear in the week of the assizes, and when himself
stood at the bar of scrutiny, and prepared for his
final never-to-be-reversed sentence.   He dies suddenly to the worst sense and event of sudden death,
who so manages his sickness, that even that state shall
not be innocent, but that he is surprised in the guilt
of a new account.   It is a sign of a reprobate spirit,
and an habitual, prevailing, ruling sin, which exacts
obedience when the judgment looks him in the face.
At least go to God with the innocence and fair deportment of thy person in the last scene of thy life;
that when thy soul breaks into the state of separation,
it may carry the relishes of religion and sobriety to the
place of its abode and sentence.*

7. When these things are taken care for, let the
sick man so order his affairs, that he have but very
little conversation with the world, but wholly (as he
can) attend to religion, and antedate his conversation
in heaven, always having intercourse with God, and
still conversing with the Holy *Jesus*, kissing his wounds,
admiring his goodness, begging his mercy, feeding on
him with faith, and drinking his blood.   To which purpose it were very fit (if all circumstances were answerable) that the narrative of the passion of Christ be read
or discoursed to him at length, or in brief according to
the style of the four Gospels.   But in all things let
his care and *society* be as little secular as is possible.

>   * Whoso him bethoft
>   Inwardly and oft,
>   How hard it were to flit
>   From bed unto the pit,
>   From pit unto pain
>   That ne'er shall cease again,
>   He would not do one sin
>   All the world to win.
>
>   Inscript. Marmor. in Eccles. Paroch. de
>   Feversham in agro Cantiano.

CHAP. IV.

OF THE PRACTICE OF THE GRACES PROPER TO THE STATE
OF SICKNESS, WHICH A SICK MAN MAY PRACTISE ALONE.

SECT. I.

Of the Practice of Patience.

Now we suppose the man entering upon his scene
of sorrows and *passive graces*. It may be he went
yesterday to a wedding, merry and brisk, and there
he felt his sentence, that he must return home and
die; for men very commonly enter into the snare
singing, and consider not whither their fate leads
them; nor feared that then the angel was to strike
his stroke, till his knees kissed the earth, and his
head trembled with the weight of the rod which God
put into the hand of an exterminating angel. But
whatsoever the ingress was, when the man feels his
blood boil, or his bones weary, or his flesh diseased
with a load of a dispersed and disordered humour, or
his head to ache, or his faculties discomposed; then
he must consider, that all those discourses he hath
heard concerning patience, and resignation, and conformity to *Christ's* sufferings, and the melancholic
lectures of the cross, must all of them now be reduced
to practice, and pass from an ineffective contem-

K 4   plation

plation to such an exercise as will really try whether
we were true disciples of the cross, or only believed the
doctrines of religion when we were at ease, and that
they never passed through the ear to the heart, and
dwelt not in our spirits. But every man should consider, God does nothing in vain, that he would not
to no purpose send us preachers, and give us rules,
and furnish us with discourse, and lend us books,
and provide sermons, and make examples, and
promise his spirit, and describe the blessedness of holy
sufferings, and prepare us with daily alarms, if he did
not really purpose to order our affairs so that we
should need all this, and use it all. There were no
such thing as the grace of patience, if we were not to
feel a sickness, or enter into a state of sufferings;
whither when we are entered, we are to practise by
the following rules.

The Practice and Acts of Patience, by way of Rule.

1. AT the first address and presence of sickness
stand still and arrest thy spirit, that it may, without
amazement or affright, consider that this was that
thou lookedst for, and wert always certain should
happen, and that now thou art to enter into the actions of a new religion, the agony of a strange constitution : but at no hand suffer thy spirits to be dispersed with fear, or wildness of thought, but stay
their looseness and dispersion by a serious consideration of the present and future employment. For so
doth the *Lybian lion*, spying the fierce huntsman, he
first beats himself with the strokes of his tail, and
curls up his spirits, making them strong with union
and recollection, till being struck with a *Mauritanian*
spear, he rushes forth into his defence and noblest
contention; and either escapes into the secrets of his
own dwelling, or else dies the bravest of the forest.
Every

Every man, when shot with an arrow from God's
quiver, must then draw in all the auxiliaries of reason,
and know that then is the time to try his strength,
and to reduce the words of his religion into action,
and consider that if he behaves himself weakly and
timorously, he suffers never the less of sickness; but
if he returns to health, he carries along with him the
mark of a coward, and a fool; and if he descends
into his grave, he enters into the state of the *faith-*
less and *unbelievers.* Let him set his heart firm upon this resolution, *I must bear it inevitably, and I*
will by God's grace do it nobly.

2. *Bear in thy sickness all along the same thoughts,*
propositions, and discourses, concerning thy person,
thy life and death, thy soul and religion, which thou
hadst in the best days of thy health, and when thou
didst discourse wisely concerning things spiritual.
For it is to be supposed (and if it be not yet done,
let this rule remind thee of it, and direct thee) that
thou hast cast about in thy health, and considered
concerning thy change, and *the evil day,* that thou
must be sick and die, that thou must need a comforter, and that it was certain thou shouldst fall into a
state in which all the cords of thy anchor should be
stretched, and the very rock and foundation of faith
should be attempted. And whatsoever fancies may
disturb you, or whatsoever weaknesses may invade
you, yet consider, when you were better able to
judge and govern the accidents of your life, you con-
cluded it necessary to trust in God, and *possess your*
souls with patience. Think of things as they think
that stand by you, and as you did when you stood by
others: that it is a blessed thing to be patient; that
a quietness of spirit hath a certain reward; that still
there is infinite truth and reality in the promises of
the Gospel; that still thou art in the care of God, in
the condition of a son, and *working out thy salvation*
with labour and pain, *with fear and trembling:* that
now

now the sun is under a cloud, but it still sends forth the same influence: and be sure to make no new principles upon the stock of a quick and an impatient sense, or too busy an apprehension; keep your old principles, and upon their stock, discourse and practise on toward your conclusion.

3. *Resolve to bear your sickness like a child*, that is, without considering the evils and the pains, the sorrows and the danger; but go straight forward, and let thy thoughts cast about for nothing, but how to make advantages of it by the instrument of religion. He that from a high tower looks down upon the precipice, and measures the space through which he must descend, and considers what a huge fall he shall have, shall feel more by the horror of it, than by the last dash on the pavement: and he that tells his groans and numbers his sighs, and reckons one for every gripe of his belly, or throb of his distempered pulse, will make an *artificial sickness* greater than the *natural*. And if thou beest ashamed that a child should bear an evil better than thou, then take his instrument, and allay thy spirit with it; reflect not upon thy evil, but contrive as much as you can for duty, and in all the rest *inconsideration* will ease your pain.

4. If thou fearest thou shalt need, observe and draw together all such things as are apt to charm thy spirit, and ease thy fancy in the sufferance. It is the counsel of *Socrates; it is* (said he) *a great danger, and you must by discourse and arts of reasoning inchant it into slumber and some rest.** It may be thou wert moved much to see a person of honour to die untimely; or thou didst love the religion of that death-bed, and it was dressed up in circumstances fitted to thy needs, and hit thee on that part where thou wert most sensible; or some little saying in a sermon, or passage of a book was chosen and singled

---

* Χαλὸς γὰρ ὁ κίνδυνϙ, καὶ χρὴ τὰ τοιαῦτα ὥσπερ ἐπάδειν ἑαυτῷ.

out

out by a peculiar apprehension, and made consent lodge a while in thy spirit, even then when thou didst place death in thy meditation, and didst view it in all its dress of fancy.   Whatsoever that was which at any time did please thee in thy most passionate and fantastic part, let not that go, but bring it home at that time especially: because when thou art in thy weakness, such little things will easier move thee than a more severe discourse and a better reason.   For a sick man is like a scrupulous; his case is gone beyond the cure of arguments, and it is a *trouble* that can only be helped by chance, or a lucky saying: and *Ludovico Corbinelli* was moved at the death of *Henry* the Second, more than if he had read the saddest elegy of all the unfortunate princes in Christendom, or all the sad sayings of scripture, or the threnes of the funeral prophets. I deny not but this course is most proper to weak persons; but it is a state of weakness for which we are now providing remedies and instruction, a strong man will not need it: but when our sickness hath rendered us weak in all senses, it is not good to refuse a remedy because it supposes us to be sick.   But then, if to the catalogue of weak persons we add all those who are ruled by fancy, we shall find that *many persons in their health,* and *more in their sickness,* are under the dominion of fancy, and apt to be helped by those little things which themselves have found fitted to their apprehension, and which no other man can minister to their needs, unless by chance, or in an heap of other things.   But therefore every man should remember by what instruments he was at any time much moved, and try them upon his spirit in the day of his calamity.

5. *Do not choose the kind of thy sickness, or the manner of thy death ;* but let it be what God please; so it be no greater than thy spirit or thy patience; and for that you are to rely upon the promise of God, and to secure thyself by prayer and industry: but in
all

all things else let God be thy chooser, and let it be thy
work to submit indifferently, and attend thy duty. It
is lawful to beg of God that thy sickness may not be
sharp or noisome, infectious or unusual, because
these are circumstances of evil which are also proper
instruments of temptation: and though it may well
concern the prudence of thy religion to fear thyself,
and keep thee from violent temptations, who hast so
often fallen in little ones; yet even in these things be
sure to keep some degrees of indifferency; that is, if
God will not be intreated to ease thee, or to change
thy trial, then be importunate that thy spirit and its
interest be secured, and *let him do what seemeth good
in his eyes.* But as in the degrees of sickness thou
art to submit to God, so in the kind of it (supposing
equal degrees) thou art to be altogether incurious,
whether God call thee by a consumption or an asthma,
by a dropsy or a palsy, by a fever in thy humours,
or a fever in thy spirits; because all such nicety of
choice is nothing but a colour or legitimate impatience,
and to make an excuse to murmur privately, and
for circumstances, when in the sum of affairs we
durst not own impatience. I have known some persons vehemently wish, that they might die of a consumption, and some of these had a plot upon heaven,
and hoped by that means to secure it after a careless
life; as thinking a lingering sickness would certainly
infer a lingering and a protracted repentance; and by
that means they thought they should be safest.
Others of them dreamed it would be an easier death;
and have found themselves deceived, and their patience hath been tired with a weary spirit, and an
useless body, by often conversing with healthful persons, and vigorous neighbours, by uneasiness of the
flesh, and sharpness of their bones, by want of
spirits, and a dying life; and in conclusion, have
been directly debauched by peevishness and a fretful
sickness. And these men had better have left it to
the

the *wisdom* and *goodness* of God, for they both are infinite.

6. *Be patient in the desires of religion, and take care that the forwardness of exterior actions do not discompose thy spirit; while thou fearest that by less serving God in thy disability, thou runnest backward in the accounts of pardon, and the favour of God.* Be content that the time which was formerly spent in prayer, be now spent in vomiting and carefulness and attendances : since God hath pleased it should be so, it does not become us to think hard thoughts concerning it. Do not think that God is only to be found in a great prayer, or a solemn office ; he is moved by a sigh, by a groan, by an act of love. And therefore when your pain is great and pungent, lay all your strength upon it, to bear it patiently : when the evil is something more tolerable, let your mind think some pious, though short meditation ; let it not be very busy and full of attention, for that will be but a new temptation to your patience, and render your religion tedious and hateful. But record your desires, and present yourself to God by general acts of will and understanding, and by habitual remembrances of your former vigorousness, and by verification of the same grace, rather than proper exercises. If you can do more, do it; but if you cannot, let it not become a scruple to thee. We must not think man is tied to the forms of health, or that he who swoons and faints is obliged to his usual forms and hours of prayer : *If we cannot labour, yet let us love.* Nothing can hinder us from that but our own uncharitableness.

7. Be obedient to thy physician in those things that concern him, if he be a person fit to minister unto thee. *God is he only that needs no help*, and God hath created the physician for thine *: therefore use

---

* Ipsi ceu vi Deo nullo est opus; apud *Senecam. Scaliger* rectè emendat, Ipsi ceu Deo, &c. Ex Græco scilicet, Μόν☉ Θεὸς ἀνελλιπὴς καὶ ἀνενδεής.

him *temperately*, without violent confidences; and *sweetly*, without uncivil distrustings, or refusing his prescriptions upon humours or impotent fear. A man may refuse to have his arm or leg cut off, or to suffer the pains of *Marius's* incision: and if he believes that to die is the less evil, he may compose himself to it without hazarding his patience, or introducing that which he thinks a worse evil. But that which in this article is to be reproved and avoided, is, that some men will choose to die out of fear of death, and send for physicians, and do what themselves list, and call for counsel, and follow none. When there is reason they should decline him, it is not to be accounted to the stock of a sin; but where there is no just cause, there is a direct impatience.

Hither is to be reduced, that we be not too confident of the physician, or drain our hopes of recovery from the fountain through so imperfect channels; laying the wells of God dry, and digging to ourselves *broken cisterns*. Physicians are the ministers of God's mercies and providence, in the matter of health and ease, of restitution or death; and when God shall enable their judgments, and direct their counsels, and prosper their medicines, they shall do thee good; for which you must give God thanks, and to the physician the honour of a blessed *instrument*. But this cannot always be done. And * *Lucius Cornelius*, the lieutenant in *Portugal*, under *Fabius* the consul, boasted in the inscription of his monument, that he had lived an healthful and vegete age till his last sickness, but then complained he was forsaken by his physician, and railed upon *Æsculapius*, for not accepting his vow and passionate desire of preserving his life longer; and all the effect of that im-

---

* *L. Cornel.* Legatus sub *Fabio* Consule vividam naturam et virilem animum servavi, quoad animam efflavi; et tandem desertus ope medicorum et *Æsculapii* Dei ingrati, cui me voveram sodalem perpetuo futurum, si fila aliquantulum optata protulisset.　　*Vetus Inscriptio in Lusitania.*

patience

patience and the folly, was, that it is recorded to following ages, that he died without reason and without religion. But it was a sad sight to see the favour of all *France* confined to a physician and a barber; and the king (*Lewis* XI.) to be so much their servant, that he should acknowledge and own his life from them, and all his ease to their gentle dressing of his gout * and friendly ministeries: for the king thought himself undone and robbed if he should die; his portion here was fair, and he was loath to exchange his possession for the interest of a bigger hope.

8. *Treat thy nurses and servants sweetly, and as it becomes an obliged and a necessitous person.* Remember that thou art very troublesome to them, that they trouble not thee willingly; that they strive to do thee ease and benefit, that they wish it, and sigh, and pray for it, and are glad if thou likest their attendance; that whatsoever is amiss is thy disease, and the uneasiness of thy head or thy side, thy distemper or thy disaffections; and it will be an unhandsome injustice to be troublesome to them, because thou art so to thyself; to make them feel a part of thy sorrows, that thou mayst not bear them alone; evilly to requite their care by thy too curious and impatient wrangling and fretful spirit. That tenderness is vicious and unnatural, that shrieks out under the weight of a gentle cataplasm; and he will ill comply with *God's rod*, that cannot endure *his friend's greatest kindness;* and he will be very angry (if he durst) with God's smiting him, that is peevish with his servants that go about to ease him.

9. *Let not the smart of your sickness make you to call violently for death:* you are not patient, unless

---

* ——— Nunc omnibus anxius aris
Illacrymat, signátque fores, et pectore tergit
Limina ; nunc frustrà vocat exorabile numen.
               Papin. l. v.

you be content to live.* God hath wisely ordered that we may be the better reconciled with death, because it is the period of many calamities; but wherever the general hath placed thee, stir not from thy station until thou beest called off; but abide so, that death may come to thee by the design of him who intends it to be thy advantage. God hath made sufferance to be thy work; and do not impatiently long for evening, lest at night thou findest the reward of him that was weary of his work: for he that is weary before his time is an unprofitable servant, and is either idle or diseased.

10. That which remains in the practice of this grace, is, that the sick man should do acts of patience by way of prayer and ejaculations; in which he may serve himself of the following collection.

SECT. II.

Acts of Patience by way of Prayer and Ejaculation.

† *I* WILL *seek unto God, and unto God will I commit my cause:*

Which doth great things and unsearchable; marvellous things without number:

To set up on high those that be low; that those which mourn may be exalted to safety.

So the poor hath hope, and iniquity stoppeth her mouth.

Behold, happy is the man whom God correcteth: therefore despise not thou the chastening of the Almighty:

For he maketh sore, and bindeth up; he woundeth, and his hands make whole.

---

* 'Αποκαρτερειν Græci vocant cùm Mors propter Impatientiam petitur.
† Job v. 8, 9. 11. 16, 17, 18, 19. 26.

He

He shall deliver thee in six troubles; yea, in seven there shall no evil touch thee.

Thou shalt come to thy grave in a full age, like as a shock of corn cometh in its season.

* *I remember thee upon my bed, and meditate on thee in the night-watches. Because thou hast been my help, therefore under the shadow of they wings will I rejoice. My soul followeth hard after thee; for thy right hand hath upholden me.*

† *God restoreth my soul: He leadeth me in the path of righteousness for his name's sake. Yea, though I walk through the valley of the shadow of death, I will fear no evil; for thou art with me; thy rod and thy staff they comfort me.*

‡ *In the time of trouble he shall hide me in his pavilion: In the secret of his tabernacle shall he hide me, he shall set me upon a rock.*

§ *The Lord hath looked down from the height of his sanctuary; from the heaven did the Lord behold the earth: to hear the groaning of his prisoners; to loose those that are appointed to death.*

¶ *I cried unto God with my voice, even unto God with my voice, and he gave ear unto me. In the day of my trouble I sought the Lord; my sore ran in the night and ceased not; my soul refused to be comforted. I remembered God, and was troubled: I complained, and my spirit was overwhelmed. Thou holdest mine eyes waking: I am so troubled that I cannot speak. Will the Lord cast me off for ever? And will he be favourable no more? Is his promise clean gone for ever? Doth his promise fail for evermore? Hath God forgotten to be gracious? Hath he in anger shut up his tender mercies? And I said, this is my infirmity: but I will remember the years of the right hand of the Most High.*

* Ps. lxii. 6, 7, 8.   †Ps. xxiii. 3, 4.   ‡ Ps. xxvii. 5.   § Ps. cii. 19, 20.
Ps. lxxvii. 1, 2, 3, 4. 7, 8, 9, 10.

L

* *No temptation hath taken me, but such as is common to man: but God is faithful, who will not suffer me to be tempted above what I am able; but will with the temptation also make a way to escape, that I may be able to bear it.*

† *Whatsoever things were written aforetime, were written for our learning; that we through patience and comfort of the scriptures might have hope. Now the God of patience and consolation grant me to be so minded.*

‡ *It is the Lord, let him do what seemeth good in his eyes.*

Surely the word that the Lord hath spoken is very good; but thy servant is weak: O remember mine infirmities; and lift thy servant up that leaneth upon thy right hand.

§ *There is given unto me a thorn in the flesh, the messenger of Satan, to buffet me. For this thing I besought the Lord thrice, that it might depart from me. And he said unto me, My grace is sufficient for thee: For my strength is made perfect in weakness. Most gladly therefore will I glory in my infirmities, that the power of Christ may rest upon me. For when I am weak, then am I strong.*

¶ *O Lord, thou hast pleaded the causes of my soul; thou hast redeemed my life. And I said, my strength and my hope is in the Lord; remembering mine affliction and my misery, the wormwood and the gall. My soul hath them still in remembrance, and is humbled in me.*

This I recall to my mind, therefore have I hope.

It is of the Lord's mercies that we are not consumed, because his compassions fail not. They are new every morning; great is thy faithfulness. The

---

* 1 Cor. x. 13.   † Rom. xv. 4, 5.   ‡ 1 Sam. iii. 18.
§ 2 Cor. xii. 7, 8, 9, 10.
¶ Lam. iii. 58. 18, 19, 20, 21, 22, 23, 24, 25, 26. 31, 32, 33. 39.

Lord

Lord is my portion, saith my soul; therefore will I hope in him.

The Lord is good unto them that wait for him, to the soul that seeketh him.   It is good that a man should both hope and quietly wait for the salvation of the Lord.   For the Lord will not cast off for ever.   But though he cause grief, yet will he have compassion according to the multitude of his mercies.   For he doth not afflict willingly, nor grieve the children of men.

*   * Wherefore doth a living man complain?   A man for the punishment of his sins?   O that thou wouldst hide me in the grave* [of Jesus], *that thou wouldst keep me secret, until thy wrath be past;   that thou wouldst appoint me a set time,   and remember me !*

*   † Shall we receive good at the hand of God, and shall we not receive evil.*

The sick man may recite, or hear recited, the following *Psalms*, in the intervals of his agony.

I.

*   ‡ O Lord, rebuke me not in thine anger, neither chasten me in thy hot displeasure.*

*   Have mercy upon me, O Lord, for I am weak :   O Lord, heal me, for my bones are vexed.*

*   My soul is also sore vexed : but thou, O Lord, how long ?*

*   Return, O Lord, deliver my soul :   O save me, for thy mercy's sake.*

*   For in death no man remembereth thee :   in the grave who shall give thee thanks ?*

*   I am weary with my groaning, all the night make I my bed to swim :   I water my couch with my tears.*

* Job, xiv. 13.   † Job, ii. 10.   ‡ Psal. vi.

L 2

Mine

Mine eye is consumed because of grief; it waxeth old because of all my [sorrows.]

Depart from me, all ye workers of iniquity; for the Lord hath heard the voice of my weeping.

The Lord hath heard my supplication: the Lord will receive my prayer.

Blessed be the Lord, who hath heard my prayer, and hath not turned his mercy from me.

II.

* *In the Lord put I my trust: how say ye to my soul, Flee as a bird to your mountain?*

The Lord is in his holy temple, the Lord's throne is in heaven: his eyes behold, his eye-lids try the children of men.

† *Preserve me, O God; for in thee do I put my trust.*

O my soul, thou hast said unto the Lord, Thou art my Lord; my goodness extendeth not to thee.

The Lord is the portion of mine inheritance and of my cup: thou maintainest my lot.

I will bless the Lord, who hath given me counsel: my reins also instruct me in the night seasons.

I have set the Lord always before me: because he is at my right hand, I shall not be moved.

Therefore my heart is glad, and my glory rejoiceth; my flesh also shall rest in hope.

Thou wilt shew me the path of life: in thy presence is the fulness of joy; at thy right hand there are pleasures for evermore.

‡ *As for me, I will behold thy face in righteousness: I shall be satisfied, when I awake, with thy likeness.*

---

* Psal. xi. 1. 4.   † Psal. xvi. 1, 2. 5. 7, 8, 9. 11.   ‡ Psal. xvii. 15.

III.

* *HAVE mercy upon me, O Lord, for I am in trouble: mine eye is consumed with grief; yea, my soul and my belly.*

For my life is spent with grief, and my years with sighing: my strength faileth because of mine iniquity, and my bones are consumed.

I am like a broken vessel.

But I trusted in thee, O Lord: I said, thou art my God.

My times are in thy hand: make thy face to shine upon thy servant: save me for thy mercy's sake.

† *When thou saidst, Seek ye my face; my heart said unto thee, Thy face, Lord, will I seek.*

Hide not thy face far from me; put not thy servant away in thine anger: thou hast been my help; leave me not, neither forsake me, O God of my salvation.

I had fainted, unless I had believed to see the goodness of the Lord in the land of the living.

‡ *O how great is thy goodness which thou hast laid up for them that fear thee; which thou hast wrought for them that trust in thee before the sons of men!*

Thou shalt hide them in the secret of thy presence, from the pride of man: thou shalt keep them secretly in a pavilion from the strife of tongues, [from the calumnies and aggravation of sins by devils.]

I said in my haste, I am cut off from before thine eyes: nevertheless thou heardest the voice of my supplications when I cried unto thee.

O love the Lord, all ye his saints; for the Lord preserveth the faithful, and plenteously rewardeth the proud doer.

Be of good courage, and he shall strengthen your heart, all ye that hope in the Lord.

---

* Ps. xxxi. 9, 10. 12. 14, 15, 16.   † Ps. xxvii. 8, 9. 13,
Ps. xxxi. 19, 20. 22, 23, 24.

The

The Prayer to be said in the beginning of a Sickness.

O ALMIGHTY GOD, merciful and gracious, who in thy justice didst send sorrow and tears, sickness and death into the world, as a punishment for man's sins, and hast comprehended all under sin, and this sad covenant of sufferings, *not to destroy us, but that thou mightest have mercy upon all,* making thy justice to minister to mercy, *short afflictions to an eternal weight of glory;* as thou hast turned my sins into sickness, so turn my sickness to the advantages of holiness and religion, of mercy and pardon, of faith and hope, of grace and glory. Thou hast now called me *to the fellowship of sufferings;* Lord, by the instrument of religion let my present condition be so sanctified, that my sufferings may be united to the sufferings of my Lord, that so thou mayest pity me and assist me. Relieve my sorrow, and support my spirit: direct my thoughts, and sanctify the accidents of my sickness, and that the punishment of my sin may be the school of virtue: in which, since thou hast now entered me, Lord, make me a holy proficient; that I may behave myself as a son under discipline, humbly and obediently, evenly and penitently, that I may come by this means nearer unto thee; that if I shall go forth of this sickness by the gate of life and health, I may return to the world with great strengths of spirit to run a new race of a stricter holiness, and a more severe religion: or if I pass from hence with the out-let of death, I may enter into the bosom of my Lord, and may feel the present joys of a certain hope of that sea of pleasures in which all thy saints and servants shall be comprehended to eternal ages. Grant this, for *Jesus Christ's* sake, our dearest Lord and Saviour. *Amen.*

An Act of Resignation, to be said by a sick Person in all the evil Accidents of his Sickness.

O ETERNAL GOD, thou hast made me and sustained me, thou hast blessed me in all the days of my life, and hast taken care of me in all variety of accidents; and nothing happens to me in vain, nothing without thy Providence : and I know thou smitest thy servants in mercy, and with designs of the greatest pity in the world. Lord, I humbly lie down under thy rod; do with me as thou pleasest; do thou choose for me, not only the whole state and condition of being, but every little and great accident of it. Keep me safe by thy grace, and then use what instrument thou pleasest of bringing me to thee. Lord, I am not solicitous of the passage, so I may get thee. Only, O Lord, remember my infirmities, and let thy servant rejoice in thee always, and feel, and confess, and glory in thy goodness. O be thou as delightful to me in this my medicinal sickness, as ever thou wert in any of the dangers of my prosperity : let me not peevishly refuse thy pardon at the rate of a severe discipline. I am thy servant and thy creature, thy purchased possession and thy son : I am all thine : and because thou hast mercy in store for all that trust in thee, I cover mine eyes, and in silence wait for the time of my redemption. *Amen.*

A Prayer for the Grace of Patience.

MOST merciful and gracious Father, who in the redemption of lost mankind by the passion of thy most holy Son, hast established a covenant of sufferings. I bless and magnify thy name, that thou hast adopted me into the inheritance of sons, and hast given me a portion of my elder brother. Lord, the cross falls heavy, and sits uneasy upon my shoulders;

L 4   my

my *spirit is willing, but* my *flesh is weak :* I humbly
beg of thee, that I may now rejoice in this thy dispensation and effect of Providence. 1 know and am
persuaded that thou art then as gracious when thou
smitest us for amendment or trial, as when thou re-
lievest our wearied bodies in compliance with our
infirmity. I rejoice, O Lord, in thy rare and mysterious mercy, who by sufferings hast turned our misery
into advantages unspeakable : for so thou makest us
like to thy Son, and givest us a gift that the angels
never did receive : for they cannot die in conformity
to, and imitation of their Lord and ours ; but blessed
be thy name, we can ; and dearest Lord, *let it be so.*
Amen.

II.

THOU who art the God of patience and consolation, strengthen me in the inner man, that I may
bear the yoke and burthen of the Lord, without any
uneasy and useless murmurs and ineffective unwillingness. Lord, I am unable to stand under the cross,
unable of myself ; but thou, O Holy *Jesus,* who didst
feel the burthen of it, who didst sink under it, and
wert pleased to admit a man to bear part of the load
when thou underwentest all for him, be thou pleased
to ease this load by fortifying my spirit, that I may
be strongest when I am weakest, and may be able
to do and suffer every thing thou pleasest, through
Christ which strengthens me. Lord, if thou wilt
support me, I will for ever praise thee : if thou wilt
suffer the load to press me yet more heavily, I will
cry unto thee, and complain unto my God ; and at
last I will lie down and die, and by the mercies and
intercession of the Holy *Jesus,* and the conduct of
thy blessed spirit, and the ministry of angels, pass
into those mansions where holy souls rest, and weep
no more. Lord, pity me ; Lord, sanctify this my
sickness ;

sickness; Lord, strengthen me; Holy *Jesus,* save me and deliver me.   Thou knowest how shamefully I have fallen with pleasure : in thy mercy and very pity let me not fall with pain too.   O let me never *charge God foolishly,* nor offend thee by my impatience and uneasy spirit, nor weaken the hands and hearts of those that charitably minister to my needs : but let me pass through *the valley of tears,* and *the valley of the shadow of death,* with safety and peace, with a meek spirit and a sense of the divine mercies : and though thou breakest me in pieces, my hope is, thou wilt gather me up in the gatherings of eternity. Grant this, eternal God, gracious Father, for the merits and intercession of our merciful high priest, who once suffered for me, and for ever intercedes for me, our most gracious and ever blessed Saviour, *JESUS.*

A Prayer to be said when the sick Man takes Physic.

O MOST blessed and eternal *Jesus,* thou who art the great physician of our souls, and *the sun of righteousness, arising with healing in thy wings,* to thee is given, by thy heavenly Father, the government of all the world, and thou disposest every great and little accident to thy Father's honour, and to the good comfort of them that love and serve thee : be pleased to bless the ministry of thy servant, in order to my ease and health, direct his judgment, prosper the medicines, and dispose the chances of my sickness fortunately, that I may feel the blessing and loving kindness of the Lord in the ease of my pain and the restitution of my health; that I being restored to the society of the living, and to thy solemn assemblies, may praise thee and thy goodness secretly among the faithful, and in the congregation of thy redeemed ones, here in the outer-courts of the Lord, and hereafter in thy eternal temple for ever and ever. *Amen.*

SECT. III.

Of the Practice of the Grace of Faith in the Time of Sickness.

Now is the time in which faith appears most
necessary, and most difficult. It is the foundation of
a good life, and the foundation of all our hopes: it
is that without which we cannot live well, and without which we cannot die well: it is a grace that then
we shall need to support our spirits, to sustain our
hopes, to alleviate our sickness, to resist temptations,
to prevent despair. Upon the belief of the articles
of our religion, we can do the works of a holy life;
but upon belief of the promises, we can bear our
sickness patiently, and die cheerfully. The sick man
may practise it in the following instances.

1. *Let the sick man be careful that he do not admit of any doubt concerning that which he believed
and received from common consent, in his best health
and day of election and religion.* For if the devil
can but prevail so far as to unfix and unrivet the
resolution and confidence or fulness of assent, it is
easy for him so to unwind the spirit, that from *why*
to *whether or no,* from *whether or no* to *scarcely not,*
from *scarcely not* to *absolutely not at all,* are steps of a
descending and falling spirit: and whatsoever a man
is made to doubt of by the weakness of his understanding in a sickness, it will be hard to get an instrument strong or subtle enough to reinforce and
insure. For when the strengths are gone by which
faith held, and it does not stand firm by the weight of
its own bulk and great constitution, nor yet by the
cordage of a tenacious root; then it is prepared for a
ruin, which it cannot escape in the tempests of a
sickness, and the assaults of a devil.   * Discourse and
argument, * the line of tradition, and * a never-fail-
ing

ing experience, * the spirit of God, and * the truth of miracles, * the word of prophecy, and * the blood of martyrs, * the excellency of the doctrine, and * the necessity of men, * the riches of the promises, and * the wisdom of the Revelations, * the reasonable- ness and * sublimity, * the concordance and the * usefulness of the articles, and * their compliance with all the needs of man, and * the government of commonwealths, are like the strings and branches of the roots by which faith stands firm and unmove- able in the spirit and understanding of a man. But in sickness the understanding is shaken, and the ground is removed in which the root did grapple, and support its trunk: and therefore there is no way now, but that it be left to stand upon the old con- fidences, and by the firmament of its own weight.* It must be left to stand, because it always stood there before : and as it stood all his life-time in the *ground of understanding*, so it must now be supported with *will*, and a *fixed resolution*. But disputation tempts it, and shakes it with trying, and overthrows it with shaking.† Above all things in the world, let the sick man fear a proposition which his sickness hath put into him contrary to the discourses of health, and a sober untroubled reason.

2. *Let the sick man mingle the recital of his creed together with his devotions, and in that let him account his faith ; not in curiosity and factions, in the confessions of parties and interests*‡ : for some over-forward zeals are so earnest to profess their little and uncertain articles, and glory so to die in a

---

* ——— Non jam validis radicibus hærens,
  Pondere fixa suo. ———

† Sanctiúsque ac reverentius visum, de actis Deorum credere quàm scire. *Tacit.*

‡ Fides tua te salvum faciet; non exercitatio Scripturarum. Fides in regula posita est; (scil. in Symbolo quod jam recitaverat) habet legem, et salutem de observatione legis: exercitatio autem in curiositate consistit, habens gloriam solam de peritiæ studio. Cedat curiositas Fidei; cedat Gloria Saluti. *Tert.* de Præscript.

particular

particular and divided communion, that in the profession of their faith, they lose or discompose their
charity.* Let it be enough that we secure our interest
of heaven, though we do not go about to appropriate
the mansions to our sect † : for every good man hopes
to be saved as he is a Christian, and not as he is a
Lutheran, or of another division. However, those
articles upon which he can build the exercise of any
virtue in his sickness ‡, or upon the stock of which
he can improve his present condition, are such as
consist in *the greatness* and *goodness,* the *veracity*
and *mercy of God* through *Jesus Christ* ‖ : nothing
of which can be concerned in the fond disputations
which faction and interest hath too long maintained
in Christendom.

3. *Let the sick man's faith especially be active
about the promises of grace, and the excellent things
of the gospel ;* those which can comfort his sorrows,
and enable his patience ; those upon the hopes of
which he did the duties of his life, and for which he
is not unwilling to die; such as the *intercession* and
advocation of Christ, remission of sins, the resurrection, the mysterious arts and mercies of man's redemption, *Christ's* triumph over death and all the
powers of hell, the covenant of grace, or the blessed
issues of repentance; and above all, the article of
eternal life, upon the strength of which 11,000 virgins
went cheerfully together to their martyrdom, and
20,000 Christians were burnt by *Dioclesian* on a

---

* S. *Augustinus* vocat Symbolum comprehensionem Fidei vestræ atque
perfectionem, cordis signaculum, et nostræ militiæ sacramentum. *Amb.*
lib. iii. de Veland. Virgin. *Aug.* serm. cxv.

† Non per difficiles nos Deus ad beatam vitam quæstiones vocat. In
absoluto nobis et facili est æternitas; Jesum suscitatum à mortuis per
Deum credere, et ipsum esse Dominum confiteri. S. *Hilar.* lib. x. de
Trinit.

‡ Hæc est fides Catholica, de symbolo suo dixit *Athanasius,* vel quicunque
author est. *Athanas.* de fide *Nicena.*

‖ Ἡ γὰρ ἐν αὐτῇ παρὰ τῶν πατέρων κατὰ τὰς θείας γραφὰς ὁμολογηθεῖσα
πίστις αὐτάρκη ἐστὶ πρὸς ἀνατροπὴν μὲν πάσης ἀσεβείας, σύστασιν δὲ τῆς εὐσεβείας
ἐν Χριστῷ. Ep. ad Epict.

Christmas-

Christmas-Day *, and whole armies of *Asian* Christians offered themselves to the tribunals of *Arius
Antonius,* and whole colleges of severe persons were
instituted, who lived upon religion, whose *dinner* was
the *eucharist,* whose *supper* was *praise,* and their
nights were *watches,* and their *days* were *labour;*
for the hope of which then men counted it gain to
lose their estates, and gloried in their sufferings, and
rejoiced in their persecutions, and were glad at their
disgraces.   This is the article that hath made all the
martyrs of *Christ* confident and glorious; and if it
does not more than sufficiently strengthen our spirits
to the present suffering, it is because we understand
it not, but have the appetites of beasts and fools.
But if the sick man fixes his thoughts, and lets his
habitation to dwell here, he swells his hope, and
masters his fears, and eases his sorrows, and overcomes
his temptations.

4. *Let the sick man endeavour to turn his faith
of the articles into the love of them:* and that will
be an excellent instrument, not only to refresh his
sorrows, but to confirm his faith in defiance of all
temptations.   For a sick man and a disturbed understanding are not competent and fit instruments to
judge concerning the reasonableness of a proposition.
But therefore let him consider and love it, because it
is useful and necessary, profitable and gracious.
And when he is once in love with it, and then also
renews his love to it, when he feels the need of it, he
is an interested person, and for his own sake will
never let it go, and pass into the shadows of doubting,
or the utter darkness of infidelity.   *An act of love* will
make him have a mind to it; and we easily believe
what we love, but very uneasily part with our belief,
which we for so great an interest have chosen, and
entertained with a great affection.

* *Tertul.* ad *Scapul.*

5. *Let*

5. *Let the sick person be infinitely careful that his faith be not tempted by any man, or any thing; and when it is in any degree weakened, let him lay fast hold upon the conclusion,* upon the article itself, and by earnest prayer beg of God to guide him in certainty and safety. For let him consider, that the article is better than all its contrary or contradictory, and he is concerned that it be true, and concerned also that he do believe it: but he can receive no good at all if Christ did not die, if there be no resurrection, his creed hath deceived him: therefore all that he is to do is to secure his hold, which he can do no way but *by prayer* and *by his interest.* And by this argument or instrument it was that *Socrates* refreshed the evil of his condition, when he was to drink his *Aconite:* "If the soul be immortal, "and perpetual rewards be laid up for wise souls, "then I lose nothing by my death: but if there be "not, then I lose nothing by my opinion; for it sup-"ports my spirit in my passage, and the evil of being "deceived cannot overtake me when I have no "being." * So it is with all that are tempted in their faith. If those articles be not true, then the men are nothing; if they be true, then they are happy: and if the articles fail, there can be no punishment for believing; but if they be true, my *not believing* destroys all my portion in them, and possibility to receive the excellent things which they contain. By faith we *quench the fiery darts of the devil:* but if our faith be quenched, wherewithal shall we be able to endure the assault? Therefore seize upon the article, and secure the great object and the great instrument; that is, the *hopes of pardon and eternal life, through Jesus Christ:* and do this by all means, and by any instrument, artificial or inartificial, by argument or by stratagem, by perfect resolution, or by

* In *Phædon.*

discourse,

discourse, by the hand and ears of premises or the foot of the conclusion, by right or by wrong, because we understand it, or because we love it, *super totam materiam,* because I will and because I ought, because it is safe to do so, and because it is not safe to do otherwise : because if I do, I may receive a good ; and because if I do not, I am miserable : either for that I shall have a portion of sorrows, or that I can have no portion of good things without it.

SECT. IV.

Acts of Faith, by way of Prayer and Ejaculation, to be said by sick Men in the Days of their Temptation.

* LORD, *whither shall I go ? thou hast the words of eternal life.*

I believe in God the Father Almighty, and in Jesus Christ his only Son our Lord, &c.

And I believe in the Holy Ghost, &c.

† *Lord, I believe : help thou my unbelief.*

‡ *I know and am persuaded by the Lord Jesus, that none of us liveth to himself, and no man dieth to himself: for whether we live, we live unto the Lord ; and whether we die, we die unto the Lord : whether we live therefore or die, we are the Lord's.*

§ *If God be for us, who can be against us ?*

He that spared not his own son, but delivered him up for us all ; how shall he not with him give us all things ?

Who shall lay any thing to the charge of God's elect ? It is God that justifieth. Who is he that

---

* John, vi. 68.   † Mark, ix. 24.   ‡ Rom. xiv. 14. 7, 8.
§ Rom. viii. 31, 32, 33, 34.

con-

condemneth? It is Christ that died; yea, rather that is risen again, who is even at the right-hand of God, who also maketh intercession for us.

* If any man sin, we have an advocate with the Father, Jesus Christ the righteous: and he is the propitiation for our sins.

† This is a faithful saying, and worthy of all acceptation, that Jesus Christ came into the world to save sinners.

O grant that I may obtain mercy, that in me *Jesus Christ* may shew forth all long suffering, that I may believe in him to life everlasting.

‡ I am bound to give thanks unto God always, because God hath from the beginning chosen me to salvation, through sanctification of the spirit, and belief of the truth: whereunto he called me by the gospel, to the obtaining of the glory of the Lord Jesus Christ.

Now our Lord Jesus Christ himself, and God even our Father which hath loved us, and hath given us everlasting consolation, and good hope through grace, comfort my heart, and stablish me in every good word and work.

§ The Lord direct my heart into the love of God, and into the patient waiting for Christ.

‖ O that our God would count me worthy of this calling, and fulfil all the good pleasure of his goodness, and the work of faith with power. That the name of our Lord Jesus Christ may be glorified in me, and I in him, according to the grace of our God and the Lord Jesus Christ.

¶ Let us who are of the day be sober, putting on the breast-plate of faith and love: and for an helmet, the hope of salvation. For God hath not appointed us to wrath, but to obtain salvation by our Lord Jesus Christ, who died for us, that whether we wake

---

* 1 John, ii. 1, 2.   † 1 Tim. i. 15.   ‡ 2 Thess. ii. 13, 14. 16, 17.
§ 2 Thess. iii. 5.   ‖ 2 Thess. i. 11, 12.   ¶ 1 Thess. v. 8, 9, 10, 11.

or

or sleep, we should live together with him. Wherefore comfort yourselves together, and edify one another.

* *There is no name under heaven whereby we can be saved, but only the name of the Lord Jesus. And every soul which will not hear that prophet, shall be destroyed from among the people.*

† *God forbid that I should glory, save in the cross of Jesus Christ. I desire to know nothing but Jesus Christ and him crucified. For to me to live is Christ, and to die is gain.*

‡ *Cease ye from man, whose breath is in his nostrils : for wherein is he to be accounted of? But the just shall live by faith.*

‖ *Lord, I believe that thou art the Christ, the Son of God, the Saviour of the world, the resurrection and the life ; and he that believeth in thee, though he were dead, yet shall he live.*

§ *Jesus said unto her, Said I not to thee, that if thou wouldst believe, thou shouldst see the glory of God?*

¶ *O death, where is thy sting? O grave, where is thy victory? The sting of death is sin, and the strength of sin is the law. But thanks be to God, who giveth us the victory, through our Lord Jesus Christ. Lord, make me stedfast and unmoveable, always abounding in the work of the Lord : for I know that my labour is not in vain in the Lord.*

The Prayer for the Grace and Strengths of Faith.

O HOLY and eternal *Jesus,* who didst die for me and for all mankind, abolishing our sin, reconciling us to God, adopting us into the portion of thine heritage, and establishing with us a covenant of faith and obedience, making our souls to rely upon

---

* Acts, iv. 12.   Acts, iii. 23.   † Gal. vi. 14.   1 Cor. ii. 2.   Phil. i. 21.
‡ Isa. ii. 22.   Hab. ii. 4.   ‖ John, xi. 27.   John, iv. 42.   John, xi. 25.
§ John, xi. 40.   ¶ 1 Cor. xv. 55, 56, 57, 58.

spiritual

spiritual strengths, by the supports of a holy belief, and the expectation of rare promises, and the infallible truths of God: O let me for ever dwell upon the rock, leaning upon thy arm, believing thy word, trusting in thy promises, waiting for thy mercies, and doing thy commandments; that the devil may not prevail upon me, and my own weaknesses may not abuse or unsettle my persuasions, nor my sins discompose my just confidence in thee and thy eternal mercies. Let me always be thy servant and thy disciple, and die in the communion of thy church, of all faithful people. Lord, I renounce whatsoever is against thy truth; and if secretly I have or do believe any false proposition, I do it in the simplicity of my heart and great weakness; and if I could discover it, would dash it in pieces by a solemn disclaiming it: for thou art *the way, the truth, and the life.* And I know that whatsoever thou hast declared, that is the truth of God: and I do firmly adhere to the religion thou hast taught, and glory in nothing so much as that I am a Christian, that thy name is called upon me. O my God, *though I die, yet will I put my trust in thee. In thee, O Lord, have I trusted, let me never be confounded.* Amen.

SECT. V.

Of the Practice of the Grace of Repentance in the Time of Sickness.

Men generally do very much dread sudden death, and pray against it passionately; and certainly it hath in it great inconveniences accidentally to men's estates, to the settlement of families, to the culture and trimming of souls, and it robs a man of the blessings which

which may be consequent to sickness, and to the passive graces and holy contentions of a Christian*, while he descends to his grave without an adversary, or a trial : and a good man may be taken at such a disadvantage, that a sudden death would be a great evil, even to the most excellent person, if it strikes him in an unlucky circumstance. But these considerations are not the only ingredients into those men's discourse who pray violently against sudden deaths; for possibly, if this were all, there may be in the condition of sudden death something to make recompence for the evils of the over-hasty accident. For certainly, it is a less temporal evil to fall by the rudeness of a sword, than the violences of a fever, and the axe is a much less affliction than a strangury ; and though a sickness tries our virtues, yet a sudden death is free from temptation : a sickness may be more glorious, and a sudden death more safe. *The deadest deaths are best,* the shortest and least premeditate, so *Cæsar* said · and *Pliny* called a short death *the · greatest fortune of a man's life.*† For even good men have been forced to an undecency of deportment by the violences of pain ‡ : and *Cicero* observes concerning *Hercules,* that he was broken in pieces with pain, even then when he sought for immortality by his death, being tortured with a plague knit up in the lappet of his shirt. And therefore as a sudden death certainly loses the rewards of a holy sickness, so it makes that a man shall not so much hazard and lose the rewards of a holy life.

But the secret of this affair is a worse matter : men live at that rate, either of an habitual wickedness, or else a frequent repetition of single acts of killing and

---

* Descendisti ad Olympia, sed nemo præter te : coronam habes, victoriam non habes.

† Mitiùs ille perit subitâ qui mergitur undâ,
  Quàm sua qui liquidis brachia lassat aquis. *Ovid.*

‡ Etiam innocentes mentiri cogit dolor.

deadly

deadly sins, that a sudden death is the ruin of all
their hopes, and a perfect consignation to an eternal
sorrow. But in this case also so is a lingering sickness: for our sickness may change us from life to
health, from health to strength, from strength to the
firmness and confirmation of habitual graces; but it
cannot change a man from death to life, and begin and
finish that process, which sits not down but in the bosom of blessedness. He that washes in the morning,
when his bath is seasonable and healthful, is not only
made clean, but sprightly, and the blood is brisk and
coloured like the first springing of the morning; but
they that wash their dead cleanse the skin, and leave
paleness upon the cheek, and stiffness in all the joints.
A repentance upon our death-bed is like washing the
corpse, it is cleanly and civil, but makes no change
deeper than the skin.* But God knows it is a custom so
to wash them that are going to dwell with dust, and to
be *buried in the lap of their kindred* earth; but all their
life-time wallow in pollutions without any washing at
all; or if they do, it is like that of the *Dardina*†, who
washed but thrice all their time, when they are born,
and when they marry, and when they die; when they
are baptized, or against a solemnity, or for the day of
their funeral: but these are but ceremonious washings,
and never purify the soul, if it be stained and hath
sullied the whiteness of its baptismal robes.

God intended we should live a holy life; he contracted with us in *Jesus* Christ for a holy life‡, he
made no abatements of the strictest sense of it, but
such as did necessarily comply with human infirmities

---

* Lavor honestâ horâ et salubri quæ mihi et calorem et sanguinem servet:
Rigere et pallere post lavacrum mortuus possum. *Tertul.* Apol. c. 42.
——— Cognatâ fæce sepulti.

† Δαρδανεῖς τὰς ὑπὸ της Ἰλλυρίδος ἀκάω τρὶς λύεσθαι μονὸν παρὰ πάντα τόν
ἑαυτῶν βίον, ἐξ ὠδίνων, καὶ γαμᾶντας, καὶ ἀποθανόντας. *Ælian.* lib. iv. Var. Hist.
cap. 1.

‡ Vide *Aug.* lib. v. Hom. 4. et Serm. 57. de Tempore. *Faustum* ad *Pau-
linum,* Ep. 1. in Biblioth. Pp. tom. v. Vet. Edit. Concil. Arelat. 1. c. 3. Carth.
4. cap. 7, 8.

or impossibilities; that is, he understood it in the
sense of repentance, which still is so to renew our
duty, that it may be a holy life in the second sense;
that is, some great portion of our life to be spent in
living as Christians should.   A resolving to repent
upon our death-bed, is the greatest mockery of God in
the world, and the most perfect contradictory to all his
excellent designs of mercy and holiness: for therefore
he threatened us with hell if we did not, and he promised heaven if we did live a holy life: and a late repentance promises heaven to us upon other conditions,
even when we have lived wickedly.   * It renders a
man useless and intolerable to the world, taking off the
great curb of religion, of fear and hope, and permitting
all impiety with the greatest impunity and encourage-
ment in the world.   † By this means we see so many
παῖδας πολυχρονίας, as *Philo* calls them, or, as the prophet, *pueros centum annorum,* children of almost an
hundred years old, upon whose grave we may write
the inscription which was upon the tomb of *Similis* in
Xiphilin, here he lies who was so many years, but
lived but seven. ‡   And the course of nature runs
counter to the perfect designs of piety; and God who
gave us a life to live to him, is only served at our
death, when we die to all the world; § and we under-
value the great promises made by the Holy *Jesus,* for
which the piety, the strictest unerring piety of ten thousand ages is not a proportionable exchange: yet we
think it a hard bargain to get heaven, if we be forced
to part with one lust, or live soberly twenty years, but
like *Demetrius Afer,* (who having lived a slave all his

---

* ————— Quis luce supremâ
  Dimisisse meas serò non ingemit horas ?   *Sil. Ital.* l. xv.
† Si contra rerum naturæ munera nota,
  Corvus maturis frugibus ova refert.

‡ In Adrian. Σίμιλις μὲν ἐνταῦθα κεῖται βιὼς κατα ἔτη τόσα, ζήσας δὲ ἔτη
ἑπλα'.

§ *Vid.* The Life of Christ, Disc. of Repentance; Rule of Holy Living, ch. 4.
sect. 9. of Repentance; and Vol. of Serm. Serm. 5, 6.

life-

life-time*, yet desiring to descend to his grave in
freedom, begged manumission of his Lord) we lived
in the bondage of our sin all our days, and hope to
die the Lord's freed men. But above all, this course
of a delayed repentance must of necessity therefore be
ineffective, and certainly mortal, because it is an entire destruction of the very formality and essential
constituent reason of religion, which I thus demonstrate.

When God made man, and propounded to him an
immortal and a blessed state, as the end of his hopes,
and the perfection of his condition, he did not give it
him for nothing, but upon certain condition; which
although they could add nothing to God, yet they were
such things which man could value, and they were his
best: and God had made appetites of pleasure in
man, that in them the scene of his obedience should
lie. For when God made instances of man's obedience, he, 1. either commanded such things to be done
which man did naturally desire, or 2. such things
which did contradict his natural desires, or 3. such
which were indifferent. Not the first and the last;
for it could be no effect of love or duty towards God,
for a man to eat when he was impatiently hungry, and
could not stay from eating; neither was it any contention of obedience or labour of love, for a man to look
eastward once a day, or turn his back when the north
wind blew fierce and loud. Therefore for the trial
and instance of obedience, God made his laws so,
that they should lay restraint upon man's appetites, so
that man might part with something of his own, that
he may give to God his will, and deny it to himself for
the interest of his service: and chastity is the denial of
a violent desire, and justice is parting with money
that might help to enrich me, and meekness is a huge

* Ne tamen ad Stygias famulus descenderet umbras
Ureret implicitum cùm scelerata lues,
Cavimus————

contra-

contradiction to pride and revenge; and the wandering of our eyes, and the greatness of our fancy, and our imaginative opinions are to be lessened, that we may serve God. There is no other way of serving God, we have nothing else to present unto him; we do not else give him any thing or part of ourselves, but when we for his sake part with what we naturally desire; and difficulty is essential to virtue, and without choice there can be no reward, and in the satisfaction of our natural desires there is no election, we run to them as beasts to the river or the crib. If therefore any man shall teach or practise such religion that satisfies all our natural desires in the days of desire and passion, of lust and appetites, and only turns to God when his appetites are gone, and his desires cease, this man hath overthrown the very being of virtues, and the essential constitution of religion. Religion is no religion, and virtue is no act of choice, and reward comes by chance, and without condition, if we only are religious when we cannot choose, if we part with our money when we cannot keep it, with our lust when we cannot act it, with our desires when they have left us. *Death is a certain mortifier;* but that mortification is deadly, not useful to the purposes of a spiritual life. * When we are compelled to depart from our evil customs, and leave to live that we may begin to live, then we die to die; that life is the prologue to death, and thenceforth we die eternally.

S. *Cyril* speaks of certain people that chose to worship the sun because he was a day-god; for believing that he was quenched every night in the sea, or that he had no influence upon them that light up candles and lived by the light of fire, they were confident they might be Atheists all night and live as they list. Men who divide their little portion of time between religion and pleasures, between God and God's enemy, think

* Cogimur à suetis animum suspendere rebus,
  Atque ut vivamus vivere desinimus.   *Corn. Gall.*

M 4

that

that God is to rule but in his certain period of time, and that our life is the stage of passion and folly, and the day of death for the work of our life. But as to God *both the day and night are alike,* so are the first and last of our days, all are his due, and he will account severally with us for the follies of the first, and the evil of the last. * The evils and the pains are great which are reserved for those who defer their restitution to God's favour till their death. And therefore *Antisthenes* said well, *It is not the happy death, but the happy life that makes man happy.* It is in piety as in fame and reputation; † he secures a good name but loosely, that trusts his fame and celebrity only to his ashes; and it is more a civility than the *base* of a firm reputation, that men speak honour of their departed relatives; but if their life be virtuous, it forces honour from contempt, and snatches it from the hand of envy, and it shines through the crevices of detraction, and as it anointed the head of the living, so it embalms the body of the dead. ‡ From these premises it follows, that when we discourse of a *sick man's repentance,* it is intended to be, not a beginning, but the prosecution, and consummation of the covenant of repentance, which Christ stipulated with us in baptism, and which we needed all our life, and which we began long before this last arrest, and in which we are now to make farther progress, that we may arrive to that integrity and fulness of duty, *that our sins may be blotted out when the times of refreshing shall come from the presence of the Lord.* §

---

      * Gnossius, hæc Rhadamanthus habet durissima regna,
        Castigátque, auditque dolos, subigitque fateri
        Quæ quis apud superos furto lætatus inani
        Distulit in seram commissa piacula mortem.   *Æneid.* vi.
      † ——— Cineri gloria sera venit.
      ‡ Tu mihi, quod rarum est, vivo sublime dedisti
        Nomen, ab exsequiis quod dare fama solet.
      § Acts, iii. 19.

SECT. VI.

Rules for the Practice of Repentance in Sickness.

1. *LET the sick man consider at what gate his sickness entered;* and if he can discover the particular, let him instantly, passionately, and with great contrition, dash the crime in pieces, lest he descend into his grave in the midst of a sin, and thence remove into an ocean of eternal sorrow. But if he only suffers the common fate of man, and knows not the particular inlet, he is to be governed by the following measures.

2. *Inquire into the repentance of thy former life* particularly: whether it were of a great and perfect grief, and productive of fixed resolutions of holy living, and reductive of these to act; how many days and nights we have spent in sorrow or care, in habitual and actual pursuances of virtue; what instrument we have chosen and used for the eradication of sin; how we have judged ourselves, and how punished; and, in sum, whether we have by the grace of repentance changed our life from criminal to virtuous, from one habit to another, and whether we have paid for the pleasure of our sin by smart or sorrow, by the effusion of alms, or pernoctations of abodes in prayers, so as the spirit hath been served in our repentance as earnestly and as greatly as our appetites have been provided for in the days of our shame and folly.

3. Supply the imperfections of thy repentance by a general or universal sorrow for the sins not only since the last communion or absolution, but of thy whole life; for all sins, known and unknown, repented and unrepented, of ignorance or infirmity, which thou knowest, or which others have accused thee of; thy clamorous and thy whispering sins, the sins of scandal and the sins of a secret conscience, of the flesh and of

8

the

the spirit. For it would be but a sad arrest to thy soul wandering in strange and unusual regions, to see a scroll of uncancelled sins represented and charged upon thee for want of care and notices, and that thy repentance shall become invalid because of its imperfections.

4. To this purpose it is usually advised by spiritual persons, that *the sick man make an universal confession*, or a renovation and repetition of all the particular confessions and accusations of his whole life; that now at the foot of his account he may represent the sum total to God and his conscience, and make provisions for their remedy and pardon, according to his present possibilities.

5. Now is the time to *make reflex acts of repentance ;* that as by a general repentance we supply the want of the just extension of parts; so by this we may supply the proper measures of the intention of degrees. In our health we can consider concerning our own acts whether they be real or hypocritical, essential or imaginary, sincere or upon interest, integral or imperfect, commensurate or defective. And although it is a good caution of securities, after all our care and diligence still to suspect ourselves and our own deceptions, and for ever to beg of God pardon and acceptance in the union of Christ's passion and intercession : yet in proper speaking, *reflex* acts of repentance, being a suppletory after the imperfection of the *direct*, are then most fit to be used when we cannot proceed in, and prosecute the direct actions. To repent because we cannot repent, and to grieve because we cannot grieve, was a device invented to serve the turn of the mother of *Peter Gratian :* but it was used by her, and so advised to be, in her sickness, and last actions of repentance. For in our perfect health and understanding if we do not understand our first act, we cannot discern our second ; and if we be not sorry for our sins, we cannot be sorry for want of sorrows : it

is

is a contradiction to say we can ; because want of sorrow, to which we are obliged, is certainly a great sin : and if we can grieve for that, then also for the rest ; if not for all, then not for this. But in the days of weakness the case is otherwise : for then our actions are imperfect, our discourse weak, our internal actions not discernible, our fears great, our work to be abbreviated, and our defects to be supplied by spiritual arts : and therefore it is proper and proportionate to our state and to our necessity, to beg of God pardon for the imperfections of our repentance, acceptance of our weaker sorrows, supplies out of the treasures of grace and mercy. And thus repenting of the evil and unhandsome adherences of our repentance, in the whole integrity of the duty it will become *a repentance not to be repented of.*

6. Now is the time beyond which the sick man must *at no hand defer to make restitution of all his unjust possessions**, or other men's rights, and satisfactions for all injuries and violences, according to his obligation and possibilities. For although many circumstances might impede the acting it in our life-time, and it was permitted to be deferred in many cases, because by it justice was not hindered, and oftentimes piety and equity were provided for : yet because this is the last scene of our life, he that does not act it so far as he can, or put it into certain conditions and order of effecting, can never do it again ; and therefore then to defer it, is to omit it, and leaves the repentance defective in an integral and constituent part.

7. Let the sick man be diligent and watchful, that the principle of repentance be *contrition*, or sorrow for sins commenced upon the love of God. For although sorrow for sins upon any motive may lead us to God by many intermedial passages, and is the threshold of returning sinners : yet it is not good nor effective upon our death-bed ; because repentance is not

---

* Ou pendre, ou rendre, ou les peines d'enfers attendre.

then

then to begin, but must then be finished and com-
pleted ; and it is to be a supply and reparation of all
the imperfections of that duty, and therefore it must by
that time be arrived to *contrition*, that is, it must have
grown from fear to love, from the passions of a servant to the affections of a son.   The reason of which
(besides the precedent) is this, Because when our repentance is in this state, it supposes the man also in a
state of grace, a well-grown Christian : for to hate sin
out of the love of God, is not the felicity of a new
convert, or an infant grace, (or if it be, that love also
is in its infancy;) but it supposes a good progress, and
the man habitually virtuous, and tending to perfection :
and therefore contrition, or repentance so qualified,
is useful to great degrees of pardon, because the man
is a gracious person, and that virtue is of good degree, and consequently a fit employment for him that
shall work no more, but is to appear before his Judge
to receive the hire of his day.   And if his repentance
be contrition even before this state of sickness, let it be
increased by spiritual arts, and the proper exercises of
charity.

Means of exciting Contrition or Repentance of Sins, proceeding from the Love of God.

To which purpose the sick man may consider, and
is to be reminded (if he does not), that there are in
God all the motives and causes of amability in the
world : that God is so infinitely good, that there are
some of the greatest and most excellent spirits of heaven, whose work, and whose felicity, and whose perfections, and whose nature it is to flame and burn in the
brightest and most excellent love : that to love God is
the greatest glory of heaven : that in him there are
such excellencies, that the smallest rays of them communicated to our weaker understandings, are yet sufficient

cient to cause ravishments, and transportations, and satisfactions, and *joys unspeakable and full of glory*: that all the wise Christians of the world know and feel such causes to love God, that they all profess them- selves ready to die for the love of God : and the apos- tles and millions of the martyrs did die for him : and although it be harder to live in his love than die for it, yet all the good people that ever gave their names to Christ, did for his love endure the crucifying their lusts, the mortification of their appetites, the contra- dictions and death of their most passionate, natural desires : that kings and queens have quitted their dia- dems, and many married saints have turned their mutual vows into the love of *Jesus*, and married him only, keeping a virgin chastity in a married life, that they may more tenderly express their love to God : that all the good we have derives from God's love to us, and all the good we can hope for is the effect of his love, and can descend only upon them that love him : that by his love it is that we receive the Holy *Jesus*, and by his love we receive the holy spirit, and by his love we feel peace and joy within our spirits, and by his love we receive the mysterious sacrament. And what can be greater, than that from the goodness and love of God we receive *Jesus Christ*, and the Holy Ghost and adoption, and the inheritance of sons, and to be co-heirs with *Jesus*, and to have pardon of our sins, and a divine nature, and restraining grace, and the grace of sanctification, and rest and peace within us, and a certain expectation of glory ? Who can choose but love him, who, when we had provoked him exceed- ingly, sent his son to die for us, that we might live with him : who does so desire to pardon us and save us, that he hath appointed his holy son continually to intercede for us ? That his love is so great, that he offers us great kindness, and intreats us to be happy, and makes many decrees in heaven concerning the in- terest of our soul, and the very provision and support

of

of our persons : that he sends an angel to attend upon
every of his servants, and to be their guard and their
guide in all their dangers and hostilities : that for our
sakes he restrains the devil, and puts his mightiness in
fetters and restraints, and chastises his malice with
degrees of grace and safety : that he it is that makes
all the creatures serve us, and takes care of our sleeps,
and preserves all plants and elements, all minerals and
vegetables, all beasts and birds, all fishes and insects,
for food to us and for ornament, for physic and instruction, for variety and wonder, for delight and for
religion : that as God is all good in himself, and all
good to us, so sin is directly contrary to God, to reason, to religion, to safety and pleasure and felicity :
that it is a great dishonour to a man's spirit to have
been made a fool by a weak temptation and an empty
lust; and to have rejected God, who is so rich, so
wise, so good, and so excellent, so delicious, and so
profitable to us : that all the repentance in the world
of excellent men does end in contrition, or a sorrow
for sins proceeding from the love of God; because
they that are in the state of grace, do not fear hell
violently, and so long as they remain in God's favour,
although they suffer the infirmities of men, yet they are
God's portion; and therefore all the repentance of
just and holy men, which is certainly the best, is a repentance not for lower ends, but because they are the
friends of God, and they are full of indignation, that
they have done an act against the honour of their patron, and their dearest Lord and Father : that it is a
huge imperfection and a state of weakness, to need to
be moved with fear or temporal respect, and they that
are so, as yet are either immerged in the affections of
the world, or of themselves; and those men that bear
such a character are not yet esteemed laudable persons, or men of good natures, or the sons of virtue :
that no repentance can be lasting that relies upon any
thing but the love of God ; for temporal motives may
cease,

cease, and contrary contingencies may arise, and fear of hell may be expelled by natural or acquired hardnesses, and is always the least when we have most need of it, and most cause for it; for the more habitual our sins are, the more cauterised our conscience is, the less is the fear of hell, and yet our danger is much the greater: that although fear of hell or other temporal motives may be the first inlet to a repentance, yet repentance in that constitution and under those circumstances cannot obtain pardon, because there is in that no union with God, no adhesion to Christ, no endearment of passion of spirit, no similitude, or conformity to the great instrument of our peace, our glorious Mediator: for as yet a man is turned from his sin, but not converted to God; the first and last of our returns to God being love, and nothing but love: for obedience is the first part of love, and fruition is the last; and because he that does not love God cannot obey him, therefore he that does not love him cannot enjoy him.

Now that this may be reduced to practice, the sick man may be advertised, that in the actions of repentance he separate low, temporal, sensual and self-ends from his thoughts, and so do his repentance, that he may still reflect honour upon God, that he confess his justice in punishing, that he acknowledge himself to have deserved the worst of evils, that he heartily believe and profess that if he perish finally, yet that God ought to be glorified by that sad event, and that he hath truly merited so intolerable a calamity: that he also be put to make acts of election and preference, professing that he would willingly endure all temporal evils rather than be in the disfavour of God or in the state of sin; for by this last instance he will be quitted from the suspicion of leaving sin for temporal respects, because he, by an act of imagination of feigned presence of the object to him, entertains the temporal evil that he may leave the sin; and therefore, unless he be an hypocrite, does not leave the sin to be quit of
the

the temporal evil. And as for the other motive of leaving sin out of the fear of hell, because that is an evangelical motive conveyed to us by the spirit of God, and
is immediate to the love of God ; if the schoolmen had
pleased, they might have reckoned it as the hand-
maid, and *of the retinue of contrition :* but the more the
considerations are sublimed above this, of the greater
effect and the more immediate to pardon will be the
repentance.

8. *Let the sick persons do frequent actions of repentance by way of prayer for all those sins which
are spiritual, and in which no restitution or satisfaction material can be made, and whose contrary acts
cannot in kind be exercised.* For penitential prayers
in some cases are the only instances of repentance that
can be. An envious man, if he gives God hearty
thanks for the advancement of his brother, hath done
an act of mortification of his envy, as directly as corporal austerities are an act of chastity, and an enemy
to uncleanness: and if I have seduced a person that is
dead or absent, if I cannot restore him to sober counsels by my discourse and undeceiving him, I can only
repent of that by way of prayer : and intemperance is
no way to be rescinded or punished *by a dying man,*
but by hearty prayers. Prayers are a great help in
all cases; in some they are proper acts of virtue, and
direct enemies to sin : but although alone and in long
continuance, they alone can cure some one or some
few little habits, yet they can never alone change the
state of the man ; and therefore are intended to be a
suppletory to the imperfections of other acts ; and by
that reason are the proper and most pertinent employment of a *clinick* or *death-bed penitent.*

9. In those sins whose proper cure is *mortification
corporal,* the sick man is to supply that part of his
repentance by a patient submission to the rod of sickness : for sickness does the work of penances, or sharp
afflictions and dry diet, perfectly well: to which if we
                                                    also

also put our wills, and make it our act by an after-election, by confessing the justice of God, by bearing it sweetly, by begging it may be medicinal, there is nothing wanting to the perfection of this part, but that God confirm our patience, and hear our prayers. When * the guilty man runs to punishment, the *injured* person is prevented, and hath no whither to go but to forgiveness.

10. I have learned but of one suppletory more for the perfection and proper exercise of a sick man's repentance ; but it is such a one as will go a great way in the abolition of our past sins, and making our peace with God, even after a less severe life ; and that is, that the sick man do some heroical actions in the matter of charity or religion, of justice or severity. — There is a story of an infamous thief, who having begged his pardon of the emperor *Mauricius*, was yet put into the hospital of S. *Sampson*, where he so plentifully bewailed his sins in the last agonies of his death, that the physician who attended found him unexpectedly dead, and over his face a handkerchief bathed in tears; and soon after somebody or other pretended a revelation of this man's beatitude. It was a rare grief that was noted in this man, which begot in that age a confidence of his being saved; and *that confidence* (as things then went) was quickly called *a revelation.* But it was a stranger severity which is related by *Thomas Cantipratanus*, concerning a young gentleman condemned for robbery and violence, who had so deep a sense of his sin, that he was not content with a single death, but begged to be tormented and cut in pieces, joint by joint, with intermedial senses, that he might by such a smart signify a greater sorrow. Some have given great estates to the poor and to religion; some have built colleges for holy persons ; many have suffered martyrdom : and though those that died

---

* Quid debent læsi facere, ubi rei ad pœnam confugiunt ?

N   under

under the conduct of the *Maccabees* in defence of their country and religion, had pendants on their breasts consecrated to the idols of the *Jamnences*, yet that they gave their lives in such a cause with so great a duty, (the biggest things they could do or give,) it was esteemed to prevail hugely towards the pardon and acceptation of their persons. An heroic action of virtue is a huge compendium of religion: for if it be attained to by the usual measures and progress of a Christian, from inclination to act, from act to habit, from habit to abode, from abode to reigning, from reigning to perfect possession, from possession to extraordinary emanations, that is to heroic actions, then it must needs do the work of man, by being so great towards the work of God. But if a man comes thither *per saltum*, or on a sudden, (which is seldom seen,) then it supposes the man always well inclined, but abused by accident of hope, by confidence or ignorance; then it supposes the man for the present in a great fear of evil, and a passionate desire of pardon; it supposes his apprehensions great, and his time little; and what the event of that will be, no man can tell. But it is certain that *to some purposes* God will account for our religion on our death-bed, not by the measure of our time, but the eminency of affection (as said *Celestine* the first); that is, * supposing the man in the state of grace, or in the revealed possibility of salvation, then an heroical act hath the reward of a longer series of good actions, in an even and ordinary course of virtue.

11. *In what can remain for the perfecting a sick man's repentance, he is to be helped by the ministeries of a spiritual guide.*

---

* Vera ad Deum Conversio in ultimis positorum mente potiùs est æstimanda quàm tempore. *Cel. P.* Ep. 2. C. 9. (Vera Conversio) scil. ab infidelitate ad fidem Christi per Baptismum.

SECT. VII.

Acts of Repentance by way of Prayer and Ejaculation, to be used especially by Old Men in their Age, and by all Men in their Sickness.

* *Let us search and try our ways and turn again to the Lord. Let us lift up our hearts with our hands unto God in the heavens. We have transgressed and rebelled, and thou hast not pardoned. Thou hast covered with anger, and persecuted us; thou hast slain, thou hast not pitied. O cover not thyself with a cloud; but let our prayer pass through.*

† *I have sinned, what shall I do unto thee, O thou preserver of men? why hast thou set me as a mark against thee, so that I am a burthen to myself? And why dost thou not pardon my transgression, and take away mine iniquity? For now shall I sleep in the dust, and thou shalt seek me in the morning, but I shall not be.*

‡ *The Lord is righteous, for I have rebelled against his commandments. Hear, I pray, all ye people, behold my sorrow. Behold, O Lord, I am in distress, my bowels are troubled, my heart is turned within me: For I have grievously rebelled.*

§ *Thou, O Lord, remainest for ever; thy throne from generation to generation. Wherefore dost thou forget us for ever, and forsake us so long time? Turn thou us unto thee, O Lord, and so shall we be turned: Renew our days as of old. O reject me not utterly, and be not exceeding wrath against thy servant.*

¶ *O remember not the sins of my youth, nor my transgressions; but according to thy mercies remember thou me, for thy goodness sake, O Lord. Do ‖ thou*

---

* Lam. iii. 40, 41, 42, 43, 44. † Job. vii. 20, 21. ‡ Lam. i. 18. 40.
§ Lam. v. 19, 20, 21, 22. ¶ Ps. xxv. 7. ‖ Ps. cix. 21, 22, 23.

for

for me, O God the Lord, for thy name's sake : because thy mercy is good, deliver thou me. For I am poor and needy, and my heart is wounded within me. I am gone like the shadow that declineth. I am tossed up and down as the locust.

* *Then Zaccheus stood forth and said, Behold, Lord, half of my goods I give to the poor ; and if I have wronged any man, I restore him fourfold.*

† *Hear my prayer, O Lord, and consider my desire. Let my prayer be set forth in thy sight as the incense, and let the lifting up of my hands be an evening sacrifice.*

‡ *And enter not into judgment with thy servant: for in thy sight shall no man living be justified. Teach me to do* the thing that pleaseth thee, *for thou art my God :* let thy loving *spirit lead me forth into the land of righteousness.*

§ *I will* [speak] *of mercy and judgment : unto thee, O Lord, will I* [make my prayer.] *I will behave myself wisely in a perfect way : O when wilt thou come unto me ? I will walk in my house with a perfect heart. I will set no wicked thing before mine eyes. I hate the work of them that turn aside, it shall not cleave to me.*

‖ *Hide thy face from my sins, and blot out all mine iniquities. Create in me a clean heart, O God, and renew a right spirit within me. Deliver me from blood-guiltiness, O God,* [from malice, envy, the follies of lust, and violences of passion, &c.] *thou God of my salvation ; and my tongue shall sing aloud of thy righteousness.*

The sacrifice of God is a broken heart ; a broken and a contrite heart, O God, thou wilt not despise.

Lord, I have done amiss ; I have been deceived : let so great a wrong as this be removed, and let it be so no more.

---

* Luke, xix. 8.
‡ Ps. cxliii. 2. 10.
† Ps. cxliii. 1.   Ps. cxli. 2.
§ Ps. ci. 1, 2, 3.   ‖ Ps. li. 9, 10. 14. 17.

The Prayer for the Grace and Perfection of Repentance.

I.

O ALMIGHTY GOD, thou art the great Judge of all the world, the Father of our Lord *Jesus Christ,* the Father of mercies, the Father of men and angels; thou lovest not that a sinner should perish, but delightest in our conversion and salvation, and hast in our Lord *Jesus Christ* established the covenant of repentance, and promised pardon to all them that confess their sins and forsake them : O my God, be thou pleased to work in me what thou hast commanded should be in me.   Lord I am a dry tree, who neither have brought forth fruit unto thee and unto holiness, nor have wept out salutary tears, the instrument of life and restitution, but have behaved myself like an unconcerned person in the ruins and breaches of my soul.   But * *O God, thou art my God, early will I seek thee ; my soul thirsteth for thee in a barren and thirsty land, where no water is.*   Lord, *give me the grace of tears* and pungent sorrow, let my heart be as a land of rivers of waters, and my head a fountain of tears : turn my sin into repentance, and let my repentance proceed to pardon and refreshment.

II.

SUPPORT me with thy graces, strengthen me with thy spirit, soften my heart with the fire of thy love and the dew of heaven, with penitential showers : make my care prudent, and the remaining portions of my days like the perpetual watches of the night, full of caution and observance, strong and resolute, patient and severe.   I remember, O Lord, that I did sin with gree-

* Psalm lxiii. 1.

N 3   diness

diness and passion, with great desires, and an unabated choice: O let me be as great in my repentance as ever I have been in my calamity and shame; let my hatred of sin be as great as my love to thee, and both as near to infinite as my proportion can receive.

III.

O LORD, I renounce all affection to sin, and would not buy my health nor redeem my life with doing any thing against the laws of my God, but would rather die than offend thee. O dearest Saviour, have pity upon thy servant, let me by thy sentence be doomed to perpetual penance during the abode of this life; let every sigh be the expression of a repentance, and every groan an accent of spiritual life, and every stroke of my disease a punishment of my sin, and an instrument of pardon: that at my return to the land of innocence and pleasure I may eat of the votive sacrifice of the supper of the *Lamb, that was from the beginning of the world slain* for the sins of every sorrowful and returning sinner. O grant me sorrow here, and joy hereafter, through *Jesus* Christ, who is our hope, *the resurrection* of the dead, the justifier of a sinner, and the glory of all faithful souls. *Amen.*

A Prayer for Pardon of Sins, to be said frequently in Time of Sickness, and in all the Portions of Old Age.

I.

O ETERNAL and most gracious Father, I humbly throw myself down at the foot of thy mercy-seat, upon the confidence of thy essential mercy, and thy commandment, that we should *come boldly to the throne of grace, that we may find mercy in time of need.* O my God, hear the prayers and cries of a sinner, who calls earnestly for mercy. Lord, my needs are greater than

than all the degrees of my desire can be : unless thou
hast pity upon me, I perish infinitely and intolerably ;
and then there will be one voice fewer in the choir of
singers, who shall recite thy praises to eternal ages.
But, * *O Lord*, in mercy *deliver my soul. O save me
for thy mercy's sake. For in* the second *death there is
no remembrance of thee ; in* that *grave who shall give
thee thanks ?*

II.

O just and dear God, my sins are innumerable,
they are upon my soul in multitudes, they are a burthen too heavy for me to bear; they already bring
sorrow and sickness, shame and displeasure, guilt and
a decaying spirit, a sense of thy present displeasure and
fear of worse, of infinitely worse.   But it is to thee so
essential, so delightful, so usual, so desired by thee to
show thy mercy, that although my sin be very great,
and my fear proportionable, yet thy mercy is infinitely
greater than all the world, and my hope and my comfort rise up in proportion towards it, that I trust the
devils shall never be able to reprove it, nor my own
weakness discompose it. Lord, thou hast sent thy son
to die for the pardon of my sins; thou hast given me
thy holy spirit, as a seal of adoption to consign the
article of remission of sins ; thou hast for all my sins
still continued to invite me to conditions of life by thy
ministers the prophets : and thou hast with variety of
holy acts softened my spirit, and possessed my fancy,
and instructed my understanding, and bended and inclined my will, and directed or over-ruled my passions
in order to repentance and pardon : and why should
not thy servant beg passionately, and humbly hope for
the effects of all these thy strange and miraculous acts
of loving kindness? Lord, I deserve it not, but I hope
thou wilt pardon all my sins : and I beg it of thee for

* Psalm vi. 4, 5.

Jesus

Jesus Christ his sake, whom thou hast made the great endearment of thy promises, and the foundation of our hopes, and the mighty instrument whereby we can obtain of thee whatsoever we need and can receive.

III.

O MY GOD, how shall thy servant be disposed to receive such a favour, which is so great that the ever-blessed *Jesus* did die to purchase it for us ; so great, that the fallen angels never could hope, and never shall obtain it ? Lord, *I do from my soul forgive all that have sinned against me :* O forgive me my sins, as I forgive them that have sinned against me. Lord, *I confess my sins unto thee daily,* by the accusations and secret acts of conscience ; and if we confess our sins, thou hast called it a part of justice to forgive us our sins, and to cleanse us from all unrighteousness. Lord, *I put my trust in thee ;* and thou art ever gracious to them that put their trust in thee. *I call upon my God for mercy ;* and thou art always more ready to hear than we to pray. But all that I can do, and all that I am, and all that I know of myself, is nothing but sin, and infirmity, and misery : therefore I go forth of myself, and throw myself wholly into the arms of thy mercy through *Jesus* Christ, and beg of thee for his death and passion's sake, by his resurrection and ascension, by all the parts of our redemption, and thy infinite mercy, in which thou pleasest thyself above all the works of the creation, to be pitiful and compassionate to thy servant in the abolition of all my sins : so shall I praise thy glories with a tongue not defiled with evil language, and a heart purged by thy grace, quitted by thy mercy, and absolved by thy sentence, from generation to generation. *Amen.*

An Act of Holy Resolution of Amendment of Life in case of Recovery.

O MOST just and most merciful Lord God, who hast sent evil diseases, sorrow and fear, trouble and uneasiness, briars and thorns into the world, and planted them in our houses, and round about our dwellings, to keep sin from our souls, or to drive it thence; I humbly beg of thee that this my sickness may serve the ends of the spirit, and be a messenger of spiritual life, and instrument of reducing me to more religious and sober courses. I know, O Lord, that I am unready and unprepared in my accounts, having thrown away great portions of my time in vanity, and set myself hugely back in the accounts of eternity; and I had need live my life over again, and live it better: but thy counsels are in the great deep, and thy footsteps in the water; and I know not what thou wilt determine of me. If I die, I throw myself into the arms of the Holy *Jesus,* whom I love above all things: and if I perish, I know I have deserved it; but thou wilt not reject him that loves thee: but if I recover, I will live by thy grace, and help to do the work of God, and passionately pursue my interest of heaven, and serve thee in the labour of love, with the charities of a holy zeal, and the diligence of a firm and humble obedience. Lord, I will dwell in thy temple, and in thy service; religion shall be my employment, and alms shall be my recreation, and patience shall be my rest, and *to do thy will* shall be *my meat and drink,* and *to live shall be Christ,* and then *to die shall be gain.*

O spare me a little that I may recover my strength, before I go hence and be no more seen. Thy will be done on earth as it is in heaven.

SECT. VIII.

An Analysis or Resolution of the Decalogue, and the special Precepts of the Gospel, describing the Duties enjoined, and the Sins forbidden respectively; for the Assistance of Sick Men in making their Confessions to God and his Ministers, and the rendering their Repentance more particular and perfect.

I. *Thou shalt have none other Gods but me.*]

Duties commanded are, 1. To love God above all things. 2. To obey him and fear him. 3. To worship him with prayers, vows, thanksgivings, presenting to him our souls and bodies, and all such actions and expressions which the consent of nations, or the laws and customs of the place where we live have appropriated to God. 4. To design all to God's glory. 5. To enquire after his will. 6. To believe all his word. 7. To submit to his providence. 8. To proceed toward all our lawful ends by such means as himself hath appointed. 9. To speak and think honourably of God, and recite his praises, and confess his attributes and perfections.

They sin against this commandment, 1. Who love themselves or any of the creatures inordinately and intemperately. 2. They that despise or neglect any of the Divine precepts. 3. They that pray to unknown or false gods. 4. They that disbelieve or deny there is a God. 5. They that make vows to creatures: 6. or say prayers to the honour of men or women, or angels; as *paternosters* to the honour of the Virgin *Mary*, or St. *Peter*, which is a taking a part of that honour which is due to God, and giving it to the creature: it is a religion paid to men and women out of God's proper portion, out of prayers directed to God immediately; and it is an act contrary

trary to that religion which makes God the last end of all things : for this through our addresses to God passes something to the creatures, as if they stood beyond him; for by the intermedial worship paid to God, they ultimately do honour to the man, or angel. 7. They that make consumptive oblations to the creatures, as the *Collyridians*, who offered cakes, and those that burnt incense or candles to the Virgin *Mary*. 8. They that give themselves to the devil, or make contracts with him, and use phantastic conversation with him. 9. They that consult witches and fortune-tellers. 10. They that rely upon dreams and superstitious observances. 11. That use charms, spells, superstitious words and characters, verses of Psalms, the consecrated elements to cure diseases, to be shot free, to recover stolen goods, or enquire into secrets. 12. That are wilfully ignorant of the laws of God, or love to be deceived in their persuasions, that they may sin with confidence. 13. They that neglect to pray to God. 14. They that arrogate to themselves the glory of any action of power, and do not give the glory to God, as *Herod*. 15. They that doubt or disbelieve any article of the creed, or any proposition of scripture, or put false glosses to serve secular or vicious ends against their conscience, or with violence any way done to their reason. 16. They that violently or passionately pursue any temporal end with an eagerness greater than the thing is in prudent account. 17. They that make religion to serve ill ends, or do good to evil purpose, or evil to good purposes. 18. They that accuse God of injustice and unmercifulness, remissness or cruelty; such as are the presumptuous, and the desperate. 19. All hypocrites and pretenders to religion, walking in forms and shadows, but denying the power of Godliness. 20. All impatient persons, all that repine or murmur against the prosperities of the wicked, or the calamities of the godly, or their own afflictions. 21. All

All that blaspheme God, or speak dishonourable
things of so sacred a majesty. 22. They that tempt
God, or rely upon his protection against his rules,
and without his promise, and besides reason, entering
into danger from which, without a miracle, they cannot be rescued. 23. They that are bold in the midst
of judgment, and fearless in the midst of the Divine
vengeance, and the accents of his anger.

II. Comm. *Thou shalt not make to thyself any
graven Image, nor worship it.*]

The moral duties of this commandment are, 1. To
worship God with all bodily worship and external
forms of address, according to the custom of the
church we live in. 2. To believe God to be a spiritual and pure substance, without any visible form or
shape. 3. To worship God in ways of his own ap-
pointing, or by his proportions, or measures of nature
and right reason, or public and holy customs.

They sin against this commandment, 1. That make
any image or pictures of the Godhead, or fancy any
likeness to him. 2. They that use images in their
religion, designing or addressing any religious worship
to them; for if this thing could be *naturally tolerable,*
yet it is too near *an intolerable* for a jealous God to
suffer. 3. They that deny to worship God with lowly
reverence of their bodies, according as the church
expresses her reverence to God externally. 4. They
that invent or practise superstitious worshippings, invented by man against God's word, or without reason,
or besides the public customs or forms of worshipping,
either foolishly or ridiculously, without the purpose
of order, decency, proportion to a wise or a religious
end, in prosecution of some virtue or duty.

III. Comm. *Thou shalt not take God's Name in vain.*]

The duties of this commandment are, 1. To honour
and

and revere the most holy name of God. 2. To in-
vocate his name directly, or by consequence, in all
solemn and permitted abjurations, or public oaths.
3. To use all things and persons upon whom his
name is called, or any ways imprinted, with a regard-
ful and separate manner of usage, different from common and far from contempt and scorn.   4. To swear
in truth and judgment.

They sin against this commandment, 1. Who swear
vainly and customarily, without just cause, without
competent authority.   2. They that blaspheme or
curse God.   3. They that speak of God without grave
cause or solemn occasion.   4. They that forswear
themselves; that is, they that do not perform their
vows to God, or that swear, or call God to witness
to a lie.   5. They that swear rashly or maliciously,
to commit a sin, or an act of revenge.   6. They that
swear by any creature falsely, or any way but as it relates to God, and consequently invokes his testimony.
7. All curious enquirers into the secrets, and intruders
into the mysteries and hidden things of God.   8. They
that curse God, or curse a creature by God.   9. They
that prophane churches, holy utensils, holy persons,
holy customs, holy sacraments.   10. They that provoke others to swear voluntarily, and by design, or
incuriously or negligently, when they might avoid it.
11. They that swear to things uncertain and unknown.

IV. Comm. *Remember that thou keep holy the
Sabbath Day.*]

The duties of this commandment are, 1. To set
apart some portions of our time for the immediate
offices of religion, and glorification of God.   2. This
is to be done according as God or his holy church hath
appointed.   3. One day in seven is to be set apart.
4. The Christian day is to be subrogated into the place
of the Jews' day.   The resurrection of Christ and the
redemp-

redemption of man was a greater blessing than to create him. 5. God on that day to be worshipped and acknowledged as our Creator, and as our Saviour. 6. The day to be spent in holy offices, in hearing Divine service, public prayers, frequenting the congregations, hearing the word of God read or expounded, reading good books, meditation, alms, reconciling enmities, remission of burthens and of offences, of debts and of work, friendly offices, neighbourhood, and provoking one another to good works; and to this end all servile works must be omitted, excepting necessary and charitable offices to men or beasts, to ourselves and others.

They sin against this commandment, 1. That do, or compel or incite others to do, servile works without the cases of necessity or charity, to be estimated according to common and prudent accounts. 2. They that refuse or neglect to come to the public assemblies of the church, to hear and assist at the Divine offices entirely. 3. They that spend the day in idleness, forbidden or vain recreations, or the actions of sin and folly. 4. They that buy and sell without the cases of permission. 5. They that travel unnecessary journeys. 6. They that act or assist in contentions or law-suits, markets, fairs, &c. They that on that day omit their private devotion, unless the whole day be spent in public. 8. They that by any cross or contradictory actions against the customs of the church, do purposely desecrate or unhallow and make the day common; as they that in despite and contempt fast upon the Lord's day, lest they may celebrate the festival after the manner of the Christians.

V. Comm. *Honour thy Father and thy Mother.*]

The duties are, 1. To do honour and reverence to and to love our natural parents. 2. To obey all their domestic commands: for in them the scene of their authority

authority lies. 3. To give them maintenance and support in their needs. 4. To obey kings and all that are
in authority. 5. To pay tribute and honours, custom
and reverence. 6. To do reverence to the aged and
all our betters. 7. To obey our masters, spiritual governors and guides, in those things which concern
their several respective interests and authority.

They sin against this commandment, 1. That despise their parents' age or infirmity. 2. That are
ashamed of their poverty and extraction. 3. That
publish their vices, errors, and infirmities, to shame
them. 4. That refuse and reject all or any of their
lawful commands. 5. Children that marry without or
against their consent, when it may be reasonably obtained. 6. That curse them from whom they receive
so many blessings. 7. That grieve the souls of their
parents by not complying in their desires, and observ-
ing their circumstances. 8. That hate their persons,
that mock them, or use uncomely jestings. 9. That
discover their nakedness voluntarily. 10. That murmur against their injunctions, and obey them involun-
tarily. 11. All rebels against their kings, or the su-
preme power, where it is legally and justly invested.
12. That refuse to pay tributes and impositions imposed legally. 13. They that disobey their masters,
murmur or repine against their commands, abuse or
deride their persons, talk rudely, &c. 14. They that
curse the king in their heart, or speak evil of the
ruler of their people. * 15. All that are uncivil and
rude towards aged persons, mockers and scorners of
them.

VI. Comm. *Thou shalt do no Murder.*]

The duties are, 1. To preserve our own lives, the
lives of our relatives and all with whom we converse,

---

* Credebant hoc grande nefas et morte piandum,
Si juvenis vetulo non assurrexerat, et si
Barbato cuicunque puer.   *Juven.* Sat. xiii.

(or

(or who can need us, and we assist,) by prudent, reasonable, and wary defences, advocations, discoveries of snares, &c. 2. To preserve our health, and the integrity of our bodies and minds, and of others. 3. To preserve and follow peace with all men.

They sin against this commandment, 1. That destroy the life of a man or woman, himself or any other. 2. That do violence to, or dismember or hurt any part of the body with evil intent. 3. That fight duels, or commence unjust wars. 4. They that willingly hasten their own or others death. 5. That by oppression or violence embitter the spirits of any, so as to make their life sad, and their death hasty. 6. They that conceal the dangers of their neighbour, which they can safely discover. 7. They that sow strife and contention among neighbours. 8. They that refuse to rescue or preserve those whom they can and are obliged to preserve. 9. They that procure abortion. 10. They that threaten or keep men in fears or hate them.

VII. Comm. *Thou shalt not commit Adultery.*]

The duties are, 1. To preserve our bodies in the chastity of a single life, or of marriage. 2. To keep all the parts of our bodies in the care and severities of chastity; so that we be restrained in our eyes as well as in our feet.

They sin against this commandment, 1. Who are adulterous, incestuous, sodomitical, or commit fornication. 2. They that commit folly alone, dishonouring their own bodies with softness and wantonness. 3. They that immoderately let loose the reins of their bolder appetite, though within the protection of marriage. 4. They that by wanton gestures, wandering eyes, lascivious dressings, discovery of the nakedness of themselves or others, filthy discourse, high diet,

amorous

amorous songs, balls and revellings, tempt and betray themselves or others to folly. 5. They that marry a woman divorced for adultery. 6. They that divorce their wives, except for adultery, and marry another.

VIII. Comm. *Thou shalt not steal.*]

The duties are, 1. To give every man his due. 2. To permit every man to enjoy his own goods and estate quietly.

They sin against this commandment, 1. That injure any man's estate by open violence or by secret robbery, by stealth or cozenage, by arts of bargaining or vexatious law-suits. 2. That refuse or neglect to pay their debts when they are able. 3. That are forward to run into debt knowingly beyond their power, without hopes or purposes of repayment. 4. Oppressors of the poor. 5. That exact usury of necessitous persons, or of any beyond the permission of equity as determined by the laws. 6. All sacrilegious persons; people that rob God of his dues, or of his possessions. 7. All that game, *viz.* at cards and dice, &c. to the prejudice and detriment of other men's estates. 8. They that embase coin and metals, and obtrude them for perfect and natural. 9. That break their promises to the detriment of a third person. 10. They that refuse to stand to their bargains. 11. They that by negligence embezzle other men's estates, spoiling or letting any thing perish which is entrusted to them. 12. That refuse to restore the pledge.

IX. Comm. *Thou shalt not bear false witness.*]

The duties are, 1. To give testimony of truth when we are called to it by competent authority. 2. To preserve the good name of our neighbours. 3. To speak well of them that deserve it.

They sin against this commandment, 1. That speak

o   false

false things in judgment, accusing their neighbours
unjustly, or denying his crime publicly when they are
asked, and can be commanded lawfully to tell it.
2. Flatterers; and, 3. Slanderers. 4. Backbiters;
and, 5. Detractors. 6. They that secretly raise jealousies and suspicion of their neighbours causelessly.

X. Comm. *Thou shalt not covet.*]

The duties are, 1. To be content with the portion
God hath given us. 2. Not to be covetous of other
men's goods.

They sin against this commandment, 1. That envy
the prosperity of other men. 2. They that desire passionately to be possessed of what is their neighbour's.
3. They that with greediness pursue riches, honours,
pleasures, and curiosities. 4. They that are too careful, troubled, distracted, or amazed, affrighted and
afflicted with being solicitous in the conduct of temporal blessings.

These are the general lines of duty by which we
may discover our failings, and be humbled, and confess accordingly; only the penitent person is to remember, that although these are the kinds of sins described after the sense of the Jewish church, which
consisted principally in the external action, or *the
deed done*, and had no restraints upon the thoughts of
men, save only in the Tenth Commandment, which
was mixed, and did relate as much to action as to
thought (as appears in the instances); yet upon us
Christians there are many circumstances and degrees
of obligation which endear our duty with greater severity and observation: and the penitent is to account
of himself and enumerate his sins, not only by external actions, or *the deed done*, but by words and by
thought; and so to reckon if he have done it directly
or indirectly, if he have caused others to do it, by
tempting or encouraging, by assisting or counselling,
by

by not dissuading when he could and ought, by fortifying their hands or hearts, or not weakening their
evil purposes ; if he have designed or contrived its
action, desired it, or loved it, delighted in the thought,
remembered the past sin with pleasure or without
sorrow.   These are the *bye-ways* of sin, and *the
crooked lanes* in which a man may wander and
be lost, as certainly as in the broad high-ways of
iniquity.

But besides this, our blessed Lord and his apostles
have added divers other precepts ; some of which have
been with some violence reduced to the decalogue,
and others have not been noted at all in the catalogues
of confession.   I shall therefore describe them
entirely, that the sick man may discover his failings,
that by the mercies of God in *Jesus* Christ, and by
the instrument of repentance, he may be presented
pure and spotless before the throne of God.

The special Precepts of the Gospel.

1. ᵃ PRAYER, frequent, fervent, holy, and persevering.   2. ᵇ Faith.   3. ᶜ Repentance.   4. ᵈ Poverty
of spirit, as opposed to ambition, and high designs.
5. And in it is ᵉ Humility, or sitting down in the
lowest place, and giving honour to go before another.
6. ᶠ Meekness, as it is opposed to waywardness, fret-
fulness, immoderate grieving, disdain and scorn.
7. Contempt of the world.   8. ᵍ Prudence, or the
advantageous conduct of religion.   9. Simplicity,
or sincerity in words and actions, pretences and
substances.   10. ʰ Hope.   11. ⁱ Hearing the word.
12. ᵏ Reading.   13. ˡ Assembling together.   14.
ᵐ Obeying them that have the rule over us in spiritual

ᵃ 1 Thess. v. 17.— Luke, xviii. 1. ᵇ Mark, xvi. 16. ᶜ Luke, xiii. 3.— Acts,
iii. 19. ᵈ Matth. v. 3. ᵉ Luke, xiv. 10.— John, xiii. 14. ᶠ Matth. v. 5.—
Col. iii. 12. ᵍ Matth. x. 16.— 1 Thess. v. 8. ʰ Rom. viii. 24. ⁱ Luke, xvi. 29.
— Mark, iv. 24. ᵏ 1 Tim. iv. 13. ˡ Heb. x. 25. ᵐ Heb. xiii. 17.— Matth.
xviii. 17.

affairs.

affairs. 15. ^a Refusing to communicate with persons excommunicate: whither also may be reduced, to reject heretics. 16. ^b Charity: viz. ^c Love to God above all things; brotherly kindness, or profitable love to our neighbours as ourselves, to be expressed in alms, ^d forgiveness, and to ^e die for our brethren. 17. ^f To pluck out the right eye, or violently to rescind all occasions of sin, though dear to us as an eye. 18. ^g To reprove our erring brother. 19. ^h To be patient in afflictions: and ⁱ longanimity is referred hither, or long sufferance; which is the perfection and perseverance of patience, and is opposed to hastiness and weariness of spirit. 20. To be ^k thankful to our benefactors: but above all, in all things, to give thanks to God. 21. ^l To rejoice in the Lord always. 22. ^m Not to quench, ⁿ not to grieve, ^o not to resist the spirit. 23. ^p To love our wives as Christ loved his church, and to reverence our husbands. 24. ^q To provide for our families. 25. ^r Not to be bitter to our children. 26. ^s To bring them up in the nurture and admonition of the Lord. 27. ^t Not to despise prophesying. 28. ^u To be gentle and easy to be intreated. 29. ^x To give no scandal or offence. 30. ^y To follow after peace with all men, and to make peace. 31. ^z Not to go to law before the unbelievers. 32. ^a To do all things that are of good report, or the actions of ^b public honesty; ^c abstaining from all appearances of evil. 33. ^d To convert souls, or turn sinners from the error of their ways. 34. ^e To confess Christ before all the world. 35. ^f To resist unto blood, if God calls us to it. 36. ^g To rejoice in tribulation for

a 2 Thess. iii. 6.—2 ep. John, 10.— Tit. iii. 10. b Col. iii. 14.—1 Tim. i. 5.—2 Tim. ii. 22. c Mark, xii. 30. d Matth. vi. 14. e 1 John, iii. 16. f Matth. xviii. 9. g Matth. xviii. 15. h Jam. i. 4.— Luke, xxi. 19. i Heb. xii. 3.— Gal. vi. 9. k Eph. v. 20.— 2 Thess. i. 3. Luke, vi. 32.— 2 Tim. iii. 2. l 1 Thess. v. 16.— Phil. iii. 1. and iv. 4. m 1 Thess. v. 19. n Eph. iv. 30. o Acts, vii. 51. p Eph. v. 33. q 1 Tim. v. 8. r Col. iii. 21. s Eph. vi. 4. t 1 Thess. v. 20. u 2 Tim. ii. 24. x Matth. xviii. 7.— 1 Cor. x. 32. y Heb. xii. 14. z 1 Cor. vi. 1. a Phil. iv. 8. b 2 Cor. viii. 21. c 1 Thess. v. 22. d Jam. v. 19, 20. e Matth. x. 32. f Heb. xii. 4. g Matth. v. 12.— James, i. 2.

Christ's

Christ's sake. 37. [a] To remember and [b] shew forth the Lord's death till his second coming, by celebrating the Lord's Supper. 38. [c] To believe all the New Testament. 39. [d] To add nothing to St. *John's* last book, that is, to pretend to no new revelations. 40. To keep the customs of the church, her festivals and solemnities, lest we be reproved as the *Corinthians* were by St. *Paul*, [e] *We have no such customs, nor the churches of God.* 41. [f] To contend earnestly for the faith. Not [g] to be contentious in matters not concerning the eternal interest of our souls: but in matters *indifferent* to *have faith to ourselves.* 42. [h] Not to make schisms or divisions in the body of the church. 43. [i] To call no man master upon earth. But to acknowledge Christ our master and law-giver. 44. [k] Not to domineer over the Lord's heritage. 45. [l] To try all things, and keep that which is best. 46. [m] To be temperate in all things. 47. [n] To deny ourselves. 48. [o] To mortify our lusts and their instruments. 49. [p] To lend, looking for nothing again, nothing by way of increase, nothing by way of recompence. 50. [q] To watch and stand in readiness against the coming of the Lord. 51. [r] Not to be angry without a cause. 52. [s] Not at all to revile. 53. [t] Not to swear. 54. [u] Not to respect persons. 55. [x] To lay hands suddenly on no man. [This especially pertains * to bishops. * To whom also, and to all the ecclesiastical order, it is enjoined, that [y] they *preach the word,* that they *be instant in season and out of season,* that they *rebuke, reprove, exhort with all long suffering and doctrine.*] 56. To keep the Lord's day, (derived into an obligation from a practice apostolical.)

* Luke, xxii. 19.   [b] 1 Cor. xi. 16.   [c] John, xx. 30, 31. — Acts, iii. 23. — Mark, i. 1. — Luke, x. 16.   [d] Rev. xxii. 18.   [e] 1 Cor. xi. 16.   [f] Jude, iii. [g] Rom. xiv. 13. 22.   [h] Rom. xvi. 17.   [i] Matth. xxiii. 8, 9, 10.   [k] 1 Pet. v. 3.   [l] 1 John, iv. 1. — 1 Thess. v. 21.   [m] 1 Cor. ix. 25. — Tit. ii. 2.   * Matt. xvi. 24.   [o] Col. iii. 5. — Rom. viii. 13.   [p] Luke, vi. 34, 35.]   [q] Mark, xiii. 34. — Matth. xxiv. 42. — and xxv. 13.   [r] Matth. v. 22. — Eph. iv. 26.   * 1 Cor. vi. 10. — Matth. v. 22.   [t] Matth. v. 34.   [u] James, ii. 1.   [x] 1 Tim. v. 22. [y] 2 Tim. iv. 2.

57. [a] To do all things to the glory of God. 58. [b] To hunger and thirst after righteousness and its rewards. 59. [c] To avoid foolish questions. 60. [d] To pray for persecutors, and to do good to them that persecute us, and despitefully use us. 61. [e] To pray for all men. 62. [f] To maintain good works for necessary uses. 63. [g] To work with our own hands, that we be not burthensome to others, avoiding idleness. 64. [h] To be perfect as our heavenly Father is perfect. 65. [i] To be liberal and frugal : for he that will call us to account for our time, will also for the spending our money. 66. [k] Not to use uncomely jestings. 67. [l] Modesty as opposed to boldness, to curiosity, to undecency. 68. [m] To be swift to hear, slow to speak. 69. [n] To worship the Holy [*Jesus*] at the mention of his holy name : as of old, God was at the mention of [*Jehovah.*]

These are the strait lines of scripture by which we may also measure our obliquities, and discover our crooked walking. If the sick man hath not done these things, or if he have done contrary to any of them, in any particular, he hath cause enough for his sorrow, and matter for his confession : of which he needs no other forms, but that he heartily deplore and plainly enumerate his follies, as a man tells the sad stories of his own calamity.

SECT. IX.

Of the Sick Man's Practice of Charity and Justice, by way of Rule.

1. LET the sick man set his house in order before

[a] Cor. x. 31. [b] Matth. v. 6. [c] Titus, iii. 9. [d] Matth. v. 44. — Rom. xii. 14. [e] 1 Tim. ii. 1. [f] Titus, iii. 14. [g] Eph. iv. 28. [h] Matth. v. 48. — [i] 1 Pet. iii. 8. — 2 Pet. i. 6, 7. — 2 Cor. viii. 7. — 2 Cor. ix. 5. [k] Eph. v. 4. [l] 1 Tim. ii. 9. [m] James, i. 19. [n] Phil. ii. 10.

he

he die ; state his cases of conscience, reconcile the fractures of his family, re-unite brethren, cause right understandings, and remove jealousies, give good counsels for the future conduct of their persons and estates, charm them into religion by the authority and advantages of a dying person ; because the last words of a dying man are like the tooth of a wounded lion, making a deeper impression in the agony than in the most vigorous strength.

2. Let the sick man discover every secret of art, or profit, physic, or advantage to mankind, if he may do it without the prejudice of a third person. * Some persons are so uncharitably envious, that they are willing that a secret receipt should die with them, and be buried in their grave, like treasure in the sepulchre of *David.* But this, which is a design of charity, must therefore not be done to any man's prejudice ; and the mason of *Herodotus* the king of *Egypt,* who kept secret his notice of the king's treasure, and when he was a dying told his son, betrayed his trust then when he should have kept it most sacredly for his own interest. In all other cases let thy charity out-live thee, that thou mayest rejoice in the mansion of rest, because by thy means many living persons are eased or advantaged.

3. Let him make his *will* with great justice and piety, that is, that the right heirs be not defrauded for collaterial respects, fancies, or indirect fondnesses ; but the inheritances descend in their legal and due channel ; and in those things where we have a liberty, that we take the opportunity of doing virtuously, that is, of considering how God may be best served by our donatives, or how the interest of any virtue may be promoted ; in which we are principally to regard the necessities of our nearest kindred and relatives, servants and friends.

* Magnifica verba mors propè admota excutit. Nam veræ voces tum demum pectore ab imo ejiciuntur. *Lucret.*

4. Let

4. Let * the *will* or *testament* be made with ingenuity, openness, and plain expression, that he may not
entail a law-suit upon his posterity and relatives, and
make them lose their charity, or entangle their estates,
or make them poorer by the gift. *He hath done me
no charity, but dies in my debt, that makes me sue for a
legacy.*

5. It is proper for the state of sickness, and an excellent anealing us to burial, that we give alms in this
state, so burying treasure in our graves that will not
perish, but rise again in the resurrection of the just.
Let the dispensation of our alms be as little intrusted
to our executors as may be, *excepting the lasting and
successive portions;* † but with our own present care
let us exercise the charity, and secure the *steward-
ship.* It was a custom amongst the old *Greeks,* to
bury horses, clothes, arms, and whatsoever was dear
to the deceased person, supposing they might need
them, and that without clothes they should be found
naked by their judges; and all the friends did use to
bring gifts, by such liberality, thinking to promote
the interest of their dead. ‡ But we may offer our
ἐντάφια ourselves best of all; our doles and funeral
meals, if they be our own early provisions, will then
spend the better: and it is good to carry our passing
penny in our hand, and by reaching that hand
to the poor, *make a friend in the everlasting habitations.*

---

* Δεῖ δὲ καὶ τὴν βασιλείαν μι ἤδη σαφηνίσανῖα καῖαλιπεῖν, ὡς ἂν μὴ ἀμφίλογος
γένοιμενη πρᾶγμαῖα ὑμῖν παρᾷσχη.   Cyrus *apud* Xenoph. l. viii. *Institut.*
† Lucian. *de Luctu.*
  Vide reg. 6. *paulo inf.*
  Herodot. *Mus.* 5.
  Plin. lib. iv. cap. 11.
  Xiphilin *in* Severo.
‡ Ἀλλὰ, κόραι, τῷ παιδὶ λεχώϊα δῶρα φέρεσαι,
    Θερμὰ καῖα ψυχρῶ δάκρυα κεῖῖε ῖάφε.
                                                    Nicharcus.
  Fallax sæpe fides, testataque vota peribunt:
    Constitues tumulum, si sapis, ipse tuum.

Man,

𝔐an, thee behoveth oft to have this in mind,
That thou givest with thine hand, that thou shalt find,
For 𝔚idows beeth slothful, and 𝔠hildren beeth unkind,
𝔈recutors beeth covetous, and keep all that they find.
If any body ask, where the 𝔇eads 𝔊oods became?
They answer,
𝔖o 𝔊od me help and 𝔥alidam, he died a poor man.
Think on this. *

He that gives with his own hand shall be sure to find it, and the poor shall find it; but he that trusts executors with his charity, and the economy and issues of his virtue, by which he must enter into his hopes of heaven and pardon, shall find but an ill account, when his executors complain he died poor. *Think on this.* To this purpose wise and pious was the counsel of *Salvian:* † " Let a dying man who hath " nothing else of which he may make an effective " oblation, offer up to God of his substance: let " him offer it with compunction and tears, with grief " and mourning, as knowing that all our oblations " have their value, not by the price, but by the af- " fection; and it is our faith that commendeth the " money, since God receives the money by the hands " of the poor, but at the same time gives, and does " not take the blessing; because he receives nothing " but his own, and man gives that which is none of " his own, that of which he is only a steward, and " shall be accountable for every shilling. Let it " therefore be offered humbly, as a creditor pays his " debts, not magnificently as a prince gives a donative: " and let him remember that such doles do not pay " for the sin, but they ease the punishment; they are " not proper instruments of redemption, but instances " of supplication, and advantages of prayer: and " when we have done well, remember that we have " not paid our debt, but shewn our willingness to " give a little of that vast sum we owe; and he that " gives plentifully according to the measure of his

* Written upon a Wall in St. *Edmund's Church* in *Lombard-Street.*
† Contra avaritiam.

" estate,

" estate, is still behind hand according to the measure
" of his sins. Let him pray to God that this late obla-
" tion may be accepted; and so it will, if it sails to
" him in a sea of penitential tears or sorrows that it is
" *so little*, and that it is *so late*."

6. Let the sick man's charity be so ordered, that it
may not come only to deck the funeral and make up
the pomp; charity waiting like one of the solemn
mourners; but let it be continued, that besides the
alms of health and sickness, there may be a rejoicing
in God for his charity long after his funerals, so as to
become more beneficial and less public; that the poor
may pray in private, and give God thanks many days
together. This is matter of prudence; and yet in this
we are to observe the same regards which we had in
the charity and alms of our lives; with this only difference, that in the funeral alms also of rich and able
persons, the public customs of the church are to be
observed, and decency and solemnity, and the expectations of the poor, and matter of public opinion, and the
reputation of religion; in all other cases let thy charity
consult with humility and prudence, that it never minister at all to vanity, but be as full of advantage and
usefulness as it may.

7. Every * man will forgive a dying person: and
therefore let the sick man be ready and sure, if he
can, to send to such persons whom he hath injured,
and beg their pardon, and do them right. For in his
case he cannot stay for an opportunity of convenient
and advantageous reconcilement: he cannot then
spin out a treaty, nor beat down the price of composition, nor lay a snare to be quit from the obligation and coercion of laws; but he must ask forgiveness downright, and make him amends as he can,
being greedy of making use of this opportunity of
doing a duty that must be done, but cannot any more,
if not now until time returns again, and tells the

---

* Πρὸς τον τελευτήσανθ' ἔκαςος, κᾀν σφόδρα ἂν ἐχθρὸς ᾖ τις, γίνεται φίλος τότε.

minutes

minutes backwards, so that yesterday shall be reckoned in the portions of the future.

8. In the intervals of sharper pains, when the sick man amasses together all the arguments of comfort, and testimonies of God's love to him and care of him, he must needs find infinite matter of thanksgiving and glorification of God: and it is a proper act of charity and love to God, and justice too that he do honour to God on his death-bed for all the blessings of his life, not only in general communications, but those by which he hath been separate and discerned from others, or supported and blessed in his own person: such as are [*In all my life-time I never broke a bone, I never fell into the hands of robbers, never into public shame, or into noisome diseases; I have not begged my bread, nor been tempted by great and unequal fortunes; God gave me a good understanding, good friends, or delivered me in such a danger, and heard my prayers in such particular pressures of my spirit.*] This or the like enumeration and consequent acts of thanksgiving are apt to produce love to God, and confidence in the day of trial; for he that gave me blessings in proportion to the state and capacities of my life, I hope also will do so in proportion to the needs of my sickness and my death-bed. This we find practised as a most reasonable piece of piety by the wisest of the heathens. So *Antipater Tarsensis* gave God thanks for his prosperous voyage into *Greece:* and *Cyrus* made a handsome prayer upon the tops of the mountains, when by a phantasm he was warned of his approaching death: *Receive, [O God] my father, these holy rites by which I put an end to many and great affairs: and I gave thee thanks for thy celestial signs and prophetic notices, whereby thou hast signified to me what I ought to do, and what I ought not. I present also very great thanks that I have perceived and acknowledged your care of me, and have never exalted myself above my condition, for any*

prosperous

prosperous accident. · *And I pray that you will grant felicity to my wife, my children and friends, and to me a death such as my life hath been.* But that of *Philagrius* in *Gregory Nazianzen* is eucharistical, but it relates more especially to the blessings and advantages which are accidentally consequent to sickness : *I thank thee, O Father and Maker of all thy children, that thou art pleased to bless and to sanctify us even against our wills, and by the outward man purgest the inward, and leadest us through crossways to a blessed ending, for reasons best known unto thee.* However, when we go from our hospital and place of little intermedial rest in our journey to heaven, it is fit that we give thanks to the *major-domo* for our entertainment. When these parts of religion are finished, according to each man's necessity, there is nothing remaining of personal duty to be done alone, but that the sick man act over these virtues by the renewings of devotion, and in the way of prayer ; and that is to be continued as long as *life,* and *voice,* and *reason* dwell with us.

SECT. X.

Acts of Charity, by way of Prayer and Ejaculation : which may be also used for Thanksgiving, in case of Recovery.

* *O* MY *soul, thou hast said unto the Lord, thou art my Lord ; my goodness extendeth not to thee : but to the saints that are in the earth, and to the excellent, in whom is all my delight. The Lord is the portion of my inheritance and of my cup ; thou maintainest my lot.*

* Psal. xvi. 2, 3. 5.

As

* *As for God his way is perfect : the word of the Lord is tried : he is a buckler to all those that trust in him. For who is God, except the Lord? Or who is a rock, save our God? It is God that girdeth me with strength, and maketh my way perfect.*

† *Be not thou far from me, O Lord : O my strength, haste thee to help me.*

Deliver my soul from the sword, my darling from the power of the dog. Save me from the lion's mouth : and thou hast heard me also from among the horns of the unicorns.

I will declare thy name unto my brethren : in the midst of the congregation will I praise thee.

Ye that fear the Lord, praise the Lord: Ye sons [of God] glorify him, and fear before him all ye sons [of men.] For he hath not despised nor abhorred the affliction of the afflicted, neither hath he hid his face from him ; but when he cried unto him he heard.

‡ *As the hart panteth after the water-brooks, so longeth my soul after thee, O God.*

My soul thirsteth for God, for the living God : when shall I come and appear before the Lord?

O my God, my soul is cast down within me. All thy waves and billows are gone over me. As with a sword in my bones I am reproached. Yet the Lord will command his loving-kindness in the day-time : and in the night his song shall be with me, and my prayer unto the God of my life.

§ *Bless ye the Lord in the congregations ; even the Lord from the fountains of Israel.*

‖ *My mouth shall shew forth thy righteousness and thy salvation all the day : for I know not the numbers thereof.*

I will go in the strength of the Lord God : I will make mention of thy righteousness, even of thine only. O

* Psal. xviii. 30, 31, 32.   † Psal. xxii. 19, 20, 21, 22, 23, 24.
‡ Psal. xlii. 1, 2. 6, 7. 10. 8.   § Psal. lxviii. 26.
‖ Psal. lxxi. 15, 16, 17. 14. 19, 20, 21, 23.

God,

God, thou hast taught me from my youth ; and hitherto have I declared thy wondrous works. But I will hope continually, and will yet praise thee more and more.

Thy righteousness, O God, is very high, who hast done great things. O God, who is like unto thee ? Thou which hast shewed me great and sore troubles, shall quicken me again, and shalt bring me up again from the depths of the earth.

Thou shalt increase thy goodness towards me, and comfort me on every side.

My lips shall greatly rejoice when I sing unto thee ; and my soul which thou hast redeemed.

* Blessed be the Lord God, the God of Israel, who only doeth wondrous things. And blessed be his glorious name for ever ; and let the whole earth be filled with his glory. Amen, Amen.

† I love the Lord, because he hath heard my voice and my supplication. The sorrows of death compassed me : I found trouble and sorrow. Then called I upon the name of the Lord : O Lord, I beseech thee, deliver my soul. Gracious is the Lord, and righteous : yea, our God is merciful.

The Lord preserveth the simple : I was brought low, and he helped me. Return to thy rest, O my soul : the Lord hath dealt bountifully with me. For thou hast delivered my soul from death, mine eyes from tears, and my feet from falling.

Precious in the sight of the Lord is the death of his saints. O Lord, truly I am thy servant, I am thy servant ; and the son of thine handmaid ; thou shalt loose my bonds.

‡ He that loveth not the Lord Jesus, let him be a cursed.

§ O that I might love thee as well as ever any creature loved thee ! He that dwelleth in love, dwelleth in God. There is no fear in love.

---

* Psal. lxxii. 18, 19.   † Psal. cxvi. 1. 3, 4, 5, 6, 7, 8. 15, 16.
‡ 1 Cor. xvi. 22.   § 1 John, iv. 16. 18.

The Prayer.

O MOST gracious and eternal God and loving Father, who hast poured out thy bowels upon us, and
sent the son of thy love unto us to die for love, and
to make us dwell in love, and the eternal compre-
hensions of thy divine mercies; O be pleased to en-
flame my heart with a holy charity toward thee and all
the world. Lord, I forgive all that ever have offended
me, and beg that both they and I may enter into the
possession of thy mercies, and feel a gracious pardon
from the same fountain of grace : and do thou forgive
me all the acts of scandal whereby I have provoked,
or tempted, or lessened, or disturbed any person.
Lord, let me never have any portion among those
that divide the union, and disturb the peace, and
break the charities of the church and Christian communion. And though I am fallen into evil times,
in which Christendom is divided by the names of an
evil division; yet I am in charity with all Christians,
with all that love the Lord *Jesus*, and long for his
coming, and I would give my life to save the soul of
any of my brethren : and I humbly beg of thee, that
the public calamity of the several societies of the
church may not be imputed to my soul, to any evil
purposes.

II.

LORD, preserve me in the unity of thy holy
church, in the love of God and of my neighbours.
Let thy grace enlarge my heart to remember, deeply
to resent, faithfully to use, wisely to improve, and
humbly to give thanks to thee for all thy favours, with
which thou hast enriched my soul, and supported my
estate, and preserved my person, and rescued me
from danger, and invited me to goodness in all the

days

days and periods of my life. Thou hast led me through it with an excellent conduct; and I have gone astray after the manner of men; but my heart is towards thee. O do unto thy servant as thou usest to do unto those that love thy name : let thy truth comfort me, thy mercy deliver me, thy staff support me, thy grace sanctify my sorrow, and thy goodness pardon all my sins, thy angels guide me with safety in this shadow of death, and thy most holy spirit lead me into the land of righteousness, for thy name's sake, which is so comfortable, and for Jesus Christ his sake, our dearest Lord, and most gracious Saviour. *Amen.*

CHAP. V.

OF VISITATION OF THE SICK ; OR, THE ASSISTANCE THAT
IS TO BE DONE TO DYING PERSONS BY THE MINISTRY
OF THEIR CLERGY-GUIDES.

SECT. I.

GOD, who hath made no new covenant with dying
persons distinct from the covenant of the living, hath
also appointed no distinct sacraments for them, no
other manner of usages but such as are common to all
the spiritual necessities of living and healthful persons.
In all the days of our religion, from our baptism to
the resignation and delivery of our soul, God hath
appointed his servants to minister to the necessities, and
eternally to bless, and prudently to guide, and wisely
to judge concerning souls ; and the Holy Ghost, that
anointing from above, descends upon us in several
effluxes, but ever by the ministeries of the church.
Our heads are anointed with that sacred unction baptism, (not in ceremony, but in real and proper effect,)
our foreheads in confirmation, *our hands* in ordina-
tions, *all our senses* in the visitation of the sick ; and
all by the ministry of especially deputed and instructed
persons. And we who all our life-time derive blessings from the fountains of grace by the channels of
ecclesiastical ministeries, must do it then especially
when our needs are most pungent and actual. 1. We

P   cannot

cannot give up our names to Christ, but the holy man
that ministers in religion must enrol them and present
the persons, and consign the grace. When we beg for
God's spirit, the minister can best present our prayers,
and by his advocation hallow our private desires, and
turn them into public and potent offices. 2. If we
desire to be established and confirmed in the grace
and religion of our baptism, the holy man, whose hands
were anointed by a special ordination to that and its
symbolical purposes, lays his hands upon his catechu-
men, and *the anointing from above*, descends by that
ministry. 3. If we would eat the body and drink the
blood of our Lord, we must address ourselves to the
Lord's table, and he that stands there to bless and to
minister, can reach it forth, and feed thy soul ; and
without his ministry thou canst not be nourished with
that heavenly feast, nor thy body consigned to immortality, nor thy soul refreshed with the sacramental
bread from heaven, except by spiritual suppletories,
in cases of necessity, and an impossible communion.
4. If we have committed sins, the spiritual man is
appointed to restore us, and to pray for us, and to
receive our confessions, and to enquire into our wounds,
and to infuse oil and remedy, and to pronounce pardon. 5. If we be cut off from the communion of the
faithful by our own demerits, their holy hands must
reconcile us and give us peace ; they are our appointed
comforters, our instructors, our ordinary judges : and
in the whole what the children of *Israel* begged of
Moses, that * *God would no more speak to them alone,
but to his servant Moses*, lest they should be consumed ; God, in compliance with our infirmities, hath
of his own goodness established as a perpetual law
in all ages of Christianity, that God will speak to us
by his *ministers*, and our solemn prayers shall be made
to him by *their* advocation, and his blessings descend
from heaven by *their* hands, and our offices return

* Exod. xx. 19.

                                        thither

thither by *their* presidences, and our repentance shall
be managed by *them*, and our pardon in many degrees
ministered by *them*.   God comforts us by their sermons, and reproves us by their discipline, and cuts off
some by their severity, and reconciles others by their
gentleness, and relieves us by their prayers, and instructs us by their discourses, and heals our sicknesses
by their intercession presented to God, and united to
Christ's advocation : and in all this *they are no causes,*
but *servants of the will of God,* instruments of the
divine grace and order, *stewards and dispensers* of the
mysteries, and appointed to our souls to serve and
lead, and to help in all accidents, dangers, and necessities.

And they who received us in our baptism are also
to carry us to our grave, and * to take care that our end
be as our life was, or should have been : and therefore it is established as an apostolical rule, *Is any*
man sick among you? let him send for the elders of
the church, and let them pray over him, &c.†

The sum of the duties and offices respectively im-
plied in these words is in the following rules.

SECT. II.

Rules for the Manner of Visitation of Sick Persons.

1. LET the minister of religion be sent to, not only
against the agony of death, but be advised with in the
whole conduct of the sickness : for in sickness indefi-
nitely, and therefore in every sickness, and therefore
in such which are not mortal, which end in health,
which have no agony, or final temptations, St. *James*

---

* Οἷον περ᾽ αἰῶνα δεδώκατε, τοιαύτην καὶ τελευτὴν δῶναι. Xenoph. περι παιδ.
lib. viii.
† James, v. 14.

gives

gives the advice; and the sick man being bound to
require them, is also tied to do it when he can know
them, and his own necessity. It is a very great evil
both in the matter of prudence and piety, that they
fear the priest as they fear the embalmer, or the sexton's spade: and love not to converse with him, unless
they can converse with no man else; and think his
office so much to relate to the other world, that he is
not to be treated with while we hope to live in this;
and, indeed, that our religion be taken care of only
when we die: and the event is this, (of which I have
seen some sad experience,) that the man is deadly sick,
and his reason is useless, and he is laid to sleep, and
his life is in the confines of the grave, so that he can
do nothing towards the trimming of his lamp; and the
curate shall say a few prayers by him, and talk to a
dead man, and the man is not in a condition to be
helped, but in a condition to need it hugely. He cannot be called upon to confess his sins, and he is not
able to remember them, and he cannot understand an
advice, nor hear a free discourse, nor be altered from
a passion, nor cured of his fear, nor comforted upon
any grounds of reason or religion, and no man can tell
what is likely to be his fate; or if he does, he cannot
prophesy good things concerning him, but evil. Let
the spiritual man come when the sick man can be conversed withal and instructed, when he can take medicine and amend, when he understands, or can be
taught to understand the case of the soul, and the rules
of his conscience; and then his advice may turn into
advantage: it cannot otherwise be useful.

2. The intercourses of the minister with the sick
man have so much variety in them, that they are not
to be transacted at once: and therefore they do not
well that send once to see the good man with sorrow,
and hear him pray, and thank him, and dismiss him
civilly, and desire to see his face no more. To dress
a soul for funeral is not a work to be dispatched
at

at one meeting : at once he needs a comfort, and anon
something to make him willing to die; and by and by
he is tempted to impatience, and that needs a special
cure: and it is a great work to make his confessions
well and with advantages; and it may be the man is
careless and indifferent, and then he needs to understand the evil of his sin, and the danger of his person ;
and his cases of conscience may be so many and so
intricate, that he is not quickly to be reduced to peace,
and one time the holy man must pray, and another
time he must exhort, a third time-administer the holy
sacrament; and he that ought to watch all the periods
and little portions of his life, lest he should be surprised and overcome, had need be watched when he is
sick, and assisted, and called upon, and reminded of
the several parts of his duty, in every instant of his
temptation. This article was well provided for amongst
the Easterlings ; for the priests in their visitations of a
sick person did abide in their attendance and ministry
for seven days together. The want of this makes the
visitations fruitless, and the calling of the clergy contemptible, while it is not suffered to imprint its proper
effects upon them that need it in a lasting ministry.

3. St. *James* advises, that * *when a man is sick he
should send for the elders;* one sick man for many
presbyters : and so did the eastern churches, they sent
for seven : and like a college of physicians, they ministered spiritual remedies, and sent up prayers like a
choir of singing-clerks. In cities they might do so,
while the christians were few, and the priests many.
But when they that dwelt in the *Pagi* or villages
ceased to be Pagans, and were baptized, it grew to be
an impossible felicity, unless in few cases, and to some
more eminent persons; but because they need it most,
God hath taken care that they may best have it ; and
they that can, are not very prudent if they neglect it.

4. Whether they be many or few that are sent to

* Jam. v. 14. *Gabriel* in 4. sent. dist. 23.

P 3   the

the sick person, let the curate of his parish or his own
confessor be among them, that is, let him not be
wholly advised by strangers who know not his particular necessities; but he that is the ordinary judge
cannot safely be passed by in his extraordinary necessity, which in so great portions depends upon his
whole life past: and it is matter of suspicion when
we decline his judgment that knows us best, and with
whom we formerly did converse, either by choice or
by law, by private election or public constitution. It
concerns us then to make severe and profitable judgments, and not to conspire against ourselves, or procure such assistances which may handle us softly,
or comply with our weaknesses more than relieve our
necessities.

5. When the ministers of religion are come, first
let them do their ordinary offices, that is, pray for
grace to the sick man, for patience, for resignation,
for health, (if it seems good to God, in order to his
great ends.) For that is one of the ends of the advice
of the apostle. And therefore the minister is to be
sent for, not when the case is desperate, but before
the sickness is come to its *crisis* or period. Let him
discourse concerning the cause of sickness, and by a
general instrument move him to consider concerning
his condition: let him call upon him to set his soul
in order, to trim his lamp, to dress his soul, to renew acts of grace by way of prayer, to make amends
in all the evils he hath done, and to supply all the
defects of duty, as much as his past condition requires, and his present can admit.

6. According as the condition of the sickness or
the weakness of the man is observed, so the exhortation is to be less, and the prayers more, because
the life of the man was his main preparatory: and
therefore if his condition be full of pain and infirmity,
the shortness and small number of his own acts is to
be supplied by the act of the ministers and standers-by,
who

who are in such case to speak more to God for him, than to talk to him.* For *the prayer of the righteous*, when it is *fervent*, hath a promise to *prevail much* in behalf of the sick person. But exhortations must prevail with their own proper weight, not by the passion of the speaker. But yet this assistance by way of prayers, is not to be done by long offices, but by *frequent,* and *fervent*, and *holy*. In which offices, if the sick man joins, let them be short, and apt to comply with his little strength and great infirmities : if they be said in his behalf without his conjunction, they that pray may prudently use their own liberty, and take no measures but their own devotions and opportunities, and the sick man's necessities.

When he hath made this general address and preparatory entrance to the work of many days and periods, he may descend to the particular by the following instruments and discourses.

SECT. III.

Of ministering in the Sick Man's Confession of Sins and Repentance.

THE first necessity that is to be served, is that of repentance; in which the ministers can in no way serve him, but by first exhorting him to *confession of his sins*, and declaration of the state of his soul. For unless they know the manner of his life, and the degrees of his restitution, either they can do nothing at all, or nothing of advantage and certainty. His discourses, like *Jonathan's* arrows, may shoot short, or shoot over, but not wound where they should, nor

* Jam. v. 16.

P 4

open

open those humours that need a lancet or a cautery. To this purpose, the sick man may be reminded.

Arguments and Exhortations to move the Sick Man to Confession of Sins.

1. THAT God hath made a special promise to confession of sins. * *He that confesseth his sins and forsaketh them shall have mercy :* and, *if we confess our sins, God is righteous to forgive us our sins, and to cleanse us from all unrighteousness.* 2. That confession of sins is a proper act and introduction to repentance. 3. † That when the *Jews* being warned by the sermons of the *Baptist* repented of their sins, they confessed their sins to *John* in the susception of baptism. 4. That the converts in the days of the apostles returning to christianity, instantly declared their faith and their repentance ‡, by confession and *declaration of their deeds* which they then renounced, abjured, and confessed to the apostles. 5. That confession is an act of many virtues together. 6. It is the gate of repentance. 7. An instrument of shame and condemnation of our sins. 8. A *glorification of God,* so called by *Joshua* particularly in the case of *Achan.* 9. An acknowledgment that God is just in punishing; for by confessing our sins, we also confess his justice, and are assessors with God in this condemnation of ourselves. 10. That by such an act of judging ourselves, we escape the more angry judgment of God : § St. *Paul* expressly exhorting us to it upon that very inducement. 11. That confession of sins is so necessary a duty, that in all scriptures it is the immediate preface to pardon, and the certain consequent of *godly sorrow,* and an integral or constituent part of that grace, which together with *faith* makes up the whole duty of the gospel. 12. That in

* Prov. xxviii. 13. — 1 John, i. 9.　† Matth. iii. 6.　‡ Acts, xix. 18.
§ 1 Cor. xi. 31.

all

all ages of the gospel it hath been taught and practised
respectively, that all the penitents made confessions
proportionable to their repentance, that is, public or
private, general or particular. 13. That God, by
testimonies from heaven, that is, by his word, and by
a consequent rare piece of conscience, hath given ap-
probation to this holy duty. 14. That by this instrument those whose office it is to apply remedies to
every spiritual sickness, can best perform their offices. 15. That it is by all churches esteemed a duty
necessary to be done in cases of a troubled conscience.
16. That what is necessary to be done in one case,
and convenient in all cases, is fit to be done by all
persons. 17. That without confession, it cannot
easily be judged concerning the sick person whether
his conscience ought to be troubled or no, and therefore it cannot be certain that it is not necessary.
18. That there can be no reason against it, but such
as consults with flesh and blood, with infirmity and
sins ; to all which confession of sins is a direct enemy.
19. That now is that time when all the imperfections
of his repentance, and all the breaches of his duty, are
to be made up, and that if he omits this opportunity,
he can never be admitted to a salutary and medicinal
confession. 20. That St. *James* gives an express
precept, that we christians should confess our sins to
each other, that is, christian to christian, brother to
brother, the people to their minister ; and then he
makes a specification of that duty which a sick man is
to do when he hath sent for the elders of the church.
21. That in all this there is no force lies upon him,
but * *if he hide his sins he shall not be directed*, (so
said the wise man); but ere long he must appeal

---

* Si tacuerit qui percussus est, et non egerit pœniten.tiam, nec vulnus
suum fratri et magistro voluerit confiteri, magister qui linguam habet
ad curandum facilè ei prodesse non poterit. Si enim erubescat ægrotus
vulnus medico confiteri quod ignorat, medicina non curat. S. *Hieron.*
ad caput 10. Eccles. Si enim hoc fecerimus, et revelaverimus peccata
nostra non solùm Deo, sed et his qui possunt mederi vulneribus nostris atque
peccatis, delebuntur peccata nostra. *Orig.* hom. xvii. in *Lucan.*

before

before the great judge of men and angels : and his
spirit will be more amazed and confounded to be seen
among the angels of light with the shadow of the
works of darkness upon him, than he may suffer by
confessing to God in the presence of him whom God
hath sent to heal him. However, it is better to be
ashamed here than to be confounded hereafter. * *Pol
pudere præstat quam pigere totidem literis.* 22. That
confession being in order to pardon of sins, it is very
proper and analogical to the nature of the thing, that
it be made there where the pardon of sins is to be administered. And that, of pardon of sins God hath
made the minister the publisher and dispenser : and
all this is besides the accidental advantages which ac-
crue to the conscience, which is made ashamed, and
timorous, and restrained by the mortifications and
blushings of discovering to a man the faults committed in secret. 23. That the ministers of the gospel
are the *ministers of reconciliation,* are commanded *to
restore such persons as are overtaken in a fault ;* and
to that purpose they come to offer their ministry, if
they may have cognizance of the fault and person.
24. That in the matter of prudence it is not safe to
trust a man's self in the final condition and last security of a man's soul, a man being no good judge in his
own case. And when a duty is so useful in all cases,
so necessary in some, and encouraged by promises
evangelical, by scripture precedents, by the example
of both Testaments, and prescribed by injunctions
apostolical, and by the canon of all churches, and the
example of all ages, and taught us even by the proportions of duty, and the analogy to the power ministerial, and the very necessities of every man ; he that
for stubbornness or sinful shamefacedness, or prejudice, or any other criminal weakness, shall decline to
do it in the days of his danger, when the vanities of

---

* *Plaut. Trinum.*
Tam facile et pronum est superos contemnere testes.
Si mortalis idem nemo sciat. —   *Juv.* Sat. xiii. v. 75.

                                                    the

the world are worn off, and all affections to sin are wearied *, and the sin itself is pungent and grievous, and that we are certain we shall not escape shame for them hereafter, unless we be ashamed of them here, and use all the proper instruments of their pardon; this man, I say, is very near death, but very *far off from the kingdom of heaven.*

2. The spiritual man will find in the conduct of this duty many cases and varieties of accidents which will alter his course and forms of proceedings. Most men are of a *rude indifferency*, apt to excuse themselves, ignorant of their condition, abused by evil principles, content with a general and indefinite confession; and if you provoke them to it by the foregoing considerations, lest their spirits should be a little uneasy, or not secured in their own opinions, will be apt to say, *They † are sinners, as every man hath his infirmity, and he as well as any man : but God be thanked, they bear no ill-will to any man, or are no adulterers, or no rebels, or they fought on the right side ; and God be merciful unto them, for they are sinners.* But you shall hardly open their breasts farther : and to enquire beyond this, would be to do the office of an accuser.

3. But, which is yet worse, there are very many persons who have been so used to an habitual course of a constant intemperance or dissolution in any other instance, that the crime is made natural and necessary, and the conscience hath digested all the trouble, and the man thinks himself in a good estate, and never reckons any sins, but those which are the egressions and passings beyond his ordinary and daily drunkenness. This happens in the cases of drunkenness, and intemperate eating, and idleness, and uncharitableness,

---

* Qui homo culpam admisit in se, nullus est tam parvi pretii quin pudeat, quin purget sese. *Plaut. Aulul.*

† ———— Verum hoc se amplectitur uno :
  Hoc amat, hoc laudat. Matronam nullam ego tango.
                              Horat. l. i. Sat. ii. v. 53.

and

and in lying and vain jestings, and particularly in such evils which the laws do not punish, and public customs do not shame ; but which are countenanced by potent sinners, or evil customs, or good nature, and mistaken civilities.

Instruments, by way of Consideration, to awaken a careless Person, and a stupid Conscience.

In these and the like cases the spiritual man must awaken the lethargy, and prick the conscience, by representing to him, that christianity is a holy and a strict religion. That many are called, but few are chosen. That the number of them that are to be saved are but very few in respect of those that are to descend into sorrow and everlasting darkness. That we have covenanted with God in baptism to live a holy life. That the measures of holiness in christian religion are not to be taken by the evil proportions of the multitude, and common fame of looser and less severe persons ; because *the multitude* is that which *does not enter into heaven,* but *the few, the elect,* the holy servants of *Jesus.* That every habitual sin does amount to a very great guilt in the whole, though it be but in a small instance. That if the righteous scarcely be saved, then there will be no place for the unrighteous and the sinner to appear in but places of horror and amazement. That confidence hath destroyed many souls, and many have had a sad portion who have reckoned themselves in the calendar of Saints. That the promises of heaven are so great, that it is not reasonable to think that every man, and every life, and an easy religion shall possess such infinite glories. That although heaven is a gift, yet there is a great severity and strict exacting of the conditions on our part to receive that gift. That some persons who have lived strictly for forty years together, yet have miscarried by some one crime at last,

or

or some secret hypocrisy, or a latent pride, or a creeping ambition, or a phantastic spirit; and therefore much less can they hope to receive so great portions of felicities, when their life hath been a continual declination from those severities which might have created confidence of pardon and acceptation, through the mercies of God, and the merits of *Jesus*. That every good man ought to be suspicious of himself, and in his judgment concerning his own condition to fear the worst, that he may provide for the better. That we are commanded to work out our salvation with fear and trembling. That this precept was given with very great reason, considering the thousand thousand ways of miscarrying. * That St. *Paul* himself, and St. *Arsenius*, and St. *Elzearius*, and divers other remarkable saints, had at some times great apprehentions of the dangers of failing of *the mighty price of their high calling*. That the stake that is to be secured is of so great an interest, that all our industry, and all the violences we can suffer in the prosecution of it, are not considerable. That this affair is to be done but once, and then never any more unto eternal ages. That they who profess themselves servants of the institution, and servants of the law and discipline of *Jesus*, will find that they must *judge* themselves by the proportions of that law by which they were to *rule* themselves. That the laws of society and civility, and the voices of my company, are as ill *judges* as they are *guides;* but we are to stand or fall by his sentence, who will not consider or value the talk of idle men, or the persuasion of wilfully abused consciences, but of him who hath felt our infirmity in all things *but sin,* and knows where our failings are unavoidable, and where and in what degree they are excusable; but never will endure a sin should seize upon any part of our love and deliberate choice, or careless cohabitation. † That *if our conscience accuse us not,*

* Apud *Surium* die 27. *Sept.*   † 1 John, iii. 20. — 1 Cor. iv. 4.

yet

yet are we not hereby justified, for *God is greater than our consciences.* That they who are most inno-cent have their consciences most tender and sensible. That scrupulous persons are always most religious; and that to feel nothing is not a sign *of life,* but *of death.* That nothing can be hid from the eyes of the Lord, to whom the day and the night, public and pri-vate, words and thoughts, actions and designs, are equally discernible. That a lukewarm person is only secured in his own thoughts, but very unsafe in the event, and despised by God. That we live in an age in which that which is called and esteemed *a holy life,* in the days of the apostles and holy primitives would have been esteemed *indifferent,* sometimes *scandalous,* and always *cold.* That what was a truth of God then, is so now; and to what severities they were tied, for the same also we are to be accountable; and heaven is not now an easier purchase than it was then. That if he would cast up his accounts, even with a superficial eye, let him consider how few good works he hath done, how inconsiderable is the relief which he gave to the poor, how little are the extraordinaries of his religion, and how unactive and lame, how polluted and disordered, how unchosen and unpleasant were the ordinary parts and periods of it? And how many and great sins have stained his course of life; and until he enters into a particular scrutiny, let him only revolve in his mind what his general course hath been; and in the way of prudence, let him say whether it was laudable and holy, or only indifferent and excusa-ble: and if he can think it only *excusable,* and so as to hope for pardon by such suppletories of faith, and arts of persuasion, which he and others use to take in for auxiliaries to their unreasonable confidence; then he cannot but think it very fit that he search into his own state, and take a guide, and erect a tribunal *, or

---

* Illi mors gravis incubat, qui notus nimis omnibus, ignotus moritur sibi.

appear

appear before that which *Christ* hath erected for him
on earth, that he may make his access fairer when
he shall be called before the dreadful tribunal of
Christ in the clouds. For if he can be confident upon the stock of an *unpraised* or a *looser* life, and
should dare to venture upon wild accounts without
order, without abatements, without consideration,
without conduct, without fear, without scrutinies and
confessions, and instruments of amends or pardon;
he either knows not his danger, or cares not for it,
and little understands how great a horror that is, that
a man should rest his head for ever upon a cradle of
flames, and lie in a bed of sorrows, and never sleep,
and never end his groans or the gnashing of his
teeth.

This is that which some spiritual persons call
awakening of a sinner by the terrors of the law;
which is a good analogy or tropical expression to represent the threatenings of the gospel, and the danger
of an incurious and a sinning person: but we have
nothing else to do with *the terrors of the law;* for,
blessed be God, they concern us not. The terrors of
the law were the intermination of curses upon all
those that ever broke any of the least commandments,
once, or *in any instance:* and to it *the righteousness
of faith* is opposed. *The terrors of the law* admitted
no repentance, no pardon, no abatement; and were
so severe, that God never inflicted them at all according to the letter, because he admitted all to repentance that desired it with a timely prayer, unless in
very few cases, as of *Achan* or *Corah, the gatherer
of sticks upon the sabbath-day,* or the like: but the
state of threatenings in the gospel is very fearful, because the conditions of avoiding them are easy and
ready, and they happen to evil persons after many
warnings, second thoughts, frequent invitations to
pardon and repentance, and after one entire pardon
consigned in baptism. And in this sense it is necessary

sary that such persons as we now deal withal should be instructed concerning their danger.

4. When the sick man is either of himself, or by these considerations, set forward with purposes of repentance and confession of his sins in order to all its holy purposes and effects, then the minister is to assist him in the understanding the number of his sins, that is, the several kinds of them, and the various manners of prevaricating the divine commandments: for as for the number of the particulars in every kind, he will need less help; and if he did, he can have it no where but in his own conscience, and from the witnesses of his conversation. Let this be done by prudent insinuation, by arts of remembrance and secret notices, and propounding occasions, and instruments of recalling such things to his mind, which either by public fame he is accused of, or by the temptations of his condition it is likely he might have contracted.

5. If the person be truly penitent, and forward to confess all that are set before him, or offered to his sight at a half face, then he may be complied withal in all his innocent circumstances, and his conscience made placid and willing, and he be drawn forward by good-nature and civility, that his repentance in all the parts of it, and in every step of its progress and emanation, may be as voluntary and chosen as it can. For by that means if the sick person can be invited to do the work of religion, it enters by the door of his will and choice, and will pass on toward consummation by the instrument of delight.

6. If the sick man be backward and without apprehension of the good-natured and civil way, let the minister take care that by some way or other the work of God be secured: and if he will not understand when he is secretly prompted, he must be hallooed to, and asked in plain interrogatives concerning the crime of his life. He must be told of the evil things that are

are spoken of him in markets and exchanges, the proper temptations and accustomed evils of his calling and
condition, of the actions of scandal: and in all those
actions which were public, or of which any notice is
come abroad, let care be taken that the right side of
the case of conscience be turned toward him, and the
error truly represented to him by which he was
abused; as the injustice of his contracts, his oppres-
sive bargains, his rapine and violence: and if he hath
persuaded himself to think well of a scandalous action,
let him be instructed and advertised of his folly and
his danger.

7. And this advice concerns the minister of religion to follow without partiality, or fear, or interest,
in much simplicity, and prudence, and hearty sincerity; having no other consideration, but that the interest of the man's soul be preserved, and no caution
used, but that the matter be represented with just
circumstances, and civilities fitted to the person with
prefaces of honour and regard, but so that nothing of
the duty be diminished by it, that the introduction do
not spoil the sermon, and both together ruin *two souls*
[of *the speaker,* and *the hearer.*] For it may soon
be considered, if the sick man be a poor or an indifferent person in secular account, yet his soul is equally
dear to God, and was redeemed with the same highest
price, and is therefore to be highly regarded: and
there is no temptation, but that the spiritual man
may speak freely without the allays of interest or fear,
or mistaken civilities. But if the sick man be a
prince, or a person of eminence or wealth, let it be
remembered, it is an ill expression of reverence to
his authority, or of regard to his person, to let him
perish for the want of an honest, and just, and a free
homily.

8. Let the sick man, in the scrutiny of his conscience and confession of his sins, be carefully reminded to consider those sins which are only con-

Q   demned

demned *in the court of conscience,* and no where
else; for there are certain secrecies and retirements,
places of darkness, and artificial veils, with which the
devil uses to hide our sins from us, and to incorporate
them into our affections by a constant uninterrupted
practice, before they be prejudiced or discovered.
1. There are many sins which have reputation, and
are accounted honour; as *fighting a duel, answering
a blow with a blow, carrying armies into a neighbour
country, robbing with a navy, violently seizing upon
a kingdom.* 2. Others are permitted by law; as
usury in all countries: and because every excess of
it is a certain sin, the permission of so suspected a
matter makes it ready for us, and instructs the temptation. 3. Some things are not forbidden by law;
as *lying in ordinary discourse, jeering, scoffing, intemperate eating, ingratitude, selling too dear, cir-
cumventing another in contracts, importunate entreaties,* and *temptation of persons to many instances
of sin, pride, and ambition.* 4. Some others do not
reckon they sin against God, if the laws have seized
upon the person; and many that are *imprisoned for
debt, think themselves disobliged from payment;* and
when they *pay the penalty, think they owe nothing
for the scandal and disobedience.* 5. Some sins are
thought not considerable, but go under the titles of
sins of infirmity, or inseparable accidents of mortality;
such as *idle thoughts, foolish talking, looser revellings, impatience, anger,* and all the events of evil
company. 6. Lastly, many things are thought to be
no sins; such as *mispending of their time, whole days
or months of useless and impertinent employment,
long gaming, winning men's money in greater portions, censuring men's actions, curiosity, equivocating
in the prices and secrets of buying and selling, rudeness, speaking truths enviously, doing good to evil
purposes,* and the like. Under the dark shadow of
these unhappy and fruitless yew-trees, the enemy of
mankind

mankind makes very many to lie hid from themselves, sewing before their nakedness the fig-leaves of *popular* and *idol reputation*, and *impunity*, *public permission*, *a temporal penalty*, *infirmity*, *prejudice*, and *direct error in judgment*, and *ignorance*. Now in all these cases the ministers are to be inquisitive and observant, lest the fallacy prevail upon the penitent to evil pur poses of death or diminution of his good, and that those things which in his life passed without observation, may now be brought forth and *pass under saws and harrows*, that is, the severity and censure of sor row and condemnation.

9. To which I add, for the likeness of the thing, that the *matter of omission* be considered; for in them lies the bigger half of our failings. And yet in many instances they are undiscerned, because they very often *sit down by* the conscience, but never *upon it:* and they are usually looked upon as poor men do upon their not having coach and horses, or as that knowledge is missed by *boys* and *hinds* which they never had; it will be hard to make them understand their ignorance; it requires knowledge to perceive it; and therefore he that can perceive it, hath it not. But by thus pressing the conscience with omissions, I do not mean recessions or distances from states of eminency or perfection: for although they may be used by the ministers as an instrument of humility, and a chastiser of too big a confidence, yet that which is to be confessed and repented of is omission of duty in direct instances and matters of commandment, or collateral and personal obligations, and is especially to be considered by kings and prelates, by governors and rich persons, by guides of souls and presidents of learning in public charge, and by all others in their proportions.

10. The ministers of religion must take care that the sick man's confession be as minute and particular as it can, and that as few sins as may be, be intrusted

to

to the general prayer of pardon for all sins : for by being particular and enumerative of the variety of evils which have disordered his life, his repentance is disposed to be pungent and afflictive, and therefore more salutary and medicinal; it hath in it more sincerity, and makes a better judgment of the final condition of the man; and from thence it is certain the hopes of the sick man can be more confident and reasonable.

11. The spiritual man that assists at the repentance of the sick must not be inquisitive into all the circumstances of the particular sins, but be content with those that are direct parts of the crime, and aggravation of the sorrow: such as *frequency, long abode* and *earnest choice* in acting them; *violent desires, great expense, scandal* of others; *dishonour to the religion, days of devotion, religious solemnities* and *holy places;* and *the degrees of boldness and impudence, perfect resolution,* and *the habit.* If the sick person be reminded or inquired into concerning these, it may prove a good instrument to increase his contrition, and perfect his penitential sorrows, and facilitate his absolution and the means of his amendment. But the other circumstances as of the relative person in the participation of the crime, the measures or circumstances of the impure action, the name of the injured man or woman, the quality or accidental condition; these and all the like, are but questions springing from curiosity, and producing scruple, and apt to turn into many inconveniences.

12. The minister in this duty of repentance must be diligent to observe concerning the person that repents *, that he be not imposed upon by some one excellent thing that was remarkable in the sick man's former life. For there are some *people of one good*

* Nunc si depositum non inficiatur amicus,
Si reddat veterem cum totâ ærugine follem,
Prodigiosa fides et Thuscis digna libellis.   *Juven.* Sat. xiii. v. 60.

thing.

thing. Some are charitable to the poor out of kind-heartedness, and the same good-nature makes them easy and compliant with drinking persons, and they die with drink, but cannot live with charity: and their alms it may be shall deck their monument, or give them the reward of loving persons, and the poor man's thanks for alms, and procure many temporal blessings; but it is very sad that the reward should be all spent in this world. Some are really just persons, and punctual observers of their word with men, but break their promises with God, and make no scruple of that. In these and all the like cases the spiritual man must be careful to remark, that *good proceeds from an entire and integral cause* and *evil from every part:* that one sickness can make a man die; but he cannot live and be called a sound man without an entire health, and therefore if any confidence arises upon that stock, so as that it hinders the strictness of the repentance, it must be allayed with the representment of this sad truth, *that he who reserves one evil in his choice, hath chosen an evil portion,* and *coloquintida and death as in the pot:* and he that worships the God of *Israel* with a frequent sacrifice, and yet upon the anniversary will *bow in the house of Venus,* and loves to see the follies and the nakedness of *Rimmon,* may eat part of the flesh of the sacrifice, and fill his belly, but shall not be refreshed by the holy cloud arising from the altar, or the dew of heaven descending upon the mysteries.

13. And yet the minister is to estimate, that one or more good things is to be an ingredient into his *judgment concerning the state of his soul,* and the capacities of his restitution, and admission to the peace of the church: and according as the excellency and usefulness of the grace hath been, and according to the degrees and the reasons of its prosecution, so abatements are to be made in the injunctions and impositions upon the penitent. For every virtue is one

degree

degree of approach to God: and though in respect
of the acceptation it is equally none at all, that is, it
is as certain a death if a man dies with one mortal
wound as if he had twenty; yet in such persons who
have some one or more excellencies, though not an
entire piety, there is naturally a nearer approach to
the state of grace, than in persons who have done
evils, and are eminent for nothing that is good. But
in making judgment of such persons, it is to be enquired into, and noted accordingly, why the sick person was so eminent in that one good thing; whether
by *choice* and apprehension of his duty, or whether it
was a virtue from which *his state of life* ministered
nothing to dehort or discourage him, or whether it
was only *a consequent of his natural temper and constitution.* If the *first,* then it supposes him in the
neighbourhood of the state of grace, and that in other
things he was strongly tempted. The *second* is a felicity of his education, and an effect of Providence.
The *third* is a felicity of his nature and a gift of God
in order to spiritual purposes. But yet of every one
of these, advantage is to be made. If the conscience
of his *duty* was the principle, then he is ready formed
to entertain all other graces upon the same reason,
and his repentance must be made more sharp and
penal; because he is convinced to have done against
his conscience in all the other parts of his life; but
the judgment concerning his final state ought to be
more gentle, because it was a huge temptation that
hindered the man, and abused his infirmity. But if
either his *calling* or his *nature* were the parents of the
grace, he is in the state of *a moral man,* (in the just
and proper meaning of the word,) and to be handled
accordingly: that virtue disposed him rarely well to
many other good things, but was no part of the grace
of sanctification: and therefore the man's repentance
is to begin anew, for all that, and is to be finished in
the returns of health, if God grants it; but if he
denies

denies it, it is much, very much the worse for all that sweet-natured virtue.

14. When the confession is made, the spiritual man is to exercise the office of a *restorer* and a *judge,* in the following particulars and manner.

SECT. IV.

Of the ministering to the Restitution and Pardon, or Reconciliation of the sick Person, by administering the Holy Sacrament.

* *If any man be overtaken in a fault, ye which are spiritual restore such a one in the spirit of meekness;* that's *the commission:* and, † *let the elders of the church pray over the sick man; and if he have committed sins, they shall be forgiven him;* that's the *effect* of his power and his ministry. But concerning this, some few things are to be considered.

1. It is the office of the presbyters and ministers of religion to declare public criminals and scandalous persons to be such, that when the leprosy is declared, the flock may avoid the infection; and then the man is excommunicate, when the people are warned to avoid the danger of the man, or the reproach of the crime, to withdraw from his society, and *not to bid him God speed,* not to eat and celebrate *Synaxes* and *church-meetings* with such who are declared criminal and dangerous. And therefore *excommunication* is in a very great part the act of the congregation, and communities of the faithful: and ‡ St. *Paul* said to the church of the *Corinthians,* that *they had inflicted the evil* upon the incestuous person, that is, by excommunicating him. All the acts of which are as

---

* Gal. vi. 1.   † James, v. 14, 15.   ‡ 1 Cor. v. 5. 12, 13. — 2 Cor. ii. 6.

Q 4   they

they are subjected in the people, acts of *caution* and *liberty*; but no more acts of direct proper *power* or *jurisdiction*, than it was when the scholars of *Simon Magus* left his chair and went to hear St. *Peter*. But as they are actions of the rulers of the church, so they are *declarative, ministerial,* and *effective too by moral causality,* that is, by *persuasion* and *discourse,* by *argument* and *prayer,* by *homily* and *material representment,* by reasonableness of *order,* and the *super-induced necessities* of men; though not by any real change of state *as to the person,* nor by diminution of his right, or violence to his condition.

2. He that *baptizes,* and he that *ministers the holy sacrament,* and he that *prays,* does holy offices of great advantage *; but in these also, just as in the former, he exercises no jurisdiction or pre-eminence after the manner of secular authority: and the same is also true if he should deny them. He that refuseth to baptize an indisposed person, hath by the consent of all men no power or jurisdiction over the unbaptized man: and he that for the like reason refuseth to give him the communion, preserves the sacredness of the mysteries, and does charity to the indisposed man, to deny that to him which will do him mischief. And this is an act of separation, just as it is for a friend or physician to deny water to an hydropic person, or *Italian* wines to an hectic fever; or as if *Cato* should deny to salute *Bibulus,* or the *censor* of manners to do countenance to a wanton and vicious person. And though this thing was expressed by words of power, such as *separation, abstention, excommunication, deposition;* yet these words we understand by the thing itself, which was notorious and evident to be matter of prudence, security, and a free uncon-

* Homines in remissione peccatorum ministerium suum exhibent, non jus alicujus potestatis exercent: Neque enim in suo, sed in nomine Patris, Filii, et Spiritus Sancti peccata dimittuntur. Isti rogant, Divinitas donat. S. *Amb.* de Spir. S. l. iii. c. 10.

strained

strained discipline; and they passed into power by consent and voluntary submission, having the same effect of constraint, fear and authority, which we see in secular jurisdiction; not because *ecclesiastical discipline* hath a natural proper coercion as *lay tribunals* have, but because men have submitted to it, and *are bound to do so* upon the interest of two or three *Christian graces.*

3. In pursuance of this caution and provision, the church superinduced *times and manners of abstention,* and expressions of sorrow and canonical punishments, which they tied the delinquent people to suffer before they would admit them to the holy table of the Lord. For the criminal having obliged himself by his sin, and the church having declared it when she could take notice of it, he is bound to repent, to make him capable of pardon with God; and to prove that he is penitent, he is to do such actions which the church in the virtue and pursuance of repentance shall accept as a testimony of it sufficient to inform her. For as she could not bind at all (in this sense) till the crime was public, though the man had bound himself in secret; so neither can she set him free till the repentance be as public as the sin, or so as she can note it and approve it. Though the man be free as to God by his internal act; yet as the publication of the sin was accidental to it, and the church-censure consequent to it, so is the publication of repentance and consequent absolution extrinsical to the pardon, but accidentally and in the present circumstances necessary. This was the same that the *Jews* did, (though in other instances and expressions,) and do to this day to their prevaricating people; and the *Essenes* in their assemblies and private colleges of scholars, and public universities. For all these being assemblies of voluntary persons, and such as seek for advantage, are bound to make an artificial authority in their superiors, and so to secure order and government by their

their own obedience and voluntary subordination,
which is not essential and of proper jurisdiction in
the superior; and the band of it is not any coercive
power, but the denying to communicate such benefits
which they seek in that communion and fellowship.

4. These, I say, were introduced in *the special
manners and instances* by positive authority, and
have not a divine authority *commanding them;* but
there is a divine power that verifies them, and makes
these separations effectual and formidable : for because they are *declarative* and *ministerial* in the
spiritual man, and suppose a delinquency and demerit
in the other, and a sin against God, our blessed
Saviour hath declared, that what *they bind on earth
shall be bound in heaven;* that is, in plain signification, the same sins and sinners which the clergy con-
demns in the face of their assemblies, the same are
condemned in heaven before the face of God, and for
the same reason too. God's law hath sentenced it,
and these are the preachers and publishers of his law,
by which they stand condemned : and these laws are
they that condemn the sin, or acquit the penitent,
there and *here; * whatsoever they bind here shall be
bound there,* that is, the sentence of God *at the day
of judgment* shall sentence the same men whom the
church does rightly sentence here. It is spoken in
the future [*it shall be bound in heaven:*] not but
that the sinner is first bound there, or first absolved
there : but because all *binding and loosing* in the interval is imperfect and relative to the day of judgment, the day of the great sentence, therefore it is

* Summum futuri judicii præjudicium est, si quis ità deliquerit, ut à com-
municatione orationis et conventûs et omnis sancti commercii relegetur.
Tertul. Apol. c. 39.
Atque hoc idem innuitur per summam Apostoli censuram, in reos maximi
criminis, sit ἀνάθεμα μαραναϑα, i. e. excommunicatus majori excommuni-
catione; *Dominus veniet,* scil. ad judicandum eum : ad quod judicium hæc
censura Ecclesiæ est relativa et in ordine. Tum demum pœnas dabit; ad
quas, nisi resipiscat, hic consignatur.

set

set down in the time to come, and says this only, the clergy are tied by the word and laws of God to condemn such sins and sinners: and that you may not think it ineffective, because after such sentence the man lives and grows rich, or remains in health and power, therefore be sure it shall be verified in the day of judgment. This is hugely agreeable with the words of our Lord, and certain in reason: for that the minister does nothing to the final alteration of the state of the man's soul by way of sentence, is demonstratively certain, because he cannot bind a man, but such as hath bound himself, and who is bound in heaven by his sin before his sentence in the church; as also because the binding of the church is merely accidental, and upon publication only; and when the man repents he is absolved before God, before the sentence of the church, upon his contrition and dereliction only; and if he were not, the church would not absolve him. The consequent of which evident truth is this, that whatsoever impositions the church-officers impose upon the criminal, they are to avoid scandal, to testify repentance, and to exercise it, to instruct the people, to make them fear, to represent the act of God, and the secret and the true state of the sinner: and although they are not essentially necessary to our pardon, yet *they are become necessary when the church hath seized upon the sinner by public notice of the crime;* necessary (I say) for the *removing the scandal,* and *giving testimony of our contrition,* and *for the receiving all that comfort which he needs,* and can derive from the promises of pardon, as they are published by him that is commanded to preach them to all them that repent. And therefore although it cannot be necessary as to the obtaining pardon that the priest should *in private* absolve a sick man from *his private sins,* and there is *no loosing* where there was *no precedent binding,* and he that was only bound before God, can before him only be loosed : yet as to confess sins to any Christian in private may have many good ends, and to confess them to a clergyman may have many more; so to hear God's sentence at the mouth of the minister, *pardon* pronounced by God's ambassador, is of huge comfort to them that cannot otherwise be comforted, and whose infirmity needs it; and therefore it were very fit it were not neglected in the days of our fear and danger, of our infirmities and sorrow.

5. The execution of this ministry being an act of prudence and charity, and therefore relative to changing circumstances, it hath been, and in many cases *may*, and in some *must* be rescinded and altered. The time of separation may be lengthened and shortened, the condition made lighter or heavier; and for the same offence the clergyman is deposed, but yet admitted to the communion, for which one of the people, who hath no office to lose, is denied the benefit of communicating; and this sometimes when he might lawfully receive it : and a private man is *separate*, when a multitude or a prince is not, cannot, ought not. And at last, when the case of sickness and danger of death did occur, they admitted all men that desired it : sometimes without scruple or difficulty, sometimes with some little restraint in great or insolent cases *, (as in the case of apostacy, in which the council of *Arles* denied absolution, unless they received and gave public satisfaction by acts of repentance; and some other councils denied at any time to do it to such persons,) according as seemed fitting to the present necessities of the church. All which particulars declare it to be no part of a divine commandment, that any man should be denied to receive the communion if he desires it, and if he be in any probable capacity of receiving it.

6. Since † the separation was an act of liberty and a direct negative, it follows that the restitution was a

---

* *Arelat.* c. 3.　　† *Vide* 2 Cor. ii. 10. et S. *Cyprian,* Ep. lxxiii.

mere

mere doing that which they refused formerly, and to give the holy communion was the formality of ab-solution, and all the instrument and the whole matter of reconcilement; *the taking off the punishment* is *the pardoning of the sin :* for this without the other is but a word ; and if this be done, I care not whether any thing be said or no. *Vinum Dominicum minis-tratoris gratia est,* is also true in this sense; to give the chalice and cup is the grace and indulgence of the minister : and when that is done, the man hath ob-tained the peace of the church ; and to do that, is all the absolution the church can give. And they were vain disputes which were commenced some few ages since concerning *the forms of absolution,* whether they were *indicative* or *optative,* by way of *declaration* or by way of *sentence :* for at first they had no forms at all, but they said a prayer, and after the manner of the *Jews,* laid hands upon the penitent, when they prayed over him, and so admitted him to the holy communion. For since the church had no power over her children, but of excommunicating and de-nying them to attend upon *holy offices and ministeries* respectively, neither could they have any absolution, but to admit them thither from whence formerly they were forbidden : whatsoever ceremony or form did signify, this was superinduced and arbitrary, alterable and accidental; it had variety, but no ne-cessity.

7. The practice consequent to this is, that if the penitent be bound by the positive censures of the church, he is to be reconciled upon those conditions which the laws of the church tie him to, in case he can perform them: if he cannot, he can no longer be prejudiced by the censure of the church, which had no relation but to the people, with whom the dying man is no longer to converse. * For what-soever relates to God, is to be transacted in spiritual

* Caus. 26. Q. 6. and Q. 7.

5   ways,

ways, by contrition and internal graces; and the
mercy of the church is such, as to give him her peace
and her blessing, upon his undertaking to obey her
injunctions, if he shall be able : which injunctions,
if they be declared by public sentence, the minister
hath nothing to do in the affairs, but to remind him of
his obligation, and reconcile him, that is, give him the
holy sacrament.

8. If the penitent be not bound by public sentence, the minister is to make his repentance as
great, and his heart as contrite as he can, to dispose
him by the repetition of acts of grace, in the way of
prayer, and in real and exterior instances, where he
can, and then to give him the holy communion in all
the same cases in which he ought not to have denied
it to him in his health, that is, even in the beginnings
of such a repentance, which by human signs he believes to be real and holy : and after this, the event
must be left to God.   The reason of the rule depends
upon this; because there is no divine commandment
directly forbidding the rulers of the church to give
the communion to any Christian that desires it, and
professes repentance of his sins.   And all church
discipline, in every instance, and to every single person, was imposed upon him by men, who did it according to the necessities of this state and constitution of our affairs below : but we, who are but
ministers and delegates of pardon and condemnation,
must resign and give up our judgment when the man
is no more to be judged by the sentences of man, and
by the proportions of this world, but of the other :
to which if our reconciliation does advantage, we
ought in charity to send him forth with all the advantages he can receive ; for he will need them
all.   And * therefore the *Nicene* council commands,
that no man be deprived of this *necessary passport*
in article of his death, and calls this *the ancient*

* Can. 13. Vide etiam Con. *Ancyr.* c. 6. *Aurel.* 2. c. 12.

canonical

canonical law of the church; and to minister it, only
supposes the man in the communion of the church,
not always in the state, but ever in the possibilities
of sanctification. They who in the article and danger
of death were admitted to the communion, and tied
to penance if they recovered, (which was ever the
custom of the ancient church, unless in very few
cases,) were but in the threshold of repentance, in the
commencement and first introductions to a devout
life ; * and indeed then it is a fit ministry, that it be
given in all the periods of time in which the pardon of
sins is working, since it is the sacrament of that great
mystery, and the exhibition of that blood *which is shed
for the remission of sins.*

9. The minister of religion ought not to give the
communion to a sick person, if he retains the affection to any sin, and refuses to disavow it, or profess repentance of all sins whatsoever, if he be required to do it. The reason is, because it is a † certain
death to him, and an increase of his misery, if
he shall so profane the body and blood of *Christ*, as
to take it into so unholy a breast, when Satan reigns,
and sin is principal, and the spirit is extinguished,
and *Christ* loves not to enter, because he is not suffered to inhabit. ‡   But when he professes repentance,
and does such acts of it as his present condition per-
mits, he is to be presumed to intend heartily what he
professes solemnly; and the minister is only judge of
the outward act, and by that only he is to take inform-
ation concerning the inward. But whether he be
so or no, or if he be, whether that be timely, and

* O sacrum convivium in quo Christus sumitur, recolitur memoria
Passionis ejus, mens impletur gratiâ, et futuræ gloriæ nobis pignus
datur!

† Ità vide ut prosit illis ignosci quos ad pœnam ipse Deus deduxit:
quod ad me attinet, non sum crudelis, sed vereor, ne quod remisero
patiar. *Tryphæna* dixit apud *Petronium.*

‡ Sævi quoque et implacabiles Domini crudelitatem suam impediunt, si
quando pœnitentia fugitivos reduxit, dedititiis hostibus parcimus.

8   effectual

effectual and sufficient toward the pardon of sins before God, is another consideration, of which we may
conjecture here, but we shall know it at doomsday.
The spiritual man is to do his ministry by the rules of
Christ, and as the customs of the church appoint him,
and after the manner of men : the event is in the
hands of God, and is to be expected, not directly
and wholly according to his ministry, but to the
former life, or the timely * *internal repentance* and
amendment, of which I have already given accounts.
These ministeries are acts of order and great assistances, but the sum of affairs does not rely upon
them. And if any man put his whole repentance upon
this time, or all his hopes upon these ministeries, he
will find them and himself to fail.

10. It is the minister's office to invite sick and dying persons to the holy sacrament; such, whose lives
were fair and laudable, and yet their sickness sad and
violent, making them listless and of slow desires,
and slower apprehensions : that such persons who
are in the state of grace may lose no accidental advantages of spiritual improvement, but may receive
into their dying bodies the symbols and great con-
signations of the resurrection, and into their souls the
pledges of immortality; and may appear before God
their Father in the union, and with the impresses and
likeness of their elder brother. But if the persons be
of ill report, and have lived wickedly, they are not to
be invited, because their case is hugely suspicious,
though they then repent and call for mercy : but if
they demand it, they are not to be denied ; only let
the minister in general represent the evil consequents
of an unworthy participation ; and if the penitent
will judge himself unworthy, let him stand candidate
for pardon at the hands of God, and stand or fall by

---

* Quæcunque ergo de pœnitentiâ jubendo dicta sunt, non ad exteriorem,
sed ad interiorem referenda sunt, sine quâ nullus unquam Deo reconciliari
poterit. *Gratian*. de Pœnit. D. 1. Quis aliquando.

that

that unerring and merciful sentence; to which his severity of condemning himself before men will make the easier and more hopeful address. And the strictest among the Christians, who denied to reconcile lapsed persons after baptism, yet acknowledged that there were hopes reserved in the court of heaven for them, though not here : since we, who are easily deceived by the pretences of a real return, are tied to dispense God's graces as he hath given us commission *, *with fear and trembling*, and without too forward confidences ; and God hath mercies which we know not of; and therefore because we know them not, such persons were referred to God's tribunal, where he would find them, if they were to be had at all.

11. When the holy sacrament is to be administered, let the exhortation be made proper to the mystery, but fitted to the man; that is, that it be used for the advantages of faith, or love, or contrition : let all the circumstances and parts of the Divine love be represented, all the mysterious advantages of the blessed sacrament be declared; that it is the bread which came from heaven ; that it is the representation of *Christ's* death to all the purposes and capacities of faith, and the real exhibition of *Christ's* body and blood to all the purposes of the spirit ; that it is the earnest of the resurrection, and the seed of a glorious immortality ; that as by our cognation to the body of the *first Adam* we took in death, so by our union with the body of the *second Adam* we shall have the inheritance of life †; (for *as by Adam came death, so by Christ cometh the resurrection of the dead ;*) that if we, being worthy communicants of these sacred pledges, be presented to God with *Christ* within us, our being accepted of God is certain, even for the sake of his well-beloved that dwells within us ; that this is the sacrament of that body which was broken for our sins, of that blood which purifies our souls,

* 1 Cor. ii. 3.   † 1 Cor. xv. 22.

R

by

by which *we are presented to God pure and holy in the beloved ;* that now we may ascertain our hopes, and make our faith confident *; for *he that hath given us his Son, how should not he with him give us all things else ;* upon these or the like considerations the sick man may be assisted in his address, and his faith strengthened, and his hope confirmed, and his charity be enlarged.

† 12. The manner of the sick man's reception of the holy sacrament hath in it nothing differing from the ordinary solemnities of the sacrament, save only that abatement is to be made of such accidental circumstances as by the laws and customs of the church healthful persons are obliged to; such as fasting, kneeling, *&c.* Though I remember that it was noted for great devotion in the legate that died at *Trent,* that he caused himself to be sustained upon his knees, when he received the *viaticum,* or the holy sacrament, before his death : and it was greater in *Huniades,* that he caused himself to be carried to the church, that there he might receive *his Lord* in *his Lord's house ;* and it was recorded for honour, that *William* the pious archbishop of *Bourges,* a small time before his last agony, sprang out of his bed, at the presence of the holy sacrament, and upon his knees and his face recommended his soul to his Saviour. But in these things no man is to be prejudiced or censured.

13. Let not the holy sacrament be administered to dying persons, when they have no use of reason to make that duty acceptable, and the mysteries effective to the purposes of the soul. For the sacraments and ceremonies of the gospel operate not without the concurrent actions and moral influences of the suscipient. To infuse the chalice into the cold lips of the clinick may disturb his agony, but cannot re-

---

* Rom. viii. 32.

† Vid. *Rule of Holy Living,* c. iv. § 10. and *History of the Life of Jesus,* Part iii. Disc. 18.

lieve

lieve the soul, which only receives improvement by acts of grace and choice, to which the external rites are apt and appointed to minister in a capable person. All other persons, as fools, children, distracted persons, lethargical, apoplectical, or any ways senseless and incapable of human and reasonable acts are to be assisted only by prayers : for *they* may prevail even for the absent, and for enemies, and for all those who join not in the office.

SECT. V.

*Of ministering to the sick Person by the spiritual Man,
as he is the Physician of Souls.*

1. In all cases of receiving confessions of sick men, and the assisting to the advancement of repentance, the minister is to apportion to every kind of sin such spiritual remedies which are apt to mortify and cure the sin ; such as abstinence from their occasions and opportunities, to avoid temptations, to resist their beginnings, to punish the crime by acts of indignation against the person, fastings and prayer, alms and all the instances of charity, asking forgiveness, restitution of wrongs, satisfaction of injuries, acts of virtue contrary to the crimes. And although in great and dangerous sicknesses they are not directly to be imposed, unless they are direct matters of duty, yet where they are medicinal they are to be insinuated, and in general signification remarked to him, and undertaken accordingly : concerning which, when he returns to health, he is to receive particular advices. And this advice was inserted into the penitential of *England* in the time of *Theodore* archbishop of *Can-*

terbury *, and afterwards adopted into the canon of all the western churches.

2. The proper temptations of sick men, for which a remedy is not yet provided, are *unreasonable fears*, and *unreasonable confidences*, which ministers are to cure by the following considerations.

Considerations against unreasonable Fears of not having our Sins pardoned.

MANY good men, especially such who have tender consciences, impatient of the least sin to which they are arrived by a long grace, and a continual observation of their actions, and the parts of a lasting repentance, many times over-act their tenderness, and turn their caution into scruple, and care of their duty into enquiries after the event, and askings after the counsels of God, and the sentences of doomsday.

He that asks of the standers-by, or of the minister, whether they think he shall be saved or damned, is to be answered with the words of pity and reproof. Seek not after *new light* for the searching into the privatest records of God : look as much as you list into the pages of Revelation, for they concern your duty ; but the event is registered in heaven, and we can expect no other certain notices of it, but that it shall be given to them for whom it is prepared by the Father of mercies. We have light enough to tell our duty ; and *if we do that*, we need not fear what the issue will be ; and *if we do not*, let us never look for more light, or enquire after God's pleasure concerning our souls, since we so little serve his ends in those things where he hath given us light. † But yet this I add, That as pardon of sins in the Old Testament was nothing but removing the punishment which then was temporal, and therefore many times they could tell if their sins were pardoned ; and concerning

---

* Caus. 26. q. 7. ab infirmis.   † Matt. ix. 6.

pardon

pardon of sins, they then had no fears of conscience, but while the punishment was on them, for so long indeed it was unpardoned, and how long it would so remain it was matter of fear, and of present sorrow: besides this, in the gospel, pardon of sins is another thing; pardon of sins is *a sanctification* * : *Christ came to take away our sins, by turning every one of us from our iniquities;* and there is not in the nature of the thing any expectation of pardon, or sign or signification of it, but so far as the thing itself discovers itself. As we hate sin, and grow in grace, and arrive at the state of holiness, which is also a state of repentance and imperfection, but yet of sincerity of heart, and diligent endeavour; in the same degree we are to judge concerning the forgiveness of sins: for indeed that is the *evangelical forgiveness*, and it signifies our pardon, because it effects it, or rather it is in the nature of the thing; so that we are to enquire into no hidden records. Forgiveness of sins is not a secret sentence, a word or a record; but it is a state of change, and effected upon us; and upon ourselves we are to look for it, to read it and understand it. We are only *to be curious of our duty*, and confident of the article of remission of sins †; and the conclusion of these premises will be, that we shall be full of hopes of a prosperous resurrection: and our fear and trembling are no instances of our calamity, but parts of duty; we shall sure enough be wafted to the shore, although we be tossed with the winds of our sighs, and the unevenness of our fears, and the ebbings and flowings of our passions, if we sail in a right channel, and steer by a perfect compass, and look up to God, and call for his help, and do our own endeavour. There are very many reasons why men ought not to despair; and there are not very many men that ever go beyond a hope, till

cts, iii. 26.
† Est modus gloriandi in conscientia, ut noveris fidem tuam esse sinceram, spem tuam esse certam. *Aug.* Psal. 149.

they

they pass into possession. If our fears have any mixture of hope, that is enough to enable and to excite
our duty: and if we have a strong hope, when we
cast about, we shall find reason enough to have many
fears : *Let not this fear * weaken our hands ;* and if
it allay our gaieties and our confidences, it is no
harm. In this uncertainty we must abide, if we have
committed sins after baptism : and those confidences
which some men glory in are not real supports or
good foundations. The fearing man is the safest;
and if he fears on his death-bed, it is but what happens to most considering men, and what was to be
looked for all his life-time : he talked of the terrors
of death, and death is the *king of terrors ;* and therefore it is no strange thing if then he be hugely afraid :
if he be not, it is either a great felicity, or a great presumption. But if he wants some degree of comfort,
or a greater degree of hope, let him be refreshed, by
considering,

† 1. That *Christ came into the world to save sinners.* 2. That *God delights not in the confusion and
death of sinners.* 3. That *in heaven there is great
joy at the conversion of a sinner.* 4. That Christ is a
perpetual *advocate* daily interceding with his Father
for our pardon. 5. That God uses infinite arts, instruments and devices to reconcile us to himself.
6. That ‡ *he prays us to be in charity with him,* and to
be forgiven. 7. That he sends angels to keep us from
violence and evil- company, from temptations and
surprises, and his Holy Spirit to guide us in holy ways,
and his servants to warn us and remind us perpetually : and therefore since certainly he is so desirous
to save us, as appears by his word, by his oaths, by
his very nature, and his daily artifices of mercy ; it is
not likely that he will condemn us without great pro-

---

* Una est nobilitas, argumentumque coloris
  Ingenui, timidas non habuisse manus.
† 1 Tim. i. 15. Ezek. xxxiii. 11. Luke, x. v. 7. 1 John, ii. 1.
‡ 2 Cor. v. 20.

                                        vocations

vocations of his majesty, and perseverance in them.
8. That the covenant of the gospel is a covenant of
grace and of repentance, and being established with
so many great solemnities and miracles from heaven,
must signify a huge favour and a mighty change of
things; and therefore that repentance, which is the
great condition of it, is a grace that does not expire
in little accents and minutes, but hath a great latitude
of signification, and large extension of parts, under
the protection of *all which* persons are safe, even
when they fear exceedingly.   9. That there are great
degrees and differences of glory in heaven; and
therefore if we estimate our piety by proportions to
the more eminent persons and devouter people, we
are not to conclude we shall not enter into the *same
state of glory*, but that we shall not go into the *same
degrees.*   10. That although forgiveness of sins is
consigned to us in baptism, and that this baptism is
but once, and cannot be repeated; yet forgiveness of
sins is the grace of the gospel, which is perpetually
remanent upon us, and secured unto us so long as we
have not renounced our baptism: for then we enter
into the condition of repentance; and *repentance* is
not an indivisible grace, or a thing performed at once,
but is working all our lives, and therefore so is our
pardon, which ebbs and flows according as we discompose or renew the decency of our baptismal promises: and therefore it ought to be certain, that no
man despair of pardon, but he that hath voluntarily
renounced his baptism, or willingly estranged himself from that covenant.   He that sticks to it, and
still professes the religion, and approves the faith,
and endeavours to obey and to do his duty, this man
hath all the veracity of God to assure him and give
him confidence that he is not in an impossible state
of salvation, unless God cuts him off before he can
work, or that he begins to work when he can no
longer choose.   11. And then let him consider, the

more he fears, the more he hates his sin that is the
cause of it, and the less he can be tempted to it, and
the more desirous he is of heaven ; and therefore
such fears are good instruments of grace, and good
signs of a future pardon. 12. That God in the old
law, although he made a covenant of perfect obedience, and did not promise pardon at all after great
sins, yet he did give pardon, and declare it so to
them for their own and for our sakes too. So he did
to *David*, to *Manasses*, to the whole nation of the
Israelites ten times in the wilderness, even after their
apostasies and idolatries. * And in the prophets, the
mercies of God, and his remissions of sins, were
largely preached, though in the law God puts on
the robes of an angry Judge, and severe Lord. But
therefore in the gospel, where he hath established the
whole sum of affairs upon *faith and repentance*, if
God should not pardon great sinners that repent after
baptism, with a free dispensation, the gospel were far
harder than the intolerable covenant of the law.
13. That if a proselyte went into the Jewish communion, and were circumcised and baptized, he entered
into all the hopes of good things which God had promised or would give to his people ; and yet that was
but the *covenant of works*. If then the Gentile prose-
lytes, by their circumcision and legal baptism, were
admitted to a state of pardon, to last so long as they
were in the covenant, even after their admission, for
sins committed against *Moses's* law, which they then
undertook to observe exactly ; in the gospel, which
is the *covenant of faith*, it must needs be certain, that
there is a greater grace given, and an easier condition entered into, than was that of the Jewish law :
and that is nothing else, but that abatement is made
for our infirmities, and our single evils, and our
timely-repented and forsaken habits of sin, and our
violent passions, when they are contested withal, and

* Ezek. xviii.—Joel, ii.

fought

fought with, and under discipline, and in the beginnings and progresses of mortification. 14. That God hath erected in his church a whole order of men, the main part and dignity of whose work it is to *remit and retain sins*, by a perpetual and daily ministry: and this they do, not only in baptism, but in all their offices to be administered afterwards; in the holy sacrament of the Eucharist, which exhibits the symbols of that blood *which was shed for pardon of our sins*, and therefore by its continued ministry and repetition declares that *all that while* we are within the ordinary powers and usual dispensations of pardon, even so long as we are in any probable disposition to receive that holy sacrament. And the same effect is also signified and exhibited to the whole power of the keys, which if it extends to private sins, sins done in secret, it is certain it does also to public. But this is a greater testimony of the certainty of the remissibility of our greatest sins: for public sins, as they always have a sting and a superadded formality of scandal and ill example, so they are most commonly the greatest; such as murder, sacrilege, and others of unconcealed nature and unprivate action. And if God, for these worst of evils, hath appointed an office of ease and pardon, which is and may daily be administered, that will be an uneasy pusillanimity and fond suspicion of God's goodness, to fear that our repentance shall be rejected, even although we have not committed the greatest or the most of evils. 15. And it was concerning baptized Christians that St. *John* said, *If any man sin, we have an advocate with the Father, and he is the propitiation for our sins:* and concerning lapsed Christians St. *Paul* gave instruction, that, *If any man be overtaken in a fault, ye which are spiritual, restore such a man in the spirit of meekness, considering lest ye also be tempted.* The *Corinthian Christian* committed incest, and was pardoned: and *Simon Magus* after he was baptized offered

to

to commit his own sin of simony, and yet St. *Peter* bid him pray for pardon : and St. *James* tells, that, *If the sick man sends for the elders of the church, and they pray over him, and he confess his sins, they shall be forgiven him.* 16. That only one sin is declared to be irremissible, *the sin against the Holy Ghost, the sin unto death,* as St. *John* calls it, for which *we are not bound to pray ;* for all others we are: and certain it is, no man commits a sin against the Holy Ghost, if he be afraid he hath, and desires that he had not ; for such penitential passions are against the definition of that sin. 17. That all the sermons in the scripture written to Christians and disciples of *Jesus,* exhorting men to repentance, to be afflicted, to mourn and to weep, to confession of sins, are sure testimonies of God's purpose and desire to forgive us, even when we fall after baptism ; and if our fall after baptism were irrecoverable, then *all preaching were in vain,* and *our faith were also vain,* and we could not with comfort rehearse the creed, in which, as soon as ever we profess *Jesus* to have died for our sins, we also are condemned by our own conscience of a sin that shall not be forgiven ; and then all exhortations, and comforts, and fasts, and disciplines were useless and too late, if they were not given us before we can understand them ; for most commonly as soon as we can, we enter into the regions of sin ; for we commit *evil actions* before we understand, and together with our understanding they begin to be imputed. 18. That if it could be otherwise infants were very ill provided for in the church, who were baptized when they had no stain upon their brows, but the misery they contracted from *Adam :* and they are left to be angels for ever after, and live innocently in the midst of their ignorances, and weaknesses, and temptations, and the heat and follies of youth ; or else to perish in an eternal ruin. We cannot think or speak good things of God, if we entertain such evil suspicions of the mercies of the
Father

Father of our Lord *Jesus.* 19. That *the long suf-ferance and patience of God* is indeed wonderful : but therefore it leaves us in certainties of pardon, so long as there is possibility to return, if we reduce the power to act. 20. That God calls upon us to forgive our brother *seventy times seven times.* And yet all that is but like the forgiving a hundred pence for his sake who forgives us ten thousand talents : for so the Lord professed that he had done to him that was his servant and his domestic. 21. That if we can forgive a hundred thousand times, it is certain God will do so to us; our blessed Lord having commanded us to pray for pardon, as we pardon our offending and penitent brother. 22. That even in the case of very great sins, and great judgments inflicted upon the sinners, wise and good men, and precedents of religion, have declared their sense to be, that God spent all his anger, and made it expire in that temporal misery; and so it was supposed to have been done in the case of *Ananias :* but that the hopes of any penitent man may not rely upon any uncertainty, we find in holy scripture, that those Christians who had for their scandalous crimes deserved to be given over to Satan to be buffetted, yet had hopes to be saved in the day of the Lord. 23. That God glories in the titles of mercy and forgiveness, and will not have his appellatives so finite and limited as to expire in one act or in a seldom pardon. 24. That man's condition were desperate, and like that of the fallen angels, equally desperate, but unequally oppressed, considering our infinite weaknesses and ignorances, (in respect of their excellent understanding and perfect choice,) if he could be admitted to no repentance after his infant baptism : and if we may be admitted to one, there is nothing in the covenant of the gospel but he may also to a second, and so for ever, as long as he can repent, and return and live to God in a timely religion. 25. That every man is a sinner :

In

In * *many things we offend all;* and, † *If we say we have no sin, we deceive ourselves:* and therefore either all must perish, or else there is mercy for all; and so there is, upon this very stock; because *Christ* ‡ *died for sinners,* and || *God hath comprehended all under sin, that he might have mercy upon all.* 26. That if ever God sends temporal punishments into the world with purposes of amendment, and if they be not all of them certain consignations to hell, and unless every man that breaks his leg, or in punishment loses a child or wife, be certainly damned, it is certain that God in these cases is angry and loving, chastises the sin to amend the person, and smites that he may cure, and judges that he may absolve. 27. That he that *will not quench the smoaking flax, nor break the bruised reed,* will not tie us to perfection, and the laws and measures of heaven upon earth : and if in every period of our repentance he is pleased with our duty, and *the voice of our heart,* and *the hand of our desires,* he hath told us plainly that he will not only pardon all the sins of the days of our folly, but the returns and surprises of sins in the days of repentance, if we give no way, and allow no affection, and give no place to any thing that is God's enemy; *all the past sins,* and *all the seldom-returning* and *ever-repented evils* being put upon the accounts of the cross.

An exercise against Despair in the Day of our Death.

To which may be added this short exercise, to be used for the curing the temptation to direct despair, in case that the hope and faith of good men be assaulted in the day of their calamity.

I consider that the ground of my trouble is my sin ; and if it were not for that, I should not need to be troubled : but the help that all the world looks for is such as supposes a man to be a sinner. Indeed, if from myself I were to derive my title to heaven, then my

* James, iii. 2.   † 1 John, i. 8.   Rom. v. 8. || Rom. xi. 32.

sins

sins were a just argument of despair: but now that they
bring me to Christ, that they drive me to an appeal to
God's mercies, and to take sanctuary in the cross, they
ought not, they cannot infer a just cause of despair.
I am sure it is a stranger thing that God should take
upon him hands and feet, and those hands and feet
should be nailed upon a cross, than that a man should
be partaker of the felicities of pardon and life eternal:
and it were stranger yet, that God should do so much
for man, and that a man that desires it, that labours
for it, that is in life and possibilities of working his
salvation, should inevitably miss that end for which that
God suffered so much. For what is the meaning, and
what is the extent, and what are the significations of
the divine mercy in pardoning sinners? If it be
thought a great matter that I am charged with original
sin, I confess I feel the weight of it in loads of temporal infelicities, and proclivities to sin: but I fear not
the guilt of it, since I am baptized; and it cannot do
honour to the reputation of God's mercy, that it
should be all spent in remissions of what I never chose,
never acted, never knew of, could not help, concerning which I receive no commandment, no pro-
hibition. But (blessed be God) it is ordered in just
measures, that that original evil which I contracted
without my will should be taken away *without my
knowledge;* and what I suffered before I had a being,
was cleansed before I had an useful understanding.
But I am taught to believe God's mercies to be
infinite, not only *in himself,* but *to us:* for mercy is *a
relative term,* and we are its *correspondents:* of all
the creatures which God made, we only in a proper
sense are the subjects of mercy and remission. Angels
have more of *God's bounty* than we have, but not so
much of *his mercy:* and beasts have little rays of his
kindness, and effects of his wisdom and graciousness
in petty donatives; but nothing of *mercy,* for they
have no laws, and therefore no sins, and need no
mercy,

mercy, nor are capable of any. Since therefore man
alone is the correlative or proper object and vessel of
reception of an infinite mercy, and that mercy is in
giving and *forgiving*, I have reason to hope that he
will so forgive me, that my sins shall not hinder me of
heaven ; or because it is a gift, I may also upon the
stock of the same infinite mercy hope he will give
heaven to me : and if I have it either upon the title of
giving or *forgiving*, it is alike to me, and will alike
magnify the glories of the divine mercy.   * And because *eternal life is the gift of God*, I have less reason
to despair : for if my sins were fewer, and my dispro-
portions towards such a glory were less, and my evenness more, yet it is still a gift, and I could not receive
it but as a free and a gracious donative ; and so I may
still, God can still give it me : and it is not an impossible expectation to wait and look for such a gift at
the hands of *the God of Mercy ;* the best men deserve it
not, and I who am the worst may have it given me.
And I consider that God hath set no measures of his
mercy, but that we be within the covenant, that is,
repenting persons, endeavouring to serve him with an
honest single heart : and that within this covenant there
is a very great latitude, and variety of persons, and
degrees, and capacities ; and therefore that it cannot
stand with the proportions of so infinite a mercy, that
obedience be exacted to such a point (which he never
expressed), unless it should be the least, and that to
which all capacities, though otherwise unequal, are
fitted and sufficiently enabled.   But however, I find
that the spirit of God taught the writers of the New
Testament to apply to us all in general, and to every
single person in particular, some gracious words which
God in the Old Testament spake to one man upon a
special occasion in a single and temporal instance.
Such are the words which God spake to *Joshua :* † *I
will never fail thee nor forsake thee.* And upon the

* Rom. vi. 23.   † Heb. xiii. 5.

stock of that promise St. *Paul* forbids covetousness, and persuades contentedness, because those words were spoken by God to *Joshua* in another case. If the gracious words of God have so great extension of parts, and intention of kind purposes, then how many comforts have we upon the stock of all the excellent words which are spoken in the Prophets and in the Psalms? And I will never more question whether they be spoken concerning me, having such an authentic precedent so to expound the excellent words of God: all the treasures of God which are in the Psalms are my own riches, and the wealth of my hope; there will I look, and whatsoever I can need, that I will depend upon. For certainly if we could understand it, that which is infinite (as God is) must needs be some such kind of thing: it must go whither it was never sent, and signify what was not first intended; and it must warm with its light, and shine with its heat, and refresh when it strikes, and heal when it wounds, and ascertain where it makes afraid, and intend all when it warns one, and mean a great deal in a small word. And as the sun passing to its southern tropic looks with an open eye upon his sun-burnt *Æthiopians*, but at the same time sends light from his posterns, and collaterial influences from the back-side of his beams, and sees the corners of the east when his face tends towards the west, because he is a round body of fire, and hath some little images and resemblances of the infinite: so is God's mercy; when it looked upon *Moses*, it relieved St. *Paul*, and it pardoned *David*, and gave hope to *Manasses*, and might have restored *Judas*, if he would have had hope, and used himself accordingly. * But as to my own case, I have sinned grievously and frequently: but I have repented it, but I have begged pardon, I have confessed it and forsaken it. I cannot undo what was done, and I perish if God hath appointed no remedy, if there

* Vixi, peccavi, pœnitui, naturæ cessi.

be

be no remission : but then my religion falls together with my hope, and God's word fails as well as I. But I believe the article of *forgiveness of sins ;* and if there be any such thing, I may do well, for I have, and do, and will do that which all good men call repentance ; that is, I will be humbled before God, and mourn for my sin, and for ever ask forgiveness, and judge myself, and leave it with haste, and mortify it with diligence, and watch against it carefully. And this I can do but in the manner of a man ; I can but mourn for my sins, as I apprehend grief in other instances : but I will rather choose to suffer all evils than to do one deliberate act of sin. I know my sins are greater than my sorrow, and too many for my memory, and too insinuating to be prevented by all my care : but I know also, that God knows and pities my infirmities; and how far that will extend I know not, but that it will reach so far as to satisfy my needs, is the matter of my hope. But this I am sure of, that I have in my great necessity prayed humbly and with great desire, and sometimes I have been heard in kind, and sometimes have had a bigger mercy instead of it ; and I have *the hope of prayers,* and *the hope of my confession,* and *the hope of my endeavours,* and *the hope of many promises,* and *of God's essential goodness :* and I am sure that God hath heard my prayers, and verified his promises in temporal instances, for he ever gave me sufficient for my life ; and although he promised such supplies, and grounded the confidences of them upon our *first seeking the kingdom of heaven and its righteousness,* yet he hath verified it to me, who have not sought it as I ought : but therefore I hope he accepted my endeavour, or will give his great gifts and our great expectation even to the weakest endeavour, to the least, so it be a hearty piety. And sometimes I have had some cheerful visitations of God's spirit, and my cup hath been crowned with comfort, and the wine that made my heart glad danced in the chalice, and I was glad
that

that God would have me so; and therefore I hope
this cloud may pass: for that which was then a real
cause of comfort, is so still, if I could discern it, and
I shall discern it when the veil is taken from mine
eyes. And (blessed be God) I can still remember
that there are *temptations* to *despair;* and they could
not be temptations if they were not apt to persuade,
and had seeming probability on their side; and they
that despair think they do it with greatest reason; for
if they were not confident of the reason, but that it
were such an argument as might be opposed or suspected, then they could not despair. *Despair assents*
as firmly and as strongly as faith itself: but because it
is a temptation, and despair is a horrid sin, therefore
it is certain those persons are unreasonably abused,
and they have no reason to despair, for all their confidence: and therefore although I have strong reasons
to condemn myself, yet I have more reason to condemn my despair, which therefore is unreasonable because it is a sin, and a dishonour to God, and a ruin
to my condition, and verifies itself, if I do not look to
it. For as the hypochondriac person that thought
himself dead, made his dream true when he starved
himself, because dead people eat not: so despairing sinners lose God's mercies by refusing to use and
to believe them. And I hope it is a disease of judgment, not an intolerable condition, that I am falling
into, because I have been told so concerning others,
who therefore have been afflicted, because they see not
their pardon sealed after the manner of this world, and
the affairs of the spirit are transacted by immaterial
notices, by propositions and spiritual discourses, by
promises which are to be verified hereafter; and here
we must live in a cloud, in darkness under a veil,
in fears and uncertainties, and our very living by
faith and hope is a life of mystery and secrecy, the
only part of the manner of that life in which we
shall live in the state of separation. And when a

s   distemper

distemper of body or an infirmity of mind happens in
the instances of such secret and reversed affairs, we
may easily mistake the manner of our notices for the
uncertainty of the thing: and therefore it is but reason I should stay till the state and manner of my
abode be changed, before I despair: there it can be
no sin nor error, here it may be both; and if it be
that, it is also *this*; and then a man may perish for
being miserable, and be undone for being a fool. In
conclusion, my hope is in God, and I will trust him
with the event, which I am sure will be *just*, and I
hope *full of mercy*. However, now I will use all the
spiritual arts of reason and religion to make me more
and more *to love God*, that if I miscarry, *charity also
shall fail*, and something that loves God shall perish
and be damned; which if it be impossible, then I may
do well.

These considerations may be useful to men *of little
hearts* and *of great piety :* or if they be persons who
have lived without infamy, or begun their repentance
so late that it is very imperfect, and yet so early that
it was before the arrest of death. But if the man be a
vicious person, and hath persevered in a vicious life
till his death-bed; these considerations are not proper. Let him inquire in the words of the first disciples after Pentecost, *Men and brethren what shall we
do to be saved?* And if they can but entertain so much
hope as to enable them to do so much of their duty as
they can for the present, it is all that can be provided
for them: an inquiry in their case can have no other
purposes of religion or prudence. And the minister
must be infinitely careful that he do not go about to
comfort vicious persons with the comforts belonging
to God's elect, lest he prostitute holy things and make
them common, and his sermons deceitful, and vices
be encouraged in others, and the man himself find that
he was deceived, when he descends into his house of
sorrow.

But

But because *very few* men are tempted with too great fears of failing, but very many are tempted by confidence and presumption; the ministers of religion had need be instructed with spiritual armour to resist this fiery dart of the devil, when it operates to evil purposes.

SECT. VI.

Considerations against Presumption.

I HAVE already enumerated many particulars to provoke a drowsy conscience to a scrutiny and to a suspicion of himself, that by seeing cause to suspect his condition, he might more freely accuse himself, and attend to the necessities and duties of repentance : but if either before or in his repentance he grow too big in his spirit, so as either he does some little violence to the modesties of humility, or abates his care and zeal of his repentance, *the spiritual man* must allay his forwardness by representing to him, 1. That the growths in grace are long, difficult, uncertain, hindered, of many parts and great variety. 2. That an infant grace is soon dashed and discountenanced, often running into an inconvenience and the evils of an imprudent conduct, being zealous and forward, and therefore confident, but always with the least reason, and the greatest danger : like children and young fellows, whose confidence hath no other reason but that they understand not their danger and their follies. 3. That *he that puts on his armour ought not to boast, as he that puts it off;* and the apostle chides the *Galatians* for *ending in the flesh after they had begun in the spirit.* 4. That a man cannot think too meanly of himself, but very easily he may think too high. 5. That a wise man will always in a matter of great concern-

s 2   ment

ment think the worst, and a good man will condemn
himself with hearty sentence. 6. That humility and modesty of *judgment* and of *hope* are very good instruments
to procure a mercy and a fair reception at the day of
our death: but presumption or bold opinion serves no
end of God or man, and is always imprudent, ever
fatal, and of all things in the world is its own greatest
enemy : for the more any man presumes, the greater
reason he hath to fear. 7. That a man's heart is infinitely deceitful, unknown to itself, not certain in its
own acts, praying one way, and desiring another, wandering and imperfect, loose and various, worshipping
God, and entertaining sin, following what it hates, and
running from what it flatters, loving to be tempted
and betrayed ; petulant like a wanton girl, running
from, that it might invite the fondness and enrage the
appetite of the foolish young man, or the evil temptation that follows it; cold and indifferent one while,
and presently zealous and passionate, furious and indiscreet : not understood of itself or any one else, and
deceitful beyond all the arts and numbers of observation. 8. That it is certain we have highly sinned
against God, but we are not so certain that our repentance is real and effective, integral and sufficient.
9. That it is not revealed to us whether or no the time
of our repentance be not past; or if it be not, yet how
far God will give us pardon, and upon what condition,
or after what sufferings or duties, is still under a cloud.
10. That virtue and vice are oftentimes so near
neighbours, that we pass into each others borders without observation, and think we do justice when we are
cruel, or call ourselves liberal when we are loose and
foolish in expenses, and are amorous when we commend our own civilities and good nature. 12. That
we allow to ourselves so many little irregularities, that
insensibly they swell to so great a heap, that from
thence we have reason to fear an evil: for an army of
frogs and flies may destroy all the hopes of our harvest.
12. That

12. That when we do that which is lawful, and do all that we can in those bounds, we commonly and easily run out of our proportions.   13. That it is not easy to distinguish the virtues of our nature from the virtues of our choice; and we may expect the reward of *Temperance*, when it is against our nature to be drunk; or we hope to have the coronet of virgins for our morose disposition, or our abstinence from marriage upon secular ends.   14. That it may be we call every little sigh or the keeping a fish-day the duty of repentance, or have entertained false principles in the estimate and measures of virtues; and, contrary to that steward in the Gospel, we write down fourscore when we should set down but fifty.   15. That it is better to trust the goodness and justice of God with our accounts, than to offer him large bills.   16. That we are commanded by Christ to *sit down in the lowest place*, till *the master of the house bids us sit up higher*. 17. That *when we have done all that we can, we are unprofitable servants:* and yet no man does all that he can do; and therefore is more to be despised and undervalued.   18. That the self-accusing publican was justified rather than the thanksgiving and confident Pharisee.   19. That if *Adam* in Paradise, and *David* in his house, and *Solomon* in the temple, and *Peter* in Christ's family, and *Judas* in the college of apostles, and *Nicholas* among the deacons, and the angels in heaven itself did fall so foully and dishonestly; then it is prudent advice that we *be not high-minded, but fear*, and when we stand most confidently, *take heed lest we fall:* and yet there is nothing so likely to make us fall as pride and great opinions, which ruined the angels, which God resists, which all men despise, and which betray us into carelessness, and a wretchless, undiscerning, and unwary spirit.

4. Now the main parts of the ecclesiastical ministry are done, and that which remains is, that the

minister

minister *pray over him*, and remind him to do good actions as he is capable; to call upon God for pardon, to put his whole trust in him, to resign himself to God's disposing, to be patient and even, to renounce every ill word, or thought, or undecent action, which the violence of his sickness may cause him, to beg of God to give him his holy spirit to guide him in his agony, and his holy angels to guard him in his passage.

5. Whatsoever is besides this concerns the standers-by: that they do all in their ministeries diligently and temperately; that they join with much charity and devotion in the prayer of the minister; that they make no outcries or exclamations in the departure of the soul; and that they make no judgment concerning the dying person, by his dying quietly, or violently, with comfort or without, with great fears or a cheerful confidence, with sense or without, like a lamb or like a lion, with convulsions or semblances of great pain, or like an expiring and a spent candle: for these happen to all men, without rule, without any known reason, but according as God pleases to dispense the grace or the punishment, for reasons only known to himself. Let us lay our hands upon our mouth, and adore the mysteries of the divine wisdom and providence, and pray to God to give the dying man rest and pardon, and to ourselves grace to live well, and the blessing of a holy and a happy death.

SECT. VII.

Offices to be said by the Minister in his Visitation of the Sick.

In the name of the Father, of the Son, and of the Holy Ghost.

Our Father, which art in Heaven, &c.

Let

Let the Priest say this Prayer secretly.

O Eternal *Jesus*, thou great lover of souls, who hast constituted a ministry in the church to glorify thy name, and to serve in the assistance of those that come to thee, professing thy discipline and service, give grace to me, the unworthiest of thy servants, that I in this my ministry may purely and zealously intend thy glory, and effectually may minister comfort and advantages to this sick person, (whom God assoil from all his offences:) and grant that nothing of thy grace may perish to him by the unworthiness of the minister; but let thy spirit speak by me, and give me prudence and charity, wisdom and diligence, good observation and apt discourses, a certain judgment and merciful dispensation, that the soul of thy servant may pass from this state of imperfection to the perfections of the state of glory, through thy mercies, O Eternal *Jesus. Amen.*

The Psalm.

* *Out of the depths have I cried unto thee, O Lord.*

Lord, hear my voice: let thine ears be attentive to the voice of my supplications.

If thou, Lord, shouldst mark iniquities, O Lord, who should stand?

But there is forgiveness with thee, that thou mayest be feared.

I wait for the Lord, my soul doth wait; and in his word do I hope.

My soul waiteth for the Lord, more than they that watch for the morning.

Let Israel hope in the Lord; for with the Lord there is mercy, and with him is plenteous redemption.

And he shall redeem his servants from all their iniquities.

† *Wherefore should I fear in the days of evil, when the wickedness of my heels shall compass me about?*

No man can by any means redeem his brother, nor give to God a ransom for him:

---

* Psalm cxxx. † Psalm xlix. 5. 7, 8, 9, 10. 15.

(*For*

(For the redemption of their soul is precious, and it ceaseth for ever.)

That he should still live for ever, and not see corruption.

But wise men die, likewise the fool and the brutish person perish, and leave their wealth to others.

But God will redeem my soul from the power of the grave: for he shall receive me.

* *As for me, I will behold thy face in righteousness: I shall be satisfied when I awake in thy likeness.*

† *Thou shalt show me the path of life: in thy presence is the fulness of joy; at thy right hand there are pleasures for evermore.*

Glory be to the Father, &c.

As it was in the beginning, &c.

Let us pray.

Almighty God, Father of mercies, the God of peace and comfort, of rest and pardon, we thy servants, though unworthy to pray to thee, yet, in duty to thee, and charity to our brother, humbly beg mercy of thee for him to descend upon his body and his soul; one sinner, O Lord, for another, the miserable for the afflicted, the poor for him that is in need: but thou givest thy graces and thy favours by the measures of thy own mercies, and in proportion to our necessities. We humbly come to thee in the name of *Jesus*, for the merit of our Saviour, and the mercies of our God, praying thee to pardon the sins of this thy servant, and to put them all upon the accounts of the cross, and to bury them in the grave of *Jesus*, that they may never rise up in judgment against thy servant, nor bring him to shame and confusion of face in the day of final enquiry and sentence. *Amen.*

II.

Give thy servant patience in his sorrows, comfort in this his sickness, and restore him to health, if it seem

---

* Psalm xvii. 15.   † Psalm xvi. 11.

good

good to thee, in order to thy great ends, and his greatest interest. And however thou shalt determine concerning him in this affair, yet make his repentance perfect, and his passage safe, and his faith strong, and his hope modest and confident; that when thou shalt call his soul from the prison of the body, it may enter into the securities and rest of the sons of God, in the bosom of blessedness, and the custodies of *Jesus*. *Amen*.

III.

Thou, O Lord, knowest all the necessities and all the infirmities of thy servant: fortify his spirit with spiritual joys and perfect resignation, and take from him all degrees of inordinate or insecure affections to this world, and enlarge his heart with desires of being with thee, and of freedom from sins, and fruition of God.

IV.

Lord, let not any pain or passion discompose the order and decency of his thoughts and duty; and lay no more upon thy servant than thou wilt make him able to bear, and together with the temptation do thou provide a way to escape; even by the mercies of a longer and a more holy life, or by the mercies of a blessed death: even as it pleaseth thee, O Lord, so let it be.

V.

Let the tenderness of his conscience and the spirit of God call to mind his sins, that they may be confessed and repented of: because thou hast promised that if we confess our sins, we shall have mercy. Let thy mighty grace draw out from his soul every root of bitterness, lest the remains of the old man be accursed with the reserves of thy wrath: but in the union of the Holy *Jesus*, and in the charities of God and of the world, and the communion of all the saints, let his

soul

soul be presented to thee blameless, and entirely pardoned, and thoroughly washed, through *Jesus* Christ
our Lord.

*Here also may be inserted the Prayers set down after
the Holy Communion is administered.*

The Prayer of St. *Eustratius* the Martyr, to be used
by the sick or dying man, or by the priests or assistants in his behalf, which he said when he was going
to martyrdom.

I will praise thee, O Lord, that thou hast considered
my low estate, and hast not shut me up in the hands
of mine enemies, nor made my foes to rejoice over
me : and now let thy right hand protect me, and let
thy mercy come upon me ; for my soul is in trouble
and anguish because of its departure from the body.
O let not the assemblies of its wicked and cruel enemies meet it in the passing forth, nor hinder me by
reason of the sins of my passed life. O Lord, be
favourable unto me, that my soul may not behold the
hellish countenance of the spirits of darkness, but let
thy bright and joyful angels entertain it. Give glory
to thy holy name and to thy majesty : place me by thy
merciful arm before thy seat of judgment, and let not
the hand of the prince of this world snatch me from
thy presence, or bear me into hell. Mercy, sweet
Jesu. Amen.

A prayer taken out of the *Euchólogion* of the Greek
Church, to be said by or in behalf of people in their
danger, or near their death.

Βεβορβορομένος ταῖς ἁμαρλίαις, &c.

I.

Bemired with sins and naked of good deeds, I that
am the meat of worms cry vehemently in spirit : cast
not me wretch away from thy face ; place me not on
the left hand who with thy hands didst fashion me ;
but give rest unto my soul, for thy great mercies' sake,
O Lord.

Suppli-

II.

Supplicate with tears unto Christ, who is to judge my poor soul, that he will deliver me from the fire that is unquenchable. I pray you all, my friends and acquaintance, make mention of me in your prayers, that in the day of judgment I may find mercy at that dreadful tribunal.

III.

Then may the standers-by pray.

When in unspeakable glory thou dost come dreadfully to judge the whole world, vouchsafe, O gracious Redeemer, that this thy faithful servant may in the clouds meet thee cheerfully. They who have been dead from the beginning, with terrible and fearful trembling stand at thy tribunal, waiting thy just sentence, O blessed Saviour *Jesus.* None shall there avoid thy formidable and most righteous judgment. All kings and princes with servants stand together, and hear the dreadful voice of the judge condemning the people which have sinned into hell: from which sad sentence, O Christ, deliver thy servant. *Amen.*

Then let the sick man be called upon to rehearse the Articles of his faith; or, if be so weak he cannot, let him (if he have not before done it) be called to say Amen, when they are recited, or to give some testimony of his faith and confident assent to them.

After which it is proper (if the person be in capacity) that the minister examine him, and invite him to confession, and all the parts of repentance, according to the foregoing rules; after which, he may pray this prayer of absolution.

Our Lord *Jesus* Christ, who hath given commission to his church, in his name to pronounce pardon to all that are truly penitent, he of his mercy pardon and forgive thee all, thy sins, deliver thee from all evils past, present, and future, preserve thee in the faith and fear of his only name to thy life's end, and bring thee

to

to his everlasting kingdom, to live with him for ever and ever. *Amen.*

Then let the sick man renounce all heresies, and what-soever is against the truth of God, or the peace of the church, and pray for pardon for all his ignorances and errors, known and unknown.

After which let him (if all other circumstances be fitted) be disposed to receive the blessed sacrament, in which the curate is to minister according to the form prescribed by the church.

When the rites are finished, let the sick man in the days of his sickness be employed with the former offices and exercises before-described: and when the time draws near of his dissolution, the minister may assist by the following order of recommendation of the soul.

I.

O holy and most gracious Saviour *Jesus*, we humbly recommend the soul of thy servant into thy hands, thy most merciful hands; let thy blessed angels stand in ministry about thy servant, and defend him from the violence and malice of all his ghostly enemies, and drive far from hence all the spirits of darkness. *Amen.*

II.

Lord, receive the soul of this thy servant: enter not into judgment with thy servant: spare him whom thou hast redeemed with thy most precious blood: deliver him from all evil for whose sake thou didst suffer all evil and mischief; from the crafts and assaults of the devil, from the fear of death, and from everlasting death, good Lord, deliver him. *Amen.*

III.

Impute not unto him the follies of his youth, nor any of the errors and miscarriages of his life: but strengthen him in his agony, let not his faith waver, nor his hope fail, nor his charity be disordered: let

none

none of his enemies imprint upon him any afflictive or evil phantasm; let him die in peace, and rest in hope, and rise in glory. *Amen.*

IV.

Lord, we know and believe assuredly, that whatsoever is under thy custody cannot be taken out of thy hands, nor by all the violences of hell robbed of thy protection, preserve the work of thy hands, rescue him from all evil; take into the participation of thy glories him to whom thou hast given the seal of adoption, the earnest of the inheritance of the saints. *Amen.*

V.

Let his portion be with *Abraham, Isaac,* and *Jacob,* with *Job* and *David,* with the prophets and apostles, with martyrs and all thy holy saints, in the arms of Christ, in the bosom of felicity, in the kingdom of God to eternal ages. *Amen.*

These following prayers are fit also to be added to the foregoing Offices, in case there be no communion or intercourse but prayer.

Let us pray.

O Almighty and eternal God, there is no number of thy days or of thy mercies: thou hast sent us into this world to serve thee, and to live according to thy laws; but we by our sins have provoked thee to wrath, and we have planted thorns and sorrows round about our dwellings: and our life is but a span long, and yet very tedious, because of the calamities that inclose us in on every side; the days of our pilgrimage are few and evil; we have frail and sickly bodies, violent and distempered passions, long designs and but a short stay, weak understandings and strong enemies, abused fancies, perverse wills. O dear God, look upon us in mercy and pity: let not our weaknesses make us to sin against thee, nor our fear cause us to betray our duty, nor our former follies provoke thy eternal anger, nor the calamities of this world vex us into

2

tediousness

tediousness of spirit and impatience : but let thy Holy
Spirit lead us through this valley of misery with safety
and peace, with holiness and religion, with spiritual
comforts and joy in the Holy Ghost; that when we
have served thee in our generations, we may be
gathered unto our fathers, having the testimony of a
holy conscience, in the communion of the Catholic
church, in the confidence of a certain faith, and the
comforts of a reasonable, religious, and holy hope, and
perfect charity with thee our God and all the world,
that neither death nor life, nor angels, nor principali-
ties, nor powers, nor things present, nor things to come,
nor heighth, nor depth, nor any other creature may be
able to separate us from the love of God, which is in
Christ *Jesus* our Lord. *Amen.*

II.

O holy and most gracious Saviour *Jesus,* in whose
hands the souls of all faithful people are laid up till
the day of recompence, have mercy upon the body
and soul of this thy servant, and upon all thy elect
people who love the Lord *Jesus,* and long for his
coming. Lord, refresh the imperfection of their condition with the aids of the spirit of grace and comfort,
and with the visitation and guard of angels, and supply to them all their necessities known only unto thee ;
let them dwell in peace, and feel thy mercies pitying
their infirmities, and the follies of their flesh, and
speedily satisfying the desires of their spirits; and
when thou shalt bring us all forth in the day of judgment, O then show thyself to be our Saviour *Jesus,*
our advocate, and our judge. Lord, then remember
that thou hast for so many ages prayed for the pardon
of those sins which thou art then to sentence. Let not
the accusations of our consciences, nor the calumnies
and aggravation of devils, nor the effects of thy wrath
press those souls which thou lovest, which thou didst
redeem, which thou dost pray for; but enable us all
by

by the supporting hand of thy mercy to stand upright in judgment. O Lord, have mercy upon us, have mercy upon us : O Lord, let thy mercy lighten upon us, as our trust is in thee. O Lord, in thee have we trusted, let us never be confounded. Let us meet with joy, and for ever dwell with thee, feeling thy pardon, supported with thy graciousness, absolved by thy sentence, saved by thy mercy, that we may sing to the glory of thy name eternal hallelujahs. *Amen. Amen. Amen.*

Then may be added in the behalf of all that are present these ejaculations.

O spare us a little, that we may recover our strength before we go hence and be no more seen. *Amen.*

Cast us not away in the time of age ; O forsake us not when strength faileth. *Amen.*

Grant that we may never sleep in sin or death eternal, but that we may have our part of the first resurrection, and that the second death may not prevail over us. *Amen.*

Grant that our souls may be bound up in the bundle of life ; and in the day when thou bindest up thy jewels, remember thy servants for good, and not for evil, that our souls may be numbered amongst the righteous. *Amen.*

Grant unto all sick and dying Christians mercy and aids from heaven, and receive the souls returning unto thee, whom thou hast redeemed with thy most precious blood. *Amen.*

Grant unto thy servants to have faith in the Lord *Jesus*, a daily meditation of death, a contempt of the world, a longing desire after heaven, patience in our sorrows, comfort in our sicknesses, joy in God, a holy life, and a blessed death ; that our souls may rest in hope, and my body may rise in glory, and both may be beautified in the communion of saints, in the kingdom of God, and the glories of the Lord *Jesus. Amen.*

The Blessing.

* Now the God of peace that brought again from the dead our Lord *Jesus*, that great shepherd of the sheep, through the blood of the everlasting covenant, make you perfect in every good work, to do his will, working in you that which is pleasing in his sight ; to whom be glory for ever and ever. *Amen.*

The Doxology.

† To the blessed and only potentate, the King of Kings, and the Lord of Lords, who only hath immortality dwelling in the light which no man can approach unto, whom no man hath seen nor can see, be honour and power everlasting. *Amen.*

After the sick man is departed, the minister, if he be present, or the major domo, or any other fit person, may use the following prayers in behalf of themselves.

I.

Almighty God, with whom do live the spirits of them that depart hence in the Lord, we adore thy majesty, and submit to thy providence, and revere thy justice, and magnify thy mercies, thy infinite mercies, that it hath pleased thee to deliver this our brother out of the miseries of this sinful world. Thy counsels are secret, and thy wisdom is infinite : with the same hand thou hast crowned him, and smitten us; thou hast taken him into regions of felicity, and placed him among the saints and angels, and left us to mourn for our sins, and thy displeasure, which thou hast signified to us by removing him from us to a better, a far better place. Lord turn thy anger into mercy, thy chastisements into virtues, thy rod into comforts, and do thou give to all his nearest relatives comforts from heaven, and a restitution of blessings equal to those which thou

---

* Heb. xiii. 20, 21. † 1 Tim. vi. 15, 16.

hast

hast taken from them. And we humbly beseech thee of thy gracious goodness shortly to satisfy the longing desires of those holy souls who pray, and wait, and long for thy second coming. Accomplish thou the number of thine elect, and fill up the mansions in heaven, which are prepared for all them that love the coming of the Lord *Jesus*; that we, with this our brother, and all others departed this life in the obedience and faith of the Lord *Jesus*, may have our perfect consummation and bliss in thy eternal glory, which never shall have ending. Grant this for *Jesus* Christ his sake our Lord and only Saviour. *Amen.*

II.

O MERCIFUL God, Father of our Lord *Jesus*, who is the first fruits of the resurrection, and by entering into glory hath opened the kingdom of heaven to all believers, we humbly beseech thee to raise us up from the death of sin to the life of righteousness, that being partakers of the death of Christ, and followers of his holy life, we may be partakers of his spirit and of his promises; that when we shall depart this life, we may rest in his arms, and lie in his bosom, as our hope is this our brother doth. O suffer us not for any temptation of the world, or any snares of the devil, or any pains of death, to fall from thee. Lord, let thy holy spirit enable us with his grace to fight a good fight with perseverance, to finish our course with holiness, and to keep the faith with constancy unto the end; that at the day of judgment we may stand at the right hand of the throne of God, and hear the blessed sentence of *Come, ye blessed children of my Father, receive the kingdom prepared for you from the beginning of the world.* O blessed *Jesus*, thou art our judge, and thou art our advocate; even because thou art good and gracious, never suffer us to fall into the intolerable pains of hell, never to lie down in sin, and never to have our portion in the everlasting burning. Mercy, sweet *Jesu*, mercy. *Amen.*

T

A Prayer

A Prayer to be said in the case of a sudden surprise by Death, as by a mortal wound, or evil accidents in child-birth, when the forms and solemnities of preparation cannot be used.

O MOST gracious Father, Lord of Heaven and Earth, judge of the living and the dead, behold thy servants running to thee for pity and mercy in behalf of ourselves and this thy servant whom thou hast smitten with thy hasty rod, and a swift angel; if it be thy will, preserve his life, that there may be place for his repentance and restitution: O spare him a little, that he may recover his strength before he go hence and be no more seen. But if thou hast otherwise decreed, let the miracles of thy compassion and thy wonderful mercy supply to him the want of the usual measures of time, and the periods of repentance, and the trimming of his lamp: and let the greatness of the calamity be accepted by thee as an instrument to procure pardon for those defects and degrees of unreadiness which may have caused this accident upon thy servant. Lord, stir up in him a great and effectual contrition: that the greatness of the sorrow, and hatred against sin, and the zeal of his love to thee, may in a short time do the work of many days. And thou who regardest the heart and the measures of the mind more than the delay and the measures of time, let it be thy pleasure to rescue the soul of thy servant from all the evils he hath deserved, and all the evils that he fears; that in the glorifications of eternity, and the songs which to eternal ages thy saints and holy angels shall sing to the honour of thy mighty name and invaluable mercies, it may be reckoned among thy glories, that thou hast redeemed this soul from the dangers of an eternal death, and made him partaker of *the gift of God, eternal life,* through *Jesus* Christ our Lord. *Amen.*

If there be time, the prayers in the forgoing offices may be added, according as they can be fitted to the present circumstances.

SECT. VIII.

A Peroration concerning the Contingencies and Treatings of our departed Friends after Death, in order to their Burial, &c.

* When we have received the last breath of our friend, and closed his eyes, and composed his body for the grave, then seasonable is the counsel of the son of *Sirach ;* † *Weep bitterly, and make great moan, and use lamentation, as he is worthy, and that a day or two, lest thou be evil spoken of; and then comfort thyself for thy heaviness. But take no grief to heart ; for there is no turning again : thou shalt not do him good, but hurt thyself.* Solemn and appointed mournings are good expressions of our dearness to the departed soul, and of his worth, and our value of him ; and it hath its praise in nature, and in manners and ‡ public customs; but *the praise of it is not in the Gospel,* that is, it hath no direct and proper uses in religion. For if *the dead* did *die in the Lord,* then there is joy to him ; § and it is an ill expression of our affection and our charity, to weep uncomfortably at a change that hath carried my friend to the state of a huge felicity. ‖ But if the man did perish in his folly and his sins, there is indeed cause to mourn, but no hopes of being comforted ; for he shall never return to light, or to hopes of restitution. Therefore beware lest thou also come into the same place of torment ; and let thy grief sit down and rest upon thy own turf, and weep till a shower springs from thy eyes to heal

---

* Τάδε δ' ἀμφιποιησόμεθ' ὅισι μάλιςα
Κήδεός ἐςι νέκυς.　　　　　　*Iliad.* ψ.

† Ecclus. xxxviii. 17. 20.

‡ Ὡς γενναίως ἀποδεδάκρυκέ με, *dixit* Socrates *de* Ergastulario *lugente.*

§ Nemo me lacrymis decoret, nec funera fletu
　　Faxit : cur ? volito vivu per ora virúm.　　*Ennius.*

‖ Πέρσας μέντοι πάντας ἐπὶ τὸ μνῆμα τῠμὸν παρακαλεῖτε συνισθησομένας ἐμοὶ, ὅτι ἐν τῷ ἀσφαλεῖ ἤδη ἔσομαι, ὡς μηδὲν ἂν ἔτι κακὸν παθεῖν, μήτε ἢν μετὰ τῦ θείῃ γένομαι, μήτε ἢν μηδὲν ἔτι ὦ.　　　Cyrus *apud* Xenoph.

T 2　　　　　　　　　　　　the

the wounds of thy spirit : turn thy sorrow into caution, thy grief for him that is dead, to thy care for thyself, who art alive ; lest thou die and fall like one of the fools, whose life is worse than death, and their death is the consummation of all felicities.   * The church in her funerals of the dead used to sing psalms, and to give thanks for the redemption and delivery of the soul from the evils and dangers of mortality. And therefore we have no reason to be angry when God hears our prayers, who call upon him to hasten his coming, and to fill up his numbers, and to do that which we pretend to give him thanks for. And St. *Chrysostom* asks, To what purpose is it that thou singest, *Return unto thy rest, O my soul,* &c. if thou dost not believe thy friend to be in rest ? and if thou dost, why dost thou weep impertinently and unreasonably ? † Nothing but our own loss can justly be deplored : and him that is passionate for the loss of his money or his advantages, we esteem foolish and imperfect ; and therefore have no reason to love the immoderate sorrows of those who too earnestly mourn for their dead, when in the last resolution of the enquiry, it is their own evil and present or feared inconveniences they deplore : the best that can be said of such a grief is, that those mourners love themselves too well. Something is to be given to custom, something to fame, to nature, and to civilities, and to the honour of the deceased friends ; for that man is esteemed to die miserable, for whom no friend or relative sheds a tear, or pays a solemn sigh. ‡ I desire to *die a dry death,* but am not very desirous to have a *dry funeral :* some showers sprinkled upon my grave would do well and comely ; and a soft shower to turn those flowers into a springing memory or a fair rehearsal,

---

* S. *Chrysost. hom.* iv. *Heb.*
† Πάτροκλον κλαίωμεν, ὁ γὰρ γέρας ἐςὶ θανόντων.   *Iliad.* ↓ .
‡ Mors optima est, perire dum lacrymant sui.   *Sen. Hippol.*
   Μηδέ μοι ἄκλαυς☉ θάνατ☉ μόλοι, ἀλλὰ φιλοῖσι
   Καλλείποιμι θανὼν ἄλγεα καὶ ςοναχάς.

that

that I may not go forth of my doors as my servants carry the entrails of beasts.

But that which is to be faulted in this particular is, when the grief is immoderate and unreasonable : and *Paula Romana* deserved to have felt the weight of St. *Hierom*'s severe reproof, when at the death of every of her children, she almost wept herself into her grave. But it is worse yet, when people by an ambitious and a pompous sorrow, and by ceremonies invented for the * ostentation of their grief, fill heaven and earth with † exclamations, and grow troublesome because their friend is happy, or themselves want his company. It is certainly a sad thing in nature, to see a friend trembling with a palsy, or scorched with fevers, or *dried up like a potsherd* with immoderate heats and rolling upon his uneasy bed without sleep, which cannot be ‡ invited with music, or pleasant murmurs, or a decent stillness : nothing but the servants of cold death, *poppy* and *weariness,* can tempt the eyes to let their curtains down, and then they sleep only to taste of death, and make an essay of the shades below : and yet we weep not here : the period and opportunity for tears we choose when our friend is fallen asleep, when he hath laid his neck upon the lap of his mother, and let his § head down to be raised up to heaven. This grief is ill-placed and undecent. But many times it is worse : and it hath been observed that those greater and stormy passions do so spend the whole stock of grief, that they presently admit a comfort and contrary affection ; while a sorrow that is even and temperate

* Expectavimus lacrymas ad ostentationem doloris paratas ; ut ergò ambitiosus detonuit, texit superbum pallio caput, et manibus inter se usque ad articulorum strepitum contritis, &c. *Petron.*

† 'Ως δὲ πατὴρ ὃ παιδὸς ὀδύρεται ὅςεα καίων
Νυμφίω, ὅς τε θανὼν δειλὼς ἀκάχησε τοκῆας.
'Ως Ἀχιλλεὺς ἑταίροιο ὀδύρετο ὅςεα καίων,
Ἐρπύζων παρὰ πυρκαιὴν, ἀδινὰ ςεναχίζων.

‡ Non Siculæ dapes dulcem elaborabunt soporem, non avium citharæque cantus somnum reducent.

§ ——Tremulúmque caput descendere jussit
In cœlum et longam manantia labra salivam.

T 3   goes

goes on to its period with expectation and the distances of a just time. The *Ephesian woman* that the
soldier told of in *Petronius* was the talk of all the
town, and the rarest example of a dear affection to her
husband. She descend with the corpse into the
vault, and there being attended with her maiden,
resolved to weep to death, or die with famine or a
distempered sorrow ; from which resolution nor his nor
her friends, nor the reverence of the principal citizens,
who used the entreaties of their charity and their
power, could persuade her. But a soldier that
watched seven dead bodies hanging upon trees just
over-against this monument, crept in, and awhile
stared upon the silent and comely disorders of the
sorrow ; and having let the wonder awhile breathe out
at each other's eyes, at last he fetched his supper and
a bottle of wine, with purpose to eat and drink, and
still to feed himself with that sad prettiness. His pity
and first draught of wine made him bold and curious
to try if the maid would drink ; who, having many
hours since felt her resolution faint as her wearied
body, took his kindness ; and the light returned into
her eyes, and danced like boys in a festival : and fearing lest the pertinaciousness of her mistress's sorrows
should cause her evil to revert, or her shame to approach, assayed whether she would endure to hear an
argument to persuade her to drink and live. The
violent passion had laid all her spirits in wildness and
dissolution, and the maid found them willing to be
gathered into order at the arrest of any new object,
being weary of the first, of which like leeches they
had sucked their fill, till they fell down and burst. The
weeping woman took her cordial, and was not angry
with her maid, and heard the soldier talk. And he
was so pleased with the change, that he, who first
loved the silence of the sorrow, was more in love with
the music of her returning voice, especially which
himself had strung, and put in tune ; and the man began to talk amorously, and the woman's weak head and
heart

heart were soon possessed with a little wine, and grew
gay, and talked, and fell in love; and that very night,
in the morning of her passion, in the grave of her husband, in the pomps of mourning, and in her funeral
garments, married her new and stranger guest. For
so the wild foragers of *Libya* being spent with heat,
and dissolved by the too fond kisses of the sun, do
melt with their common fires, and die with faintness,
and descend with motions slow and unable to the little
brooks that descend from heaven in the wilderness;
and when they drink they return into the vigour of a
new life, and contract strange marriages; and the
lioness is courted by a panther, and she listens to his
love, and conceives a monster that all men call unnatural, and the daughter of an equivocal passion and of
a sudden refreshment. And so also was it in the cave
at *Ephesus;* for by this time the soldier began to think
it was fit he should return to his watch, and observe
the dead bodies he had in charge; but when he
ascended from his mourning bridal chamber, he found
that one of the bodies was stolen by the friends of the
dead, and that he was fallen into an evil condition,
because by the laws of *Ephesus* his body was to be
fixed in the place of it. The poor man returns to his
woman, cries out bitterly, and in her presence resolves
to die to prevent his death, and *in secret to prevent
his shame.* But now the woman's *love was raging*
like her former sadness, and grew witty, and she comforted her soldier, and persuaded him to live, lest by
losing him, who had brought her from death and a
more grievous sorrow, she should return to her old
solemnities of dying, and lose her honour for a dream,
or the reputation of her constancy without the change
and satisfaction of an enjoyed love. The man would
fain have lived, if it had been possible, and she found
out this way for him; that he should take the body of
her first husband, whose funeral she had so strangely
mourned, and put it upon the gallows in the place of
the stolen thief. He did so, and escaped the present

T 4 danger,

danger, to possess a love which might change as violently as her grief had done.   But so I have seen a
crowd of disordered people rush violently and in
heaps till their utmost border was restrained by a wall,
or had spent the fury of their first fluctuation and
watery progress, and by and by it returned to the
contrary with the same earnestness, only because it
was violent and ungoverned.   A raging passion is the
crowd, which, when it is not under discipline and the
conduct of reason, and the proportions of temperate
humanity, runs passionately the way it happens, and
by and by as greedily to another side, being swayed
by its own weight, and driven any whither by chance,
in all its pursuits having no rule, but to do all it can,
and spend itself in haste, and expire with some shame
and much undecency.

When thou hast wept awhile, compose the body to
burial ; which that it be done gravely, decently, and
charitably, we have the example of all nations to
engage us, and of all ages of the world to warrant ;
so that it is against *common honesty, and public fame
and reputation,* not to do this office.

It is good that the body be kept veiled and secret,
and not exposed to curious eyes, or the dishonours
wrought by the changes of death discerned and stared
upon by impertinent persons.   When *Cyrus* was dying,
he called his sons and friends to take their leave,
to touch his hand, to see him the last time, and gave
in charge, that when he had put his veil over his face,
no man should uncover it.   And *Epiphanius's* body
was rescued from inquisitive eyes by a miracle.   Let
it be interred after the * manner of the country, and
the laws of the place, and the dignity of the person.
For so *Jacob* was buried with great solemnity, and
Joseph's bones were carried into *Canaan* after they
had been embalmed and kept four hundred years ; and

* Νόμοις ἕπεσθαι τοῖσιν ἐγχώροις καλῶς.
Τύμβον δ' ὃ ὃ μάλα πολλὸν ἰγὼ πονέεσθαι ἀνοιγᾶ,
'Αλλ' ἐπιεικία τοῖον.   *Iliad.* ψ.

devout

devout men carried St. *Stephen to his burial, making great lamentation over him.* And *Ælian* tells *, that those who were the most excellent persons were buried in purple; and men of an ordinary courage and fortune had their graves only trimmed with branches of olive, and mourning flowers. But when *Mark Antony* gave the body of *Brutus* to his freedman to be buried honestly, he gave also his own mantle to be thrown into his funeral pile: and the magnificence of the old funeral we may see largely described by *Virgil* in the Obsequies of *Misenus,* and by *Homer* in the funeral of *Patroclus.* It was noted for piety in the men of *Jabesh Gilead,* that they showed kindness to their lord *Saul,* and buried him; and they did it honourably. And our blessed Saviour who was temperate in his expense, and grave in all the parts of his life and death as age and sobriety itself, yet was pleased to admit the cost of *Mary's* ointment upon his head and feet, because she did it against his burial: and though she little thought it had been so nigh, yet because he accepted it for that end, he knew he had made her apology sufficient: by which he remarked it to be a great act of piety, and honourable, to inter our friends and relatives according to the proportions of their condition, and so to give a testimony of our hope of their resurrection.† So far is piety, beyond it may be the ostentation and bragging of a grief, or a design to serve worse ends. Such was that of *Herod,* when he made too studied and elaborate a funeral for *Aristobulus,* whom he had murdered; and of *Regulus* for his boy, at whose pile he killed dogs, nightingales, parrots, and little horses: ‡ and such also was the

* *Lib.* vi. *Var. histor. cap.* vi.   Τὰς τελέως ἀριστεύσαντας ἐν φοινικίδι ταφῆναι.
† Cum quid sibi saxa cavata,
    quid pulchra volunt monumenta,
    nisi quòd res creditur illis
    non mortua, sed data somno?   *Prud.* hymn. in Exeq. defunct.
‡ ——— Cupit omnia ferre
    Prodigus, et totos melior succendere censns,
    Desertas exosus opes ———   *Statius,* lib. ii. Sylvar.

expense

2

82 HOLY DYING.

expense of some of the *Romans*, who hating their left
wealth, gave order by their testament to have huge
portions of it thrown into their fires, bathing their
locks, which were presently to pass through the fire,
with *Arabian* and *Egyptian* liquors, and balsam of
Judea. In this, as in every thing else, as our pity
must not pass into superstition or vain expense, so
neither must the excess be turned into parsimony, and
chastised by negligence and impiety to the memory of
their dead.

  * But nothing of this concerns the dead in real and
effective purposes; nor is it with care to be provided
for by themselves : but it is the duty of the living ; for
to them it is all one whether they be carried forth
upon a chariot or a wooden bier, whether they rot in
the air or in the earth, whether they be devoured by
fishes or by worms, by birds or by sepulchral dogs, by
water or by fire, or by delay. † When *Criton* asked
Socrates how he would be buried, he told him, I think
I shall escape from you, and that you cannot catch
me ; but so much of me as you can apprehend, use it
as you see cause for, and bury it ; but however do it
according to the laws. ‡ There is nothing in this but
opinion and the decency of fame to be served.
Where ‖ it is esteemed an honour and the manner of
blessed people to descend into the graves of their
fathers, there also it is reckoned as a curse to be buried
in a strange land, or that the birds of the air devour
them. § Some nations used to eat the bodies of their
friends, and esteemed that the most honoured sepul-
ture ; but they were barbarous. The *Magi* never
buried any but such as were torn of beasts. The
Persians besmeared their dead with wax, and the

* Totus hic locus contemnendus est in nobis, non negligendus in nostris.
                                                                    Cicero.

+ Id cinerem aut manes credis curare sepultos?
‡ Ὅπως ἄν σοι φίλον ᾖ, καὶ μάλιϛα ἤγη νόμιμον εἶναι.
‖ Fugientibus Trojanis minatus est Hector.
§ Αὐτῶ οἱ θάνατον μητίσσομαι, ἀδέ νυ τύνγε
   Γνωτοί τε γνωταί τε πυρὸς λελάχωσι θανόντα,
   Ἀλλὰ κύνις ἐρύϛσι πρὸ ἄϛε☺· ἡμιῖεροιο.

                                                    Iliad. ν.
                                                    Egyptians

Egyptians with gums, and with great art did condite the bodies, and laid them in charnel-houses. But *Cyrus* the elder would none of all this, but gave command that his body should be interred, not laid in a coffin of gold or silver, but just into the earth*, from whence all living creatures receive birth and nourishment, and whither they must return. Among Christians the honour which is valued in the behalf of the dead is, that they be buried in holy ground, that is, in appointed cemeteries, in places of religion, there where the field of God is sown with the seeds of the resurrection, † that their bodies also may be among the Christians, with whom their hope and their portion is, and shall be for ever. *Quicquid feceris, omnia hæc eodem ventura sunt.* That we are sure of; our bodies shall all be restored to our souls hereafter, and in the interval they shall all be turned into dust, by what way soever you or your chance shall dress them. *Licinus* ‡ the freed man slept in a marble tomb; but *Cato* in a little one; *Pompey* in none: and yet they had the best fate among the *Romans*, and a memory of the biggest honour. And it may happen that to want a monument may best preserve their memories, while the succeeding ages shall by their instances remember the changes of the world, and the dishonours of death, and the equality of the dead. And § *James* the Fourth, King of the *Scots*, obtained an epitaph for wanting of a tomb: and King *Stephen* is remembered

---

* Τί γὰρ τότε μακαριώτερον, τῇ γῇ μιχθῆναι, ἢ πάντα μὲν τὰ καλὰ πάντα τ᾽ ἀγαθὰ φύει τε καὶ τρέφει.   Xenoph. περὶ παιδ.
  Sit tibi terra levis, mollique tegaris arenâ,
  Ut tua non possunt, eruere ossa canes.   *Mart.*
† Nam quòd requiescere corpus
  Vacuum sine mente videmus,
  Spatium breve restat, ut alti
  Repetat collegia sensus—
  Hinc maxima cura sepulchris
  Impenditur————   *Prud.* hymn. in Exeq. defunct.
‡ Marmoreo Licinus tumulo jacet: at Cato parvo,
  Pompeius nullo: credimus esse Deos?   *Varro Atacinus.*
§ Fama orbem replet, mortem sors occulit, at tu
  Desine scrutari quod tegit ossa solum.
  Si mihi dent animo non impar fata sepulchrum;
  Angusta est tumulo terra Britanna meo.

with

with a sad story, because four hundred years after his death his bones were thrown into a river, that evil men might sell the leaden coffin. It is all one in the final event of things. *Ninus* the *Assyrian* had a monument erected whose height was nine furlongs, and the breadth ten, (saith *Diodorus :*) but *John the Baptist* had more honour when he was humbly laid in the earth between the bodies of *Abdias* and *Elizeus.* And St. *Ignatius,* who was buried in the bodies of lions, and St. *Polycarp,* who was burned to ashes, shall have their bones, and their flesh again, with greater comfort than those violent persons who slept among kings*, having usurped their thrones when they were alive, and their sepulchres when they were dead.

Concerning doing honour to the dead, the consideration is not long. † Anciently the friends of the dead used to make their funeral orations, and what they spake of greater commendation was pardoned upon the accounts of friendship; but when Christianity seized upon the possession of the world, this charge was devolved upon priests and bishops, and they first kept the custom of the world, and adorned it with the piety of truth and of religion : but they also ordered it that it should not be cheap ; for they made funeral sermons only at the death of princes, or of such holy persons *who shall judge the angels.* The custom descended, and the channels mingled with the veins of earth through which it passed : and now-a-days men that die are commended at a price, and the measure of their legacy is the degree of their virtue. But *these things ought not so to be :* the reward of the greatest virtue ought not to be prostitute to the doles of common persons, but preserved like laurel and coronets, to remark and encourage the noblest things. Persons of an ordinary life should neither be praised publicly, nor reproached in private ; for it is an office and charge of humanity to speak no evil of the dead,

---

* Cernit ibi mœstos et mortis honore carentes,
   Leucaspim, et Lyciæ ductorem classis Orontem.   *Æneid.* vi.
† Lustravitque viros, dixitque novissima verba.   *Æneid.*

(which

(which I suppose is meant concerning things not public and evident;) but then neither should our charity to them teach us to tell a lie, or to make a great flame from a heap of rushes and mushrooms, and make orations crammed with the narrative of little observances, and acts of *civil* and *necessary* and *eternal religion.*

* But that which is most considerable is, that we should do something for the dead, something that is real and of proper advantage. That we perform their will, the laws oblige us, and will see to it; but that we do all those parts of personal duty, which our dead left unperformed, and to which the laws do not oblige us, is an act of great charity and perfect kindness: and it may redound to the advantage of our friends also, that their debts be paid even beyond the inventory of their moveables.

Besides this, let us right their causes, and assert their honour. When *Marcus Regulus* had injured the memory of *Herennius Senecio, Metius Carus* asked him, *What he had to do with his dead ;* and became his advocate after death, of whose cause he was patron when he was alive. And *David* added this also, that he did kindness to *Mephibosheth* for *Jonathan's* sake: and *Solomon* pleaded his father's cause by the sword against *Joab* and *Shimei.* †And certainly it is the noblest thing in the world to do an act of kindness to him whom we shall never see, but yet hath deserved it of us, and to whom we would do it if he were present; and unless we do so, our charity is mercenary, and our friendships are direct merchandize, and our gifts are brokage: but what we do to the dead or to the living for their sakes, is *gratitude* and *virtue for virtue's sake,* and the *noblest portion of humanity.*

And yet I remember that the most excellent prince *Cyrus,* in his last exhortation to his sons upon his

---

* Χαῖρέ μοι, ὦ Πάτροκλε, καὶ εἰν Ἀΐδαο δόμοισι,
Πάντα γὰρ ἤδη τοι τελέω τὰ πάροιθεν ὑπέσην.   *Iliad.* ↓.

† Χρὴ δὲ καὶ τῶν προγόνων ποιήσασθαί τινα πρόνοιαν, καὶ μὴ παραμελῆσαι, μηδὲ τῆς περὶ ἐκείνας εὐσεβείας.   *Isoc. Plataic.*

—— Misenum in littore Teucri
Flebant, et cineri ingrato suprema ferebant. *Æneid.* vi.

death-

death-bed, charms them into peace and union of hearts
and designs, by telling them that his soul would be still
alive, and therefore fit to be revered and accounted
as awful and venerable as when he was alive: and
what we do to our dead friends is not done to persons
undiscerning, as a fallen tree, but to such who better
attend to their relatives, and to greater purposes,
though in other manner than they did here below.
And therefore those wise persons who in their funeral
orations made their doubt, with an [εἴ τις αἴσθησις τέλε-
λευτηκόσι περὶ τῶν ἐνθάδε γιγνομίνων, if the dead have any
perception of what is done below] which are the
words of *Isocrates*, in the funeral *encomium* of *Eva-
goras*, did it upon the uncertain opinion of the soul's
immortality; but made no question, if they were living, they did also understand what could concern
them. The same words *Nazianzen* uses at the exe-
quies of his sister *Gorgonia*, and in the former invec-
tive against *Julian :* but this was upon another reason ;
even because it was uncertain what the state of separation was, and whether our dead perceive any thing
of us till we shall meet in the day of judgment. If it
was uncertain then, it is certain, since that time we
have had no new revelation concerning it ; but it is ten
to one but when we die we shall find the state of affairs
wholly differing from all our opinions here, and that
no man or sect hath guessed any thing at all of it as it
is. Here I intend not to dispute, but to persuade :
and therefore *in the general,* if it be probable that
they know or feel the benefits done to them, though
but by a reflex revelation from God, or some under-
communication from an angel, or the stock of acquired
notices here below, it may the rather endear us to our
charities or duties to them respectively ; since our virtues use not to live upon abstractions, and metaphysi-
cal perfections or inducements *, but *then* thrive when
they have material arguments, such which are not too

---

* Ἦλθε δ᾽ ἐπὶ ψυχὴ Παῖροκλῆ©ͻ δειλοῖο,
　—————　καί μιν πρὸς μῦθον ἔειπεν,
Εὔδεις, αὐτὰρ ἐμεῖο λελασμέν©· ἔπλευ, Ἀχιλλεῦ;
Οὐ μέν μευ ζώον①ͻ ἀκήδεις, ἀλλὰ θανόντ©. *Iliad.* ψ.

1   far

far from sense. However it be, it is certain they are not dead; and though we no more see the souls of our dead friends than we did when they were alive, yet we have reason to believe them to know more things and better; and if our sleep be an image of death, we may also observe concerning it, that it is a state of life so separate from communication with the body*, that it is one of the ways of *Oracle* and prophecy by which the soul best declares her immortality, and the nobleness of her actions, and powers if she could get free from the body, (as in the state of separation,) or a clear dominion over it, (as in the resurrection.) To which also this consideration may be added, † that men a long time live the life of *sense*, before they use their *reason*; until they have furnished their head with experiments and notices of many things, they cannot at all discourse of any thing: but when they come to use their reason, all their knowledge is nothing but *remembrance*; and we know by proportions, by similitudes and dissimilitudes, by relations and oppositions, by causes and effects, by comparing things with things; all which are nothing but operations of understanding upon the stock of former notices, of something we knew before, *nothing but remembrances:* all the heads of topics, which are the stock of all arguments and sciences in the world, are a certain demonstration of this; and he is the wisest man that remembers most, and joins those remembrances together to the best purposes of discourse. From whence it may not be improbably gathered, that in the state of separation, if there be any act of understanding, that is, if the understanding be alive, it must be relative to the notices it had in this world, and therefore the acts of it must be discourses upon all the parts and persons of their conversation and relation, excepting only such new revelations which may be communicated to it; concerning which we know nothing. But if by seeing

* Ἡ δὲ τῦ ἀνθρώπῃ ψυχὴ τότε δήπυ θειοτάτη καταφαίνεῖαι, καὶ τότε τι τῶν μελλόντων προορᾷ, τότε γὰρ ὡς ἔοικε μάλιςα ἐλιυθερῦται. *Cyrus* apud *Xenop.* lib. viii. Instit.

† ———— Τίς ἐςι καὶ εἰν αἴδαο δόμοισι·
  Ψυχὴ καὶ εἴδωλον, ἀτὰρ φρένες ὒκ ἔνι τά΄υπαν. *Iliad.* ψ.

Socrates

Socrates I think upon *Plato*, and by seeing a picture I remember a man, and by beholding two friends I remember my own and my friend's need, (and he is wisest that draws most lines from the same centre and most discourses from the same notices;) it cannot but be very probable to believe, since the separate souls understand better, if they understand at all, that from the notices they carried from hence, and what they find there equal or unequal to those notices, they can better discover the things of their friends than we can here by our conjectures and craftiest imaginations: and yet many men here can guess shrewdly at the thoughts and designs of such men with whom they discourse, or of whom they have heard, or whose characters they prudently have perceived. I have no other end in this discourse, but that we may be engaged to do our duty to our dead; lest peradventure they should perceive our neglect, and be witnesses of our transient affections and forgetfulness. Dead persons have religion passed upon them, and a solemn reverence: and if we think a ghost beholds us, it may be we may have upon us the impressions likely to be made by *love*, and *fear*, and *religion*. However, we are sure that God sees us, and the world sees us: and if it be matter of duty towards our dead, *God will exact it;* if it be matter of kindness, *the world will;* and as *religion* is the band of that, so *fame* and *reputation* is the endearment of this.

It remains, that we who are alive should so live, and by the actions of religion attend the coming of the day of the Lord, that we neither be surprised, nor leave our duties imperfect, nor our sins uncancelled, nor our persons unreconciled, nor God unappeased: but that when we descend to our graves we may rest in the bosom of the Lord, till the mansions be prepared where we shall sing and feast eternally. *Amen.*

Te Deum Laudamus.

FINIS.

Printed by Strahan and Spottiswoode,
Printers-Street, London.

THE LITERATURE OF
DEATH AND DYING

Abrahamsson, Hans. **The Origin of Death:** Studies in African Mythology. 1951

Alden, Timothy. **A Collection of American Epitaphs and Inscriptions with Occasional Notes.** Five vols. in two. 1814

Austin, Mary. **Experiences Facing Death.** 1931

Bacon, Francis. **The Historie of Life and Death with Observations Naturall and Experimentall for the Prolongation of Life.** 1638

Barth, Karl. **The Resurrection of the Dead.** 1933

Bataille, Georges. **Death and Sensuality:** A Study of Eroticism and the Taboo. 1962

Bichat, [Marie François] Xavier. **Physiological Researches on Life and Death.** 1827

Browne, Thomas. **Hydriotaphia.** 1927

Carrington, Hereward. **Death:** Its Causes and Phenomena with Special Reference to Immortality. 1921

Comper, Frances M. M., editor. **The Book of the Craft of Dying and Other Early English Tracts Concerning Death.** 1917

Death and the Visual Arts. 1976

Death as a Speculative Theme in Religious, Scientific, and Social Thought. 1976

Donne, John. **Biathanatos.** 1930

Farber, Maurice L. **Theory of Suicide.** 1968

Fechner, Gustav Theodor. **The Little Book of Life After Death.** 1904

Frazer, James George. **The Fear of the Dead in Primitive Religion.** Three vols. in one. 1933/1934/1936

Fulton, Robert. **A Bibliography on Death, Grief and Bereavement:** 1845-1975. 1976

Gorer, Geoffrey. **Death, Grief, and Mourning.** 1965

Gruman, Gerald J. **A History of Ideas About the Prolongation of Life.** 1966

Henry, Andrew F. and James F. Short, Jr. **Suicide and Homicide.** 1954

Howells, W[illiam] D[ean], et al. **In After Days;** Thoughts on the Future Life. 1910

Irion, Paul E. **The Funeral:** Vestige or Value? 1966

Landsberg, Paul-Louis. **The Experience of Death:** The Moral Problem of Suicide. 1953

Maeterlinck, Maurice. **Before the Great Silence.** 1937

Maeterlinck, Maurice. **Death.** 1912

Metchnikoff, Élie. **The Nature of Man:** Studies in Optimistic Philosophy. 1910

Metchnikoff, Élie. **The Prolongation of Life:** Optimistic Studies. 1908

Munk, William. **Euthanasia.** 1887

Osler, William. **Science and Immortality.** 1904

Return to Life: Two Imaginings of the Lazarus Theme. 1976

Stephens, C[harles] A[sbury]. **Natural Salvation:** The Message of Science. 1905

Sulzberger, Cyrus. **My Brother Death.** 1961

Taylor, Jeremy. **The Rule and Exercises of Holy Dying.** 1819

Walker, G[eorge] A[lfred]. **Gatherings from Graveyards.** 1839

Warthin, Aldred Scott. **The Physician of the Dance of Death.** 1931

Whiter, Walter. **Dissertation on the Disorder of Death.** 1819

Whyte, Florence. **The Dance of Death in Spain and Catalonia.** 1931

Wolfenstein, Martha. **Disaster:** A Psychological Essay. 1957

Worcester, Alfred. **The Care of the Aged, the Dying, and the Dead.** 1950

Zandee, J[an]. **Death as an Enemy According to Ancient Egyptian Conceptions.** 1960